Thought Knows No Sex

D1566622

Thought Knows No Sex

Women's Rights
at Alfred University

Susan Rumsey Strong

State University of New York Press

All photographs courtesy of Herrick Memorial Library, Alfred University.

Published by State University of New York Press, Albany

For information, contact State University of New York Press, Albany, NY
www.sunypress.edu

Production by Marilyn P. Semerad
Marketing by Anne M. Valentine

Library of Congress Cataloging-in-Publication Data

Strong, Susan Rumsey, 1944–
  Thought knows no sex : women's rights at Alfred University / Susan Rumsey
Strong.
      p. cm
  Includes bibliographical references and index.
  ISBN 978-0-7914-7513-3 (hardcover : alk. paper)
  ISBN 978-0-7914-7514-0 (pbk. : alk. paper)
  1. Alfred University—Students—History.   2. Women—Education (Higher)—
New York—Alfred—History.   3. Sex discrimination in higher education—United
States—History.   4. Women's rights—United States—History.   I. Title.

LD131.A34S77 2008
378.747'84—dc22

                                                                    2007037530

10 9 8 7 6 5 4 3 2 1

I dedicate this book to my family (especially to our grandchildren, Sofia Kathryn and Michael Steven VanHook, who would have read it too if they could!), to Siena, and to the memory of my parents, Kathryn Skinner Rumsey and Dexter Phelps Rumsey, who would have been very pleased.

Contents

Illustrations

Acknowledgments

I want to thank the many people who helped with the research and preparation for this book. Drs. Lynn Gordon, Harold Wechsler, and Mary Young read early versions, helping me focus the arguments. Among the individuals who assisted in locating sources over years of research were Mercedes Hanbach, Scholes Library of Ceramics, Alfred University; Herrick Memorial Library staff, Alfred University; Linda Lewandowski, Jean B. Lang Western New York Historical Collection, Alfred State College; Lynne Belluscio, The Le Roy Historical Society, Le Roy, New York; Gould P. Colman, University Archivist, Cornell University; Caswell Nilsen, Massachusetts Historical Society, Boston; Ruth Quattlebaum, Phillips Academy Archives; Margaret Rase (granddaughter of Leona Burdick Merrill), Alfred, New York; and Lois Westlund, Milton College Archives, Wisconsin. Quotations from materials owned by the Alfred University Archives are used with the kind permission of Herrick Memorial Library, Alfred University.

Many friends offered encouragement and helped me persevere. I am grateful to Norma Higgins and Laurie McFadden, archivists at Alfred University's Herrick Memorial Library, who have carefully preserved the materials that enrich this book. Laurie McFadden also prepared the photographs for publication; all photographs are courtesy of Herrick Memorial Library. Alfred University granted me leave to prepare the manuscript. My sincere thanks to Charles Edmondson, Alfred University president, for his support. Careful reading from the SUNY Press's anonymous readers helped shape and improve the text. I would also like to thank Lisa Chesnel, former Acquisitions Editor at SUNY Press, for supporting this project.

Most of all, I am grateful to my family who encouraged me at every step. My sister, Barbara Rumsey, director of the Boothbay Region Historical Society in Boothbay Harbor, Maine, shares an interest in past lives. My children, Michael Bernard Strong and Amy Lovell Strong, both accomplished writers, read the chapters more than once, offering many suggestions and corrections. My son-in-law, David VanHook, a gifted writer himself, helped with many technical issues. Finally, my husband,

Paul Strong, was indispensable. He offered unstinting support for this lengthy enterprise, read countless versions, made many suggestions for polishing the prose, shared the pleasure of knowing the hopes and dreams of these educational pioneers, and suffered the distractions of such a project with a willing spirit. Siena Seadog, our golden retriever, watched over every word and shared our lives throughout.

Introduction

the bumptious and defiant little village

—Julia Ward Howe, "An Idyl of Mid-Summer and Middle Age"

The query was first raised by an annoyed professor at an Oberlin dinner table in 1847. Oberlin College women were not permitted to read their graduation essays in public, a policy consistent with the prevalent belief that women's role was private; public activities were unseemly. A furor arose when Lucy Stone refused to write her graduation essay because of this ban. Professor Fairchild asked his boarder, Jonathan Allen (studying there after his graduation from Alfred Academy), "How do you get along with that question at Alfred?"

"The most natural way in the world," Allen replied. "If a young woman is capable of writing a paper, she ought to be able to read it."[1]

Allen's response is deceptively simple. Why did an egalitarian environment for women appear "natural" at Alfred University when most contemporary voices proclaimed it "unnatural"? In assessing the early history of coeducation at academies and colleges, historians have often focused on conservative aspects, finding that women were separated or silenced, and emphasizing those educators who directed women to domesticity.[2] Undeniably this was often the case, yet not all institutions were conservative. Reexamination of antebellum education has brought fresh, even surprising, insights. Historians have portrayed vibrant academy life, nurturing women's abilities. In her work on women's education from 1780 to 1840, Margaret Nash asserts that it "matured in a relatively friendly atmosphere." Nancy Beadie and Kim Tolley's collected essays on the academy movement find "a culture of intellectualism and competition among young women." Through close study of the curriculum, Tolley has overturned the usual view that young girls were discouraged from studying science, discovering that "more girls than boys studied science in many

As spelling was not yet systematic in the early nineteenth century, there are numerous deviations from current usage in source documents. Most of the time I have quoted these without the distraction of [sic].

1

early nineteenth-century academies." Christine Ogren has shown that in early normal schools women and men studied together in relative equality. Identifying the state normal school as "a revolutionary institution," Ogren concluded that "the notion of separate spheres may have had a much weaker hold, at least among non-elite members of society, than many women's historians have suggested."[3]

Alfred's experience extends these findings into early college-level education. Alfred University (chartered in 1857 from an 1843 academy that grew from an 1836 select school) provides a case study of a remarkably egalitarian institution where separate spheres certainly had a "weaker hold." Historians have shown that one form of feminism may have originated in rural areas, which produced numerous women's rights adherents; such rural egalitarianism permeated this educational community. Not only does Alfred's history throughout the nineteenth century demonstrate that coeducational colleges were not uniformly conservative, it provides new perspective on several significant issues: theories of education, the relationship of academies to women's advances, the relationship of religion to reform, the rural origins of feminist activity, and the close ties between colleges and their local communities.

Founded just three years after Oberlin, Alfred is one of the nation's first coeducational colleges. Settlers sharing a religion came from New England to this frontier area in the remote Allegheny hills seventy miles south of Rochester. At Alfred women were treated "on an equality" with men, as a student asserted in 1858. At a time when public speaking was widely forbidden to women, Alfred expected its women to speak publicly and to pursue an active life. Through archival resources and by drawing on scholarly research into New York's farm life, reform movements, and spiritual fervor, this study explores the regional context for coeducation and women's activism.

In a small village in western New York, Alfred supported its women to an unusual degree. Gender mutuality, based on rural family patterns and kinship networks, was buttressed by the philosophy of natural rights. The ideology of separate spheres was not articulated; instead the community embraced a family model of shared work. Indeed, Alfred appears to have offered an egalitarian environment from its first days: women attended in large numbers, found intellectual females on the faculty, and were schooled not for subservience, but for independence. Women were on the faculty, and many alumnae worked after marriage. There it was "natural" for young women and men to wish for higher education, "natural" for women and men to be educated together, "natural" for women to speak publicly, and ultimately "natural" for them, led by their teacher, Abigail Allen, to seek suffrage.

The reform spirit was fostered by Alfred's proximity to the "Burned-over District." Alfred shared that reform spirit with Oberlin, but differed in preparing its female students for the independent life of teaching rather than dependency as ministers' wives. As a new, rural, and inexpensive institution, it offered social mobility to local young people; as a "non-elite," non-eastern institution, it particularly offered opportunities to young women.[4] Finally, the partnerships existing in the farm lives of its students and the marriages of its presidents were utilized as an ideal educational model. Late in the nineteenth century, as coeducation became the leading mode of higher education, and then suffered from public disapproval when fears of "feminization" arose at many institutions, Alfred University's faculty and students persisted in their support of coeducation. They noted the disputes elsewhere, while remaining committed to their "natural" form of higher education.

This environment nourished the equal rights beliefs of Abigail A. Maxson Allen and her husband Jonathan Allen, she a member of the faculty from 1846 to her death in 1902, he a faculty member from 1849 and president from 1867 to his death in 1892. Their advocacy was shared. Jonathan Allen asserted: "The essential powers of the spirit are neither masculine nor feminine, but human, sexless. Thought knows no sex." Uniquely among women's educators, Abigail Allen was a suffragist, speaking out and encouraging her students to do the same. "Be radical, radical to the core," she urged at a national Women's Congress, explicitly rejecting the prevailing gender ideology of separate education for the sexes' separate spheres as well as expressing her confidence that coeducation itself was natural. Alfred "has no more thought of changing, than parents who find in their families boys and girls, would think of organizing two households in which to train them," she said. In doing so, she entered a public dispute over coeducation, touching on central issues of a larger debate over women's nature and capabilities.[5]

According to most historians, the earliest coeducational colleges—notably Oberlin (founded in 1833) and Antioch (founded in 1853)—perpetuated traditional roles of subservience and subordination for their women, restricted their public speaking, and discouraged professional aspirations. They argue that the college founders' conception of women's education should not be viewed as a radical departure from social norms; rather, it lay well within separate spheres ideology, assigning women a private, domestic role, subordinate to men's public responsibilities. In her excellent history—a standard text—Barbara Solomon asserted, "consistently, one generalization holds: coeducational schools made plain both directly and indirectly what could be denied at women's colleges, that society attached greater importance to men's achievements" and "it was in the separate female academy that . . . the values of women's liberal education prevailed." Jill Ker Conway maintained that coeducational colleges offered only "compensatory education" for women, considering women "only from the point of view of the services they might provide for men."

Not until women's colleges were established, she believes, did women receive intellectual training that was not "derivative."[6]

Oberlin's women were reportedly secondary, trained for "intelligent motherhood and properly subservient wifehood." Viewed chiefly as future wives who would marry Oberlin's theological students and join their husbands' ministerial or missionary labors, they were, in Ronald Hogeland's view, "catalysts for cultivation, reservoirs for wifedom, and redemptive agents for male sensuality." Oberlin faculty carefully explained that activists such as Lucy Stone did not get their advanced ideas at Oberlin. Fairchild declared in an 1867 address that Oberlin had not created any "strong-minded women": three alumnae who might be classed as such "came to us very mature in thought, with their views of life settled and their own plans and purposes determined and announced. Whatever help in their chosen life they derived from the advantages afforded them, they have never given us any credit for their more advanced views of women's rights and duties."[7]

John Rury and Glenn Harper argued that Antioch aspired to educate women for "a limited set of domestic roles." President Horace Mann and his wife Mary were opposed to "women's rights women," those "of an ultra stamp [who] increased the difficulties for him by coming upon the premises, and promulgating their heresies against good manners." Similarly, Joan G. Zimmerman writes, "the example of Grinnell College [founded in 1861] demonstrates, rather than a broadening of opportunity for women or providing a vehicle for women significantly to alter their status in American society, the institutionalization of coeducation instead reinforced and perpetuated into the twentieth century the careful segregation of the sexes which had characterized Victorian America." Women were often treated with disdain and even hostility as the new state universities reluctantly opened to them.[8]

In this tumultuous climate, most educators, whether in coeducational or single-sex institutions, carefully distinguished women's higher education from women's rights ideology—some from personal belief, others perhaps from political necessity. As Louise Boas explains, "women educators were careful to divorce themselves from any association with those who urged that women be trained for leadership, for life in the world of man" and Solomon points out, "Ironically . . . even though feminism has been one catalyst for women's education, academic institutions serving women have often tried to repress or ignore its messages." Evidence of this repression has been found in private antebellum colleges and post-Civil War land-grant universities. Few educators espoused suffrage. An educator who was also a suffrage activist, Alfred's Abigail Allen was rare indeed.[9]

The revolutionary implications of joint study were seen by a few. Sarah Grimké, a pioneering reformer and one of the first women to break the ban on public speaking, certainly saw the possibilities. She commented on Horace Mann, the first president of Antioch College, who opposed females entering public life or the professions (other than teaching): "He will not help the cause of woman greatly, but his efforts to educate her will do a greater work than he anticipates. Prepare woman for duty and usefulness, and she will laugh at any boundaries man may set for her." An Antioch student also perceived the logical outcome. When Mann asserted that if he believed coeducation would lead to women joining the professions, "he should think he was doing very wrong in remaining at the head of a coed school," his student Olympia Brown was puzzled: "I wondered much that a professed advocate of coeducation . . . was so disinclined to face its obvious results." Historian Joan Wallach Scott concluded that joint education was indeed more radical than single-sex institutions: "coeducation as practiced in increasing numbers of institutions was far more subversive (of education, of sexuality, and of gender relations) than were the women's colleges."[10]

The men who created the research university model at the end of the nineteenth century (and their historians) dismissed the small antebellum colleges, rising up "like mushrooms," as stifling and narrow, petty products of "a great retrogression . . . a host of little institutions in which doctrinal and sectarian considerations were rated above educational accomplishment." But those pioneering schools represented a populist enthusiasm for education that America has yet to reject. And most research universities—for all their strengths—restricted the entry of women and contributed to their withdrawal from activism in the twentieth century, as the democratizing power of the antebellum college was replaced by a "gate-keeping" mentality. While "the traditional college was portrayed as an obstacle to progress" for many years, historians in fact have found "the origins of many 'university' reforms in antebellum institutions," as Julie Reuben points out in her article on writing higher education history. Scholars are now beginning to fill the historical vacuum described by Bruce Leslie in *Gentlemen and Scholars*, caused by "disproportionate attention to a few institutions."[11]

The importance of academy origins in opening women's educational opportunities, long overlooked, has only recently been explored. Nearly every coeducational college that opened before the Civil War originated as an academy. Lamenting the "dearth of published texts," Beadie asserts that "more sophisticated analysis needs to be focused on rural and small town settings." Academies were crucial, as Nash makes clear in her reassessment of early women's education. Variously elementary, secondary, and higher education institutions at a time when those terms did not yet exist, blending public and private funding before those categories became mutually exclusive, academies met local needs, expanded educational opportunities for men and women in the new republic, and drew some of their students on to college. "Despite Eastern opposition to coeducation," Midwestern academies open to both men and women rapidly proliferated.

Alfred's development from an academy thus mirrors the broader development of women's education throughout the century.[12]

Like many of the economically accessible colleges described by David Potts in his studies of nineteenth-century students and David Allmendinger in *Paupers and Scholars*, Alfred offered social mobility for "poor" young men and, a group often ignored, women from farm families. Early colleges—products of local needs and boosterism as well as denominationalism—expanded in number and diversity, served aspiring farm and middle-class families, and engaged in revision of the classical curriculum to meet the needs of a rapidly changing America. The farming origins of most faculty and students helped shape Alfred's unusual educational environment.

Influenced by the doctrine of separate spheres prevailing in prescriptive literature, most studies have emphasized a profound disjunction between nineteenth-century men's and women's lives. In her 1966 article, Barbara Welter distilled the "ideal of the perfect woman," responsible for providing the home's stability—a peaceful refuge in a threatening, rapidly changing world. Using the private writings of and public pronouncements on white, middle-class, New England women of mostly urban origins, Nancy Cott expanded the analysis to a broad "interpretive framework for a thorough social history." Their work is valuable and influential. Other scholars however have found mutuality—shared tasks and blurring of the spheres' boundaries—in several rural communities. Mutuality, expressed most clearly in the Allens' lives, also dominated the rural educational community of Alfred University, where men and women shared work, reform values, and common goals, as families shared work on their farms.[13]

Furthermore, most scholars have linked women's reform activities with the doctrine of separate spheres and urban benevolent activities, arguing that women used their assigned role as moral guardians of the home to expand their concern with public issues of morality. Yet important early manifestations of feminist activity had their roots in unusually egalitarian rural cultures that denied separate spheres ideology and were predisposed to accept the Enlightenment values of natural rights. In her study of women's activism, historian Nancy Hewitt called for re-evaluation of the "dominant thesis"—that "women's path to public prominence began at the hearth of the privatized family and the altar of religious revivalism." She argued that Rochester feminists sprang from an equal rights tradition, philosophically and socially distinct from urban benevolence, and of rural origin.[14] Similarly, Abigail Allen's vision was tied to her farming roots. Self-sufficient and hard-working, she and many women like her needed to work, expected to work, and wanted work that was meaningful and fairly compensated.

Finally, study of the Allens' religious beliefs gives insight into the varieties of educational experience. Influenced in complicated and contradictory ways by the University's connection with the Seventh Day Baptist sect, Alfred's story illuminates an apparent paradox: that a school founded in what Donald Tewksbury named the "denominational era," sustained by one small group of co-religionists and shaped by their culture and community, could maintain a secular purpose, resisting denominational control and avoiding narrow sectarianism. Moreover, this religious group valued basic education and social reform activity, routes to public action for nineteenth-century women. There was a curious balance in this school; it prided itself on its nonsectarian stance, yet was dominated throughout the nineteenth century by one sect; that sect was not doctrinal, yet the school demanded respect for its Sabbath by all; Alfred was unusually liberal in its treatment of women, although the denomination was not. The university maintained a somewhat prickly distance from the denomination and ministers were notably absent from the faculty. Historians have debated the relative influence of sectarian motives and rivalries versus local needs among antebellum colleges. To understand Alfred's environment, we must untangle these mingled motives.[15]

Evangelical Christianity has been credited with advancing women's education. David Tyack and Elisabeth Hansot have written that "many advocates of the education of women were activists in the evangelical religious movements that swept the nation in the first half of the nineteenth century," and David Noble argues, "Through the pioneering efforts of Oberlin and Mount Holyoke, religious revival paved the way for the establishment of both collegiate coeducation and colleges for women." Evangelical Christianity did support women's education but with an ambivalence so familiar in women's history. Nancy Cott and others have pointed out that religious identity allowed women to assert themselves "both in private and in public ways." Yet conservative controls remained in place: "In most ministers' interpretation evangelical Christianity confined women to pious self-expression, sex-specific duties, and subjection to men."[16]

In contrast, a few historians have observed that less conventional religious beliefs can be linked with the development of more assertive women's rights stands. Cott has suggested it was "escape from the containment of conventional evangelical Protestantism" that led to what she named the "equalitarian feminist view." Nancy Gale Isenberg and Blanche Glassman Hersh have shown that early feminists tended to have unorthodox or dissident religious views. In a muted variation of this "escape," Alfred's secular mission and avoidance of denominational control combined with Jonathan Allen's liberal theological beliefs to permit development of feminist values.[17]

This paradoxical entanglement of faith, values, and purpose so deep in Alfred's identity can be found in other early colleges. Certainly some, such as Oberlin, Knox, and Olivet, were evangelical in purpose, but the contours of early nineteenth-century education were far more complex than the "university builders" of the late nineteenth century cared to see.

A close look at individual colleges shows fascinating diversity; it also suggests that the most liberal environments did not arise from conventional evangelical Christianity. Alfred was founded in the denominational era but it was most importantly a neighborhood college that, like many others, spread the gospel of education.

Three interrelated patterns of thought, each drawing on the concept of "naturalness," were prominent in shaping both behavior and rhetoric: the tradition that the school "grew up naturally from the soil," from a select school—begun at student initiative and supported by its small community—to an academy and then a university; the belief articulated by Abigail Allen that a natural family model was the best basis for the education of men and women; and the conviction derived from natural rights philosophy that male and female intellects were equal in capacity ("thought knows no sex," as Jonathan Allen said). Each contributed to mold a distinctive educational environment.

To understand this environment, one must examine the "soil" that nourished egalitarianism, those cultural, economic, and regional factors leading Alfred's community of learning to take an early stand on slavery, women's education, the public role of women, labor issues, suffrage, and other reforms. Archival evidence and historical sources point to several contributing factors, some shared with other early colleges, some distinctive to Alfred: the farming origins of most students; the school's mission to educate the "poor"; its "special work" in training teachers (and the accompanying subordination of ministerial training); cultural and familial values of the founding denomination; regional and denominational commitment to reform; a "family model" of coeducation; and the fervent, vocal commitment to women's rights of Abigail and Jonathan Allen.

Alfred University's archives house an unusually rich collection of student publications, reminiscences, diaries, letters, presidential histories, photographs, and meticulous minutes of the student literary societies' activities that give a vivid sense of their world. Recollections gathered by Boothe Colwell Davis (Alfred president, 1895–1933) and by John Nelson Norwood (president, 1933–1945, and historian) are particularly valuable. The Jean B. Lang Western New York Historical Collection at Alfred State College also contains Seventh Day Baptist histories and newspapers as well as local diaries, photographs, and genealogical materials.

The narrative of this book follows a chronological structure excepting chapters seven and eight, which explore women's public speaking and student relationships (which were at the heart of student life throughout the period). Individual voices recount the struggle to establish a school, the exhilaration of learning, family sacrifice, friendship, and camaraderie on campus. They tell a story of the excitement, hopes, and fears felt by some of the first women to aspire to higher education. This is not a conventional institutional history, stressing organizational changes, presidential policy, and plant development. This study of Alfred University's nineteenth-century history, grounded in student experiences, explains a remarkably liberal environment by focusing on the individuals who created it and sociocultural factors contributing to it. As much as possible, and as the Allens encouraged, I have tried to let Alfred's women speak for themselves.

Chapter One

Gender and
Higher Education

What an infernal set of fools those schoolmarms must be! Well, if in order to please men they wish to live on air, let them. The sooner the present generation of women dies out, the better. We have idiots enough in the world now without such women propagating any more.

—Elizabeth Cady Stanton, in Harper,
The Life and Work of Susan B. Anthony

In the nineteenth century, American women challenged their assigned role in the social order as never before. Lecturing for antislavery societies, temperance or women's rights; fighting for suffrage and entry to college; entering the professions—all expressed a new activism in a time of rapid socioeconomic and cultural change. The nineteenth-century experience for women provided both opportunities and restrictions, betraying society's ambivalence about women's nature and role. As Gerda Lerner has pointed out, society was confused about "the woman question"; deep tensions and conflicting views were manifestations of a shifting value system.[1] Embedded as education is in the culture it serves, nowhere was this ambivalence more clearly stated than in the erratic development of women's higher education and the century-long debate over its appropriateness.

This complex debate must be understood before the unusual nature of Alfred University's environment can be grasped. Fueled by deep-seated preconceptions of assigned gender roles expressed formulaically in the ideology of separate spheres, this debate demonstrates "the powerful ways that notions of appropriate sex roles and of the organization of the gender system shaped educational discourse." Historians' exploration of the concept of separate spheres, often viewed as a reaction to sudden

11

urban growth in the previously agrarian nation, has shaped our understanding of every aspect of women's lives in the nineteenth century. Welter's influential article, "The Cult of True Womanhood," drew the
ideal—piety, purity, submissiveness, and domesticity—from women's mag-
azines, sermons, novels, and diaries of the period. Studying industrialization, Gerda Lerner identified that cult as a predominantly middle-class
ideology; "mill girls" were ignored. (As others have pointed out, the ideology held less sway in rural areas as well.) Examining diaries and letters,
Cott argued that women's sphere, while restrictive, opened a path to
"social power based on their special female qualities."[2]

Separate spheres ideology hardened the characteristics and roles ascribed to men and women into the view that the sexes possessed opposed,
if complementary, natures. Men were assumed to be rational, worldly, ag-
gressive, sexual, voters, property owners; they lived in the public world.
Women were emotional, spiritual, submissive, asexual, non-voters, non-
property owners; they inhabited a private world. These differences were
considered divinely ordained and immutable. Though historians discard
separate spheres as a single lens, it remains an important concept.

The barriers were real. The first question was not "Should women be
taught?"; it was "Could women be taught?" Female intellectual inferior-
ity had long been assumed. Scattered voices in past centuries had
protested women's subordination, but the multiple protests heard at the
end of the eighteenth century were unprecedented. The advantages, dangers, and utility of education for women were widely discussed. Would
education destroy feminine characteristics or enhance them? If women
restricted themselves to the home, what type of education was appropriate for those circumscribed duties? If women were the primary influence
on youth, what level of education was sufficient for that essential task?

The competitive nature of school life with its long tradition of
rhetorical training, debates, public demonstrations, and awards, thought
bracing for boys, was considered destructive to desired feminine traits,
such as subservience and compliance. "Would the desire of distinction, of
surpassing her friends, be the most sure [way] to suggest to a wife the
numberless little kindnesses and attentions so essential to the happiness
of a husband?" asked one educator. And even granted an intellect, what
use was a woman to make of it? For most Americans, access to education
did not suggest conferring social, political, or economic equality on
women. Florence Nightingale became so frustrated with narrow home
life before beginning her nursing crusade that she contemplated suicide.
She wrote in her private journal, "Why have women passion, intellect,
moral activity—these three—and a place in society where no one of the
three can be exercised?"[3]

These constraints became increasingly poignant as popular enthusiasm for education grew dramatically. Primary schools spread after the Revolution; by 1840, Cott reports, "almost all women in New England could

read and write, women's literacy having approximately doubled since 1780." In fact, "New England women in the years of the early republic were the most literate women in western society." As industrialization and urban growth transformed society, all concurred: human development, government, commerce, even salvation depended on education.[4]

Soon a new argument was heard: not only could women be taught, they actually made ideal teachers. Still, most early advocates of women's education—Emma Willard, Mary Lyon, Catharine Beecher, and Horace Mann—had conservative views of women's role, justifying the need for education within the domestic sphere. Willard's school "would differ as much from a school for men as women's character and duties differed from men's." Believing that "nature designed our sex for the care of children," she wanted to "place the business of teaching children, in hands now nearly useless to society; and take it from those, whose services the state wants in many other ways." Beecher convinced many that women were best at nurturing the young; she traveled the West, placing female teachers in hundreds of schools. Teacher preparation gave real impetus to women's education; coeducational and single-sex academies sprang up by the hundreds, many specializing in teacher training.[5]

The new nation's educational aspirations, opportunities, and enrollments grew rapidly. Common schools, uniformly coeducational, appeared in every new settlement. Academies and seminaries, offering secondary education, spread across the growing country; by 1850, there were more than 6,000. Republican values, community needs, denominational pride, and westward expansion produced a surge of college building after 1800. While only twenty-five colleges were chartered in the 160 years after Harvard's 1636 founding, by 1870, 582 colleges existed; by 1900, nearly 1,000.

Writing from the later perspective of the research university, influential historians denigrated this impressive surge of antebellum college building. Donald Tewksbury termed this the "denominational era," when sect after sect "will [each] have its college, generally one at least in each State." Richard Hofstadter and Frederick Rudolph criticized church affiliation as incompatible with intellectual freedom, apparently viewing these institutions as irrelevant sectarian outposts, "narrow, rigid, anti-intellectual backwaters." In his classic study, Laurence Veysey saw the college as a "somewhat quaint ministerial survival," its leaders opposed to change.[6]

Recent historians have corrected this view, finding instead vibrant and diverse institutions that were a popular expression of faith in education, responding to local needs of the new middle class. Even Tewksbury observed, "America had already become the land of neighborhood colleges." The distinctive character of American higher education was established by 1850 when Henry P. Tappan (later, University of Michigan president) said, "we have multiplied colleges so as to place them at every man's door."[7]

Tappan failed to note that colleges had also been placed at every woman's door. Unprecedented growth in female schooling occurred as women benefited from the general support for basic education, then entered the burgeoning academies. Thousands of unrecorded coeducational academies brought advanced education to young women. In New York, of two hundred incorporated academies in mid-century, 85 percent were coeducational. Of 20,000 students, half were women.[8]

Historians had long ignored academies and seminaries (barring a few leading female seminaries) for a variety of reasons: some vanished leaving no trace; others were absorbed into public school districts; still others developed into colleges and their historians rush over the somewhat embarrassing academy prelude to reach college history. Academies have been dismissed as mercifully temporary, because their standards varied greatly; as elitist, though most were not; as unfortunate preludes, erratic and undersupervised, to the modern, bureaucratized high school; or as unimportant forerunners to colleges (in fact their lack of regulation, unorthodox approaches, and responsiveness to local conditions were important factors for women's entry into higher education). Tewksbury wrote in 1932, "The general relation of the academy movement in this country to the college movement remains to be adequately studied." Theodore Sizer echoed in 1964: "a detailed study of the academies has yet to be written." Recent work is filling this gap and bringing fresh insights. Beadie and Tolley's collection of essays, Nash's analysis of academy development, and Tolley's work on girls' science education represent the first major studies in the last forty years.[9]

Academies were quasi-public institutions, funded through a combination of tuition, state payments, and local payments that provided nearly all the secondary education in antebellum America. Diverse, fluid, mostly unregulated, frequently ephemeral, they were "founded and supported, often at great sacrifice," by local families and civic leaders in almost every town.[10] Their curricula and student body overlapped with common schools at one end of the spectrum and colleges at the other. Academies took erratically prepared students of a wide age range and educated them as far as they could. Strong academies sent their graduates into the sophomore or even junior year of college. Academies were, in spirit and achievement, America's first engine for mass secondary education.

Fundamentally rural, admirably adapted to thinly scattered populations (because room and board were available), the academy was slowly replaced by the new publicly funded high school as Americans became urban dwellers in the second half of the century (students could then walk to school). However, many colleges maintained their academies or preparatory departments until the late nineteenth century, either as regional service or because student preparation was deficient. In 1850, only 69 of Oberlin's 500 students were in its college courses; in 1860, 199 of 1,311 were. In Antioch's first year, more than 200 students were enrolled in its preparatory department; only six (four men, two women) were ready for the college course, and a discouraged Mary Mann wrote a Massachusetts friend, "Our college is in fact a school." Of 300 women who enrolled at Wellesley when it opened in 1875, only 30 passed the entrance examination; a preparatory class was immediately established. As late as 1889, Bucknell's preparatory students outnumbered its college-level students three to one. Swarthmore, founded 1869, did not eliminate its preparatory program until 1894.[11]

Academies played a critical role by opening advanced education to women and establishing their ability to study equally with men. Oberlin's founders did not see coeducation as an innovation when they opened their academy in 1833 with 29 men, none yet ready for college, and 15 women. Nevertheless, it did not cross their minds that women would seek admittance to the Collegiate Department. But in 1837, four women did just that, presenting enough Greek and Latin to enter the college course. After initial confusion, hesitation, and debate, the faculty allowed them to enter.[12] Although several schools have since claimed the honor of first offering women college-level instruction, it is generally agreed that the passage of these four women from Oberlin's academy to its college-level courses marked women's first access to full collegiate education. Building on the academy movement, other coeducational colleges, including Alfred, opened in the antebellum period. By 1865, when Vassar (generally considered the first women's college) opened, more than twenty coeducational schools already provided collegiate instruction to women. Yet most histories focus on women's colleges rather than the earlier and more numerous coeducational schools.

While college education may appear to have been an inevitable step, it proved contentious. Women's separate sphere could be used to justify basic education; its utility for the important role of raising the next generation was relatively easy to accept. Academy-level education spread rapidly. But higher education was a very different matter. It traditionally led to public life and occupations closed to women. Giving women an identity outside the family created anxiety over their possible abandonment of traditional roles. As work left the home for urban shops, factories, and mills in the early nineteenth century, the home, which had been a production center, became instead a retreat. In this time of rapid change, the cult of True Womanhood prescribed religious, social, familial, and sexual stability—impossible demands on woman, "the hostage in the home." Morality, fertility, the family, societal power, Western civilization itself—some observers believed all were threatened by women's higher education.[13]

The normative curriculum when women entered higher education was "the classical course," a liberal arts curriculum based on scholastic and humanistic thinkers—"the education of a gentleman"—and the public purpose of its rhetorical tradition excluded women. In preparing the citizen and statesman for public life and public speaking, oration and debate were integral to advanced education. Since women were without the vote or public power of any sort, denied public forums, and directed to the home, such education appeared ludicrously inappropriate to some, including Harvard's powerful President Charles W. Eliot.

At the end of the century, M. Carey Thomas, President of Bryn Mawr College (founded in 1884), still struggled to legitimize equal education for women. Possessed of a ferocious intellect herself, she was determined to prove women the intellectual equals of men. Eliot infuriated Thomas with his pronouncement—incredibly, made at Wellesley College—that women were unfit to study the liberal arts. In her 1899 opening address at Bryn Mawr, Thomas attacked this "dark spot of mediaevalism," protesting Eliot's attempt to shove women's higher education "out of its path":

> President Eliot said that the president and faculty of a women's college had no guide from the past, that the great tradition of learning existing from the time of the Egyptians to the present existed only for men and that this vast body of inherited tradition was of no service in women's education, that women's colleges simply imitated men when they used the same educational methods instead of inventing new ones of their own and that furthermore it would indeed be strange if women's intellects were not at least as unlike men's as their bodies.
>
> . . . He might as well have told the president of Wellesley to invent a new Christian religion for Wellesley or new symphonies and operas, a new Beethoven and Wagner . . . new Chemistry, new philosophies, in short, a new intellectual heavens and earth.[14]

The argument frequently shifted ground: if it was conceded that women's brains might be equal to the task, their bodies were not. One physician thundered, "Women beware. You are on the brink of destruction. . . . Beware!! Science pronounces that the woman who studies is lost." Another asserted that a woman is "a moral, a sexual, a germiferous, gestative and parturient creature." These warnings culminated in the book that created the "most notorious controversy" of the century, *Sex in Education*, "the great uterine manifesto" published in 1873 by Harvard's Dr. Edward Clarke. This infamous book expressed the most profound fear: education would "unsex" women, rendering them sterile. Asserting that women were dominated by the uterus, which would be atrophied by use of the brain, Clarke declared that women's reproductive system could not tolerate extended study and that "identical education" of women was "a crime before God and humanity, that physiology protests against, and that experience weeps over."[15]

He argued that "schools and colleges . . . require girls to work their brains with full force and sustained power, at the time when their organization periodically requires a portion of their force for the performance of a periodical function, and a portion of their power for the building up of a peculiar, complicated, and important mechanism,—the engine within an engine." Energy required for hours of study was diverted from this uterine construction project. The resulting sterility in this "sexless class of termites" would destroy the family and Anglo-Saxon civilization: "It requires no prophet to foretell that the wives who are to be mothers in our republic must be drawn from trans-atlantic homes." His science left no room for argument: both the woman who studies, and her civilization, is lost.[16]

Clarke's book, which quickly went through multiple editions, stirred immediate controversy and put women's educators on the defensive; they scrambled to prove their graduates were healthy, married, and fertile. M. Carey Thomas remembered, "We were haunted in those early days by the clanging chains of that gloomy little specter.[17] In the midst of these persistent and profound disagreements, the pioneering coeducational and women's colleges had to make decisions about the appropriate education for women.

Advocates struggled to eradicate persistent views of women's intellectual disability and occupational purposelessness. Yet educational institutions expressed the ambivalence towards women's intellect manifest in society as a whole. In 1889, when Alice Freeman Palmer (past president of Wellesley College) reviewed women's higher education, she found, "After fifty years of argument and twenty-five of varied and costly experiment, it might be easy to suppose that we were still in chaos, almost as far from knowing the best way to train a woman as we were at the beginning." Palmer described the advent of coeducation, "established in some colleges at their beginning, in others after debate, and by a radical change in policy," opening of women's colleges after the Civil War, and development of the coordinate college (for instance, the Harvard "Annex," dating from 1879 and which became Radcliffe). Each system represented a variant belief in women's role, and Palmer found this variety valuable, given society's continuing uncertainty about the proper education for women: "While the public mind is so uncertain, so liable to panic, and so doubtful whether, after all, it is not better for a girl to be a goose, the many methods of education assist one another mightily in their united warfare against ignorance, selfish privileges, and antiquated ideals."[18]

The diverse, unregularized nature of nineteenth-century higher education and the blurred line between academy and college contributed much to women's opportunities. Oberlin (opened in 1833), Alfred (1836), and Antioch (1853), each with large academies, were "western" schools, and it was in the West that coeducation was more readily accepted. In the East, where established men's colleges had prior possession of the educational territory, women were barred and coeducation resisted. Women's colleges and coordinate colleges were founded there after the Civil War to provide for women. As Palmer observed, "The older, more generously endowed, more conservative seats of learning, inheriting the complications of the dormitory system, have remained closed to women."[19]

Western colleges claimed to be more egalitarian than eastern schools and in many cases they were. Frontier values and a democratic spirit "breaking the bond of custom" were friendly to coeducation. Western colleges, naturally opening later than eastern, arose from coeducational academies, which were more economical than separate institutions. The West's rural nature was also conducive: Kathryn Kerns's research on five Western New York colleges (two women's colleges and three coeducational) demonstrates that the women's colleges drew many more students from cities than did coeducational ones, suggesting that urban families (clustered in the Northeast) were influenced by separate spheres doctrine and preferred separate schooling.[20]

Even so, coeducation was often difficult to implement in the West; state universities exhibited great ambivalence. There were numerous confrontations and idiosyncratic resolutions as the new universities dealt with women's demands and powerful resistance to those demands. Many institutions battled over enrolling women, initially resisting coeducation as Michigan and Cornell did, or alternately admitting women, then separating them, as Wisconsin did. As the University of Wisconsin's President Van Hise declared, "it is necessary to remember that in the older state universities of the middle west, coeducation began, not in consequence of the theoretical belief in it upon the part of the officials of those institutions, but in spite of such belief."[21] Michigan's state university opened in 1841 with six male students. In 1855, the State Teachers Association asked that women be allowed to attend. The request was tabled, but in 1858, when informed that twelve young women would indeed seek admission, the Regents asked a committee to review the issue.

That committee gathered opinions from a number of college presidents. Women's prescribed sphere was uppermost to Harvard's James Walker, who responded that enlightened public opinion was against this experiment and that "its decision must turn in no small measure, on the question whether we propose to educate females for public or private life." The character differences between men and women seemed an insuperable barrier to Dr. Eliphalet Nott of Union College: "Delicacy of sentiment, a feeling of dependence and shrinking from the public view, are attributes sought for in the one sex, in the other decision of character, self-reliance, a feeling of personal independence, and a willingness to meet opposition and encounter difficulties." Educating men and women together would endanger "alike their virtue and their happiness."[22]

Even the presidents of Oberlin and Antioch were cautious. Horace Mann wrote from Antioch that while the advantages of joint education were "*very great. The dangers of it are terrible. . . .* I must say that I should rather forego the advantages than incur the dangers." The dangers, of course, included unsupervised "clandestine" meetings of men and women. These responses reinforced the beliefs of the University of Michigan's President Tappan, who did not relax his opposition, writing nearly ten years later: "I sometimes fear we shall have no more women in America. If the Women's Rights sect triumphs, women will try to do the work of men—they will cease to be women while they will fail to become men—they will be something mongrel, hermaphroditic. The men will lose as the women advance, we shall have a community of *defeminated* women and *demasculated* men. When we attempt to disturb God's order we produce monstrosities." The Michigan Regents denied admission to the twelve petitioners and did not open the university to coeducation until 1870, when they reluctantly bowed to the most economical solution to taxpayers' demands for educated daughters.[23]

While coeducation's proponents justifiably viewed women's entry as a victory, admission per se certainly did not guarantee equitable or even respectful treatment. Women were admitted to Wisconsin's Normal Department in 1860 and permitted to take some "college classes" with men. One student remembered, "The feeling of hostility was exceedingly intense and bitter. As I now recollect the entire body of students were without exception opposed to the admission of the young ladies." (Christine Ogren has shown that, ironically, the nearby Wisconsin state normal schools fostered a far more egalitarian environment than did the university.) When women were admitted to Missouri in 1870, they were marched to class in a group. Missouri's President Reed recalled, "Finding that the young women at 'the Normal' did no matter of harm, we very cautiously admitted them to some of the recitations and lectures in the University building itself, providing always that they were to be marched in good order, with at least two teachers, one in front and the other in the rear of the column as guards." At Cornell, fraternity members were not allowed to date Cornell women, invite them to parties, or even speak to them. Charlotte Williams Conable concluded, "The cultural message which the Cornell experience reinforced for both men and women, was that woman's proper role is as a social appendage to a man."[24]

Women and men alike were concerned about the radical implications of coeducation. Even teachers accustomed to educating young men and women together often opposed equal education at the college level. In 1857 Susan B. Anthony presented a resolution favoring coeducation to the New York State Teachers' Convention. Vehement opposition erupted on the floor: coeducation would produce "a vast social evil," "abolish marriage," and lead to "horrible quagmires" like racial mixing, Mormonism, and sexual impurity. The resolution lost by a large majority; many women present must have voted against it. Anthony's good friend, Elizabeth Cady Stanton, was infuriated: "What an infernal set of fools those schoolmarms must be! Well, if in order to please men they wish to live on air, let them. The sooner the present generation of women dies out, the better. We have idiots enough in the world now without such women propagating any more."[25]

Opposition did slowly give way, and by the end of the century, much had changed. America's twenty-five colleges entered the nineteenth century as a small homogeneous band, confident in their liberal arts curriculum, educating just a few students; no women were permitted to enroll. By century's end there were nearly a thousand colleges and universities. Development was erratic, seemingly noncontroversial in some schools, dogged by dispute in others, but by the end of the century women's higher education was firmly established and coeducation was the dominant mode. Total college enrollment reached about 238,000 (a dramatic rise from 5,000 in 1800), almost three-quarters of colleges were coeducational, and nearly 85,000 women were enrolled. The curriculum was irrevocably changed, by science and the expansion of knowledge certainly, but also by women's reach for equal rights, equal education, and a public role. As industrialization and urbanization transformed the nation, colleges "stumbled toward clarifying how they were going to fit into the world of new technology, vast material gains, and broadened opportunities."[26]

The "education of a gentleman" shifted, accommodating women. In doing so, however, the liberal arts curriculum diminished in purpose and prestige, until finally there were doubts as to whether it retained any utility for men. "Our women really have some use for the education of a gentleman, but our men have none," observed William Dean Howells.[27] The rhetorical tradition fundamental to higher education had also accommodated women. By the end of the century, women had won a public voice and through it a public role, albeit in underpaid professions not attractive to men, professions deemed compatible with women's nurturant nature—teaching, nursing, social work—and rhetoric had somehow lost its dominant place in the curriculum. Still, ambivalence over women's activities continued: a reaction against coeducation set in during the 1890s and early 1900s as women attended in greater numbers, leading to fears of "feminization."

Women's inclusion in higher education came slowly, amid controversy and fear, and often through the side door—parallel courses of study, parallel colleges, courses in an "Annex," the extracurriculum. Yet an interpretation of history that emphasizes resistance to coeducation, or resistance to higher education for women in general, masks the remarkable diversity of attitudes and experiences among pioneering colleges. Furthermore, exclusive focus on separate spheres limits interpretation, by ignoring the diversity of experiences—among social classes, single and married women, various ethnic groups, and geographic areas, each shaped by regional culture and varying stages of economic development. Alfred University's experience underlines Nancy Hewitt's assertion that "the notion of a single women's community rooted in common oppression denies the social and material realities." Linda Kerber reviewed twenty years of historians' approaches, concluding it is time to move on to more complex analyses. As exceptions multiply, evidence accumulates that separate spheres may indeed be an "exhausted" concept, as Kerber proclaimed.[28]

Yet "these challenges to the ideology of separate spheres have barely begun to have an impact on the history of women's education." In fact, rigidity of the prescriptions was far from uniform. Ogren has found that "'modern' feminist notions of female autonomy existed as an unexamined undercurrent" and gender segregation was minimal in normal schools, which drew predominantly rural students. Hewitt, Joan Jensen, and

Nancy Grey Osterud have shown that rural areas presented important variations; in these communities, cross-gender mutuality, the *denial* of separate spheres, led directly to a feminist vision. Early reformers came out of rural areas where men and women shared work and therefore the cult of domesticity had less currency. Just such a model of mutuality and reform dominated in Alfred University's rural educational community.[29]

Exclusive focus on gender polarity also ignores an important intellectual ideology that stubbornly reappeared among liberal thinkers of the time: Enlightenment values. These principles of human equality, natural rights, and self-government were in direct conflict with the ideology of domesticity. America's founders did not reconceptualize gender relationships; they "did not choose to explore with much rigor the socially radical implications of their republican ideology." Nevertheless the promise of the Enlightenment hung before women as an unresolved dilemma. Most sought to reconcile domesticity to this intellectual challenge. A few men and women embraced radical egalitarianism. In their view, the principles of the Declaration of Independence were universal and women's appropriate sphere unknown since they had been given neither education nor free rein to test their limits. This small band included Jonathan and Abigail Allen.[30]

Within these powerful and complex crosscurrents, at Alfred Academy and Alfred University there was created an institution premising equality of intellect, the value of public action for both sexes, and a "natural" model of gender relations that did not threaten, but rather strengthened, the family. While coeducation was viewed as unnatural and dangerous by many, it does not appear that it was ever viewed as other than natural at Alfred. Alfred's liberalism was unprecedented: its young women came with family support, they were encouraged to speak publicly, and women's rights leaders were welcomed to campus.

The practice of gender integration in rural areas and the belief in sexual equality of natural rights philosophy—these two threads, underemphasized by most historians, came together to create a durable vision of cooperative gender relations and women's equality at Alfred University. Founded in a period of tremendous national growth and populist optimism, this school typified the explosion of educational opportunities in the first half of the nineteenth century; at the same time, it developed a distinctive character. Two arguments were prominent in creating the unusually egalitarian environment: the belief that coeducation was in accord with nature and divine teaching, and the belief, drawn from Enlightenment values, that women had a right to equal opportunities.

Chapter Two

Seventh Day Baptist
and Farm Roots

Alfred "has ever been the school of the poor. Not many sons and daughters of the rich have entered its portals. . . . May it ever continue thus."

—Jonathan Allen, "Life and Labors of Kenyon"

S tarted at student initiative and supported by its community, the 1836
Alfred select school served a population scattered on farms surrounding the village of Alfred, New York, as well as those coming
from more distant Seventh Day Baptist towns from Rhode Island to Wisconsin. Important elements of Alfred's character were formed in its first
few years. Settling in a hilly area with poor soil, family members worked together on modest farms, creating an egalitarian spirit that defined gender
relations. Coeducational from the first day, the school carried its women
along naturally as it developed from academy to university. Young women
attended with the support of their families, often combining study with
teaching to earn tuition money. Motivated and independent, with a deep
desire to advance their education, they came to a school whose faculty reflected the spirit of the age in being deeply religious, committed to education and reform. The faculty prized self-reliant women and encouraged
them to achieve.

At the end of his life, Jonathan Allen stressed that the school's growth
had stemmed naturally from student aspirations: "Alfred University had
its origin in a response to the cry of the people for more light. It has
grown up naturally as the trees grow, from the common soil of the common wants of the people. 'Give us more light,' is the ever-increasing cry
of humanity."[1] The impetus to meet local needs was a distinctive charac-
teristic of this school. Not founded as a utopian evangelizing community

like Oneida Institute, Oberlin, or Knox College; not modeled on a female academy, like nearby Ingham University; not sponsored by a denomination, like nearby Genesee College; not founded after competing town bids, like St. Lawrence; not founded by local boosters who hoped to increase economic prosperity, like Middlebury College; instead Alfred was simply begun by a student who found a teacher to open a school.

The "common soil" from which Alfred University grew contributed to its character. Its founding, like so many schools established in the early nineteenth century, was the result of westward expansion. As Tewksbury observed, "the American college came in large part to represent the essential frontier character of our civilization." Antebellum colleges were "truly native institutions of higher education," closely associated with the migration of population from the East's coastal region.[2] The Allegany hills of Western New York were within a two million acre tract briefly owned by land speculators, Phelps and Gorham, who bought the territory in 1788 from Massachusetts and negotiated confirmation of the purchase with the Iroquois. The acreage changed hands several times as speculators failed to make immediate profits. Agents were employed to entice settlers into purchasing the wilderness at $2 to $4 an acre.

Although the land was cheap and the terms generous, the fertile soil along the Genesee River to the north was naturally settled earlier than the heavily forested hills of Allegany with their short growing season and poor transportation. Allegany County was "rugged upland, with confining valleys and short, turbulent watercourses, [that] forms part of the Appalachian plateau region, with elevations in the southeastern section of 2,400 feet." These remote hills offered only marginal farm country, similar to that being abandoned by New England families, and the rocky acreage sold slowly, usually to impoverished settlers. "The poor, without money, could contract for lands in Allegany and Cattaraugus counties on ten years' credit. Yet even with these terms 'a very considerable proportion could never pay for the lands they occupied.'"[3]

The county's first settler was Nathaniel Dike, who arrived in 1795 and cleared land on what became Dike's Creek in Wellsville. Few followed. In 1896 historian John Minard wrote: "Although the owners of these lands made strenuous efforts to attract settlers, distrust of titles, the density of the forest, the presence of bears, wolves, and panthers, and of roving bands of Indians, greatly retarded settlement until after the war of 1812."[4] Slowly, others came and Allegany County was formed in 1806 on petition of the region's scattered settlers, who found travel for county business to the distant towns of Batavia or Canandaigua burdensome. The township of Alfred, still devoid of settlers, was also constituted in 1806 along lines established by the Phelps and Gorham surveyors.

Early settlers came on foot, following Indian trails along creeks and rivers, guided by blazed trees. Streams had to be forded, as there were no bridges. Flatboats laden with belongings could be poled along the larger streams. Oxen carts could not make their way until paths had been cleared of fallen trees or widened through the brush. In 1807, the first three Alfred settlers, Clark Crandall (later prominent as associate county judge, state legislator, and first to engage in the local cheese trade), Nathan Greene, and Edward Greene, walked from Berlin, New York, a town in Rensselaer County, with numerous Seventh Day Baptists. Many of the village's settlers brought this faith with them, and although the university was founded on a nonsectarian basis, throughout the nineteenth century a majority of its trustees, faculty, and students were adherents.

Seventh Day Baptists tended to migrate in groups, preserving family relationships reaching back to Brookfield, Berlin, and Westerly (Rhode Island), or forward to Ohio and Milton, Wisconsin. They had a particular impetus to cluster—they were marked by their Saturday Sabbath, which bound them together, as it set them apart from others. Their weekly rhythm—be it for school, work, or worship—differed from nearly all Christian groups. It was more satisfactory to live in a community that shared observance of the Sabbath-driven schedule, and they tried to stay in groups large enough to dominate or at least to command respect for their practice. Alfred became one of the largest such communities. By 1858, a year after receiving the university charter, First Alfred was the largest Seventh Day Baptist church in the country. Even so, Seventh Day Baptists were only the fourth largest denomination in Allegany County.[5]

This small denomination developed early in the history of America's settlement. The first Seventh Day Baptist churches were established in England during the 1650s, after the turmoil of the Reformation. Seeking first principles based on Biblical authority, it was natural that some would return to the Seventh Day Sabbath, believing it the original Biblical intent, one neglected by most Christians to avoid sharing observance with Jews. Seventh Day Baptists, like other Baptists, espoused congregational governance—"the priesthood of all believers"—and adult baptism so that one could make a conscious profession of faith.[6]

In 1671 a few persons withdrew from the First Baptist Church in Newport, Rhode Island (the second oldest Baptist church in the colonies), forming their own church, the first Seventh Day Baptist church in this country. Members moved to new towns, and by 1678 there were twenty members in Newport, seven in Westerly (also called Hopkinton), and ten in New London, Connecticut. By 1795 the Westerly Seventh Day Baptist church was the largest of New England's 325 Baptist churches. Caroline Dall observed (after visiting Alfred in 1876), "The 'Seventh-Day Baptists' feel towards [the Westerly] church as the descendants of the Pilgrims feel towards the first church in Plymouth."[7] Westerly provided the nucleus for new churches as families began the movement west, forming communities in Bristol and New London in Connecticut, Berlin and Brookfield in New York. Many young people came to the Alfred school from Berlin and Brookfield.

Seventh Day Baptism and the larger Baptist group grew rapidly in an upsurge of anti-clericalism at the turn of the century. Migration to the frontier led to the rise of antiformalist churches (including Baptists and Methodists, emphasizing the independence of each congregation and preferring an untrained lay clergy), which flourished in areas where individual initiative was highly prized and clerical authority far distant. In 1795 there were only five Baptist churches in New York. By 1815 there were more than three hundred, and by 1830, eight hundred.[8]

In 1807, when the first settlers reached Alfred, the Seventh Day Baptist General Conference reported 1,848 communicants for the entire denomination. By 1820, there were 2,330 and about 8,000 in 1876.[9] Membership was spread over about sixty-five churches by the middle of the century. In spite of geographic separation, membership was close-knit, and the far-flung churches maintained relationships through annual meetings, exchange of delegates, and circular letters.

Emphasis on individual interpretation meant that, like other Baptists, Seventh Day Baptists resisted uniform doctrine, church authority, and ecclesiastical decree. Independence, lay clergy, opposition to hierarchy, and lack of dogma produced a people that were democratic, egalitarian, open, and enthusiastic about reform. Edwin H. Lewis, an alumnus, recounted, "I grew up with very little interest in sects, not being keen enough to see that sects are closely associated with different forms of government. . . . It gradually dawned upon me that I was born into the most democratic form of church government, so democratic that at times it approached anarchy. To be sure, we elected a pastor each year . . . but we scorned much government of any sort."[10]

Preaching was carried out by a variety of laymen, often in rotation. (At least one woman, Martha Hull Ernst, became a preacher as well.) Those showing promise were "called to improve their gifts." Some were licensed to preach and ordained as elders, but full ordination to pastor was rare; it developed later concurrently with an educated ministry. In Minard's 1896 *History of Allegany County, New York*, Ethan Lanphear vividly remembered one early preacher: "Richard Hull preached the first sermon I remember of in the schoolhouse at the "Bridge" [Baker's Bridge, now Alfred Station]. He could scarcely read or write his name at that time. He worked at farming, and made spinning wheels—large and small—quill wheels, etc. He wore no coat, linen trousers, and a vest, without a shoe to his feet. . . . Men, women and children often went to church barefooted in those days, and preachers had no salary."[11] Hull was paid in wheat for missionary labors in nearby towns.

In 1812, twenty-four men and women in the new town of Alfred organized for worship, meeting in a small house owned by the Coons, adopting articles of faith and a covenant, and choosing Stephen Coon Sr. (grandfather of Amos Coon, who brought Bethuel Church to start the select school) as leader of their fledgling church. In 1813, this organization became a branch of the Berlin church and in 1816 became independent. Membership grew rapidly as settlers flowed in, rising from 87 in 1816, to 200 in 1826, to 354 in 1830 (by 1830 only the Westerly "mother church" was larger), so that a second Alfred church opened in 1831.

Because Seventh Day Baptists preferred to settle where most or all followed their observance, cities were uncongenial, threatening loss of values and ultimately of faith. Daniel Maxson wrote from Covington, Kentucky, near Cincinnati: "Sabbaths are rather lonely. & now I think I hear Mother say 'I wonder if Daniel will get to be unsteady living in a city.' Tell her that *Ego non muto!*"[12] She cannot have been the only mother who worried that in the city her son would become "unsteady" in his faith. Nor was this unrealistic. Seventh Day Baptists rivaled the Amish, Mennonites, Shakers, and a few less well-known groups for the distinction of most tiny. No wonder they feared for their survival. "Sunday-keepers" often shifted to Saturday observance when in the minority; surely Sabbatarians could be drawn as easily the other way.

In consequence, Seventh Day Baptists tended to remain in rural areas to protect their way of life. Even in 1900, when most Americans had migrated to cities, only 9 of 106 Seventh Day Baptist churches were in towns of more than 5,000 inhabitants. In 1912 Boothe Colwell Davis (Alfred University President, 1895–1933) stated that Seventh Day Baptists "have no assured future existence, growth or prosperity independent of our rural churches. There are fundamental reasons why we can never do our greatest and our best work among city populations." Farm work was more compatible with Sabbath observance than many urban occupations, which demanded Saturday labor. As farm employment dwindled throughout the twentieth century and family farms numbered fewer and fewer, it became more difficult to maintain their communities.[13]

Practice of this faith required elementary education for all—regardless of sex or income. Basic schooling and teacher training were important, for women, men, and children were expected to study the Bible and form independent judgments. Still, only a modest level of schooling was necessary for a literate congregation, and support for a college was relatively late in developing; by 1835, Baptists had chartered six colleges (while Seventh Day Baptists lacked even an academy). In part this can be explained by the denomination's small size and scant resources.

As year followed year, more families arrived from Berlin and other Seventh Day Baptist areas, purchasing land at an "astonishingly low price" and holding the first town meeting in 1808. The Greenes' sister, Hannah Greene Fisk, "was one of the most notable women of early days . . . her home was one of the first 'taverns.' Being a professional *accoucheur*, she often rode alone on horseback through the woods whenever and wherever duty called her, her long journeys giving her many thrilling experiences with bears and wolves." In 1809 John Teater came from Oneida County; his daughter, Nancy Teater, became the town's first schoolteacher.[14]

Settlers continued to come from Berlin, Brookfield, and several towns in Connecticut and Rhode Island, joining the westward migration from New England in the first decade of the nineteenth century. Southern New England proved to be an unrewarding location for farming and many families began to push west to millions of newly opened acres in central and western New York: "During one three day period in February 1795 about 1200 sleighs freighted with men, women, children, and furniture" passed through Albany on the way to the Genesee River Valley, which they had heard offered good farm land. In fact, Yale's President Dwight declared that by 1820 New York was becoming a "colony from New England." This influx of New Englanders quadrupled New York's population in three decades, their culture and values overwhelming those of the earlier Dutch and German inhabitants as English heritage became dominant. Western New York's population grew even more quickly. Migration only slowed when New England's mills and factories were built, bringing a demand for workers.[15]

The flow of settlers into the township included many who later played important roles in the school's development. In 1817, John Allen, grandfather of future University president Jonathan Allen, arrived with his family from Rhode Island, making the journey with an ox team. He purchased two hundred acres of land and built a log house. In 1818, Amos Crandall walked from Rhode Island with his brother-in-law and took up fifty acres of land at $4 an acre. After building a log cabin, he walked back to Rhode Island. The next year he and his brother-in-law moved their families to their new home with an ox team and one horse. Crandall taught school "four winters at $10 per month, boarding himself and taking his pay in produce or labor." One winter he received only seventy-five cents in return for teaching. As chorister of the Seventh Day Baptist church, he was one of the earliest singing-school teachers and established the town's first Sabbath school.[16]

The first task for each settler was to clear land and build a log cabin. In this heavily forested area, potash, shingles, maple sugar, and lumber were the chief sources of revenue. Transporting grain on horseback thirty-one miles to Dansville, as Luke Maxson did in 1810 to sell for 31 cents a bushel, could not sustain a family. As the forests were cleared and the wolf population reduced, flax and sheep were raised, providing linen and wool for clothing. Settlement was slow, cash crops were few, and "in the haying and harvesting season it was customary for such of the men as could be spared to 'go north,' to the lower, warmer and longer-settled farms of Livingston and Genesee counties to convert their time and strength into cash, which usually went to make payments on the land or improvements." Slowly the forests gave way and settlers realized the limitations of their gravelly hillside farms: "grass, oats and potatoes [were] surer and more profitable crops than corn and wheat, so stock-raising and dairying became the chief business."[17]

The farming origins of faculty and students shaped the people who in turn created Alfred's unusual environment. Allegany County's poor soil and remote location meant that dairy farming (which lacked the sharp division of labor between the sexes of wheat farming, for example) would form its economic base. While residents viewed their remoteness as a liability, rural life patterns in the Allegany hills produced egalitarian gender roles, manifest in shared labor, cross-gender socializing, and a degree of economic independence for women. The slow pace of economic development was dictated by geography. Much of Allegany County was still unsold in 1836, nearly thirty years after the first settlers reached Alfred, and transportation into these stony hills remained difficult. When James Irish (Alfred Select School's second teacher) traveled to Alfred in November 1837, he related:

> Railroads were then unknown west of Utica, and the passage from Schenectady to Alfred had the vicissitudes incident to a wide range of locomotion. A night-ride on a locomotive, facing a snow storm, served as an introduction. Morning found me at Utica. Taking passage on what was predicted as the last westward bound packet-boat for the season, after many changes and delays, on account of the ice, we arrived at Geneva too late for the stage. In company with a couple of farmers, I took a lumber-wagon ride to their homes, near Penn Yan, by whom I was kindly entertained, and conveyed to Pen Yan in time for the stage to Bath. From there, a stage-coach being out of the question, on account of the roughness of the roads, a lumber wagon took me to Almond. Leaving my heavy luggage, I set out, with a light bundle, on foot for Alfred. Snow, that had fallen from three to six inches deep, was now reduced to slush by a drizzling fog. . . . This gave me my first inkling of Allegany mud.[18]

It was as difficult to send goods out as to travel in. The Erie Canal, completed in 1825, provided Genesee Valley settlers with an easy, inexpensive route to the expanding markets of New York City as well as overseas trade. Town after town sprang up along the canal. One of the first inland cities, Rochester developed quickly as a commercial center, but Allegany County (seventy miles south) was not a partner in this growth. In fact the canal's completion depressed trade in the Southern Tier of counties as its river depots were abandoned for the canal; bitter residents complained they had been taxed for its construction but received no benefit.

Knowing cheap transportation was essential, Allegany residents began to agitate for a railroad line in 1831. One select school student wrote in January 1838, "Most of our inhabitants have the sweet anticipation of living to see a railroad through this dispised and frostbitten country. If this should be the case it would be a great help to us about importing our grain, but it is not likely that we shall ever have any to export." Finally, the line from the Hudson River to Lake Erie was completed in 1851. "Music and dancing, banquets and speeches, were the order of the day," wrote the county historian. "And who can feel to blame them? They were really celebrating their liberation from a long bondage." At every hamlet, excited crowds, anticipating inexpensive access to markets at last, thronged the triumphal train carrying President Fillmore and Daniel Webster.[19]

Butter and cheese were made on nearly every farm. As elsewhere, dairying was a cooperative family occupation. The diaries of Maria Langworthy Whitford, who lived a few miles outside Alfred, give a vivid picture of life on the farms surrounding the school. Maria's short life embodied patterns familiar to historians of such areas: a network of relatives and friends; a woman's economic contribution through butter, weaving, and knitting; shared work with her husband. In fact, her last diary entry before her sudden death at thirty in July 1861 speaks to mutuality: "I washed window. Sam'l washed the woodwork to parlor."[20]

Maria records the heavy workload of a farm wife: "[November] 13th [1857]. Friday and a great deal to do. I loaded up two and a half bushels of apples for Sam'l to carry to Andover to sell them. I swept out and next I took care of the butter that Sam'l churned while I milked the cows, washed up the things and went out to pull some carrots, pulled three bushel, come in, got in the rest of the tallow to try, fixed some pumpkin to stew and went to ironing. Sam'l got back about 4 o'clock, got dinner, finished ironing and made my bonnet cape."[21] Despite the difficulties of travel—by foot or wagon in summer, sleigh in winter—visits were continually exchanged with relatives and friends, male and female. Some were primarily for socializing—to share quilting, apple paring, or other tasks—others to help a neighbor who was ill or tending a newborn.

Sometimes Maria churned, sometimes Samuel did. Sometimes he boiled sap, sometimes she did so he could start spring plowing. Haying and harvesting grain were typically Samuel's work, though she helped on occasion, "pitch[ing] off a load of oats after sunset" or helping "unload a load of hay." When Maria was sick, Samuel "got the breakfast himself and made some wheat bread." Three days later, Samuel "washed what cloths we could not do without." When he was sick, she "got up, made a fire and chopped pumpkin for the cows, fed them, milked, fed the hogs, carried some bran to the calves come back, got back, got breakfast etc."[22]

Allegany County's delayed development was evident in that her daily round of heavy tasks still included spinning and weaving; by 1860 such home-based manufacturing was found "only in the most remote outposts of the frontier and was almost negligible as a component of the national product." Maria contributed income by selling butter and eggs, cloth she had made, socks she had knitted, and feathers plucked from their poultry. Most of the young women and men who would enroll at the Alfred school came from just such farm lives described by Kerns, "where women's work still played an important part. . . . Daughters coming from such farms would be much more likely to view the family as a production unit and work as compatible with marriage, even after their schooling had taught them to strive for careers beyond the farm."[23]

Elaboration of separate spheres, defining distinctly distanced gender roles, occurred in urban areas (with the rising middle class) in response to industrialization with its separation of work from home. During this period "the gap between the worlds of men and women became wider than possible at any other time in American history."[24] Much previous scholarship has pointed to the divisions of urban gender roles. Yet some historians have demonstrated that in rural areas shared tasks induce mutuality. A more egalitarian gender vision can be linked to economies in which women had significant roles. Furthermore, most scholars have linked women's reform activities with the urban doctrine of separate spheres. But the earliest reformers came from just such communities as Alfred—rural, homogeneous, with a relatively high degree of cooperation between the sexes. Important manifestations of feminism, such as some Quaker cultures and Alfred University's, had their roots in unusually egalitarian rural communities. Thus gender-integrated farm life could lead to women's enhanced economic role on the one hand and early feminist values on the other. Both can be tied to development of the Allens' equal rights convictions.

Joan Jensen's exploration of the sexual division of labor within households has illuminated how geography, class, and local economy shaped women's roles. She examined the lives of Chester County, Pennsylvania, farm women from 1750 to 1850, arguing that the message of domesticity was slow to reach rural readers, and when it did reach them, they did not necessarily heed its call. "Although the ideal of true womanhood began its urban ascent in the decade of the 1830s, [these] records offer evidence that the practice of rural women was still far different from the urban vision of domesticity."[25]

Nanticoke Valley, in central New York, was much like Allegany County in that its steep slopes and thin soils supported dairying rather than wheat; butter was its most important product. Butter, traditionally made by women, made their economic contribution visible. Nancy Grey Osterud's study of Nanticoke Valley farm women showed that men and women shared dairy work, "the least gender marked of any farm or household operation," with mutual give and take. Separate spheres ideology could not easily take hold in an economy where home and work, public and private, were blended. "For most preindustrial and precommercial farm families, the public and private was blurred and indistinct." "Rural women did not occupy a 'separate sphere' during the late nineteenth century," Osterud concluded. Rather, they sought mutuality in marriage, reciprocity in labor, and integration in sociability.[26]

Such mutuality nourished the earliest feminists. Nancy Hewitt, Jensen, and Osterud have urged historians to turn their attention to the links between rural egalitarianism and reform values. Alfred's fervent commitment to reform, which developed in just such a context, supports the work of scholars who have shown rural women were among the first to venture into the public sphere. Still, as Osterud noted, "many historians have failed to recognize rural women's actions as feminist because women did not organize separately from men or proclaim that women's and men's interests were opposed, but rather espoused a vision and practice of gender integration."[27]

Taking issue with numerous historians who posited an urban origin for reform growing out of separate spheres ideology, Nancy Hewitt criticized the "intricate argument" necessary to explain the paradox that "pious, pure, domestic, submissive, and sororal women" were transformed by a complex series of steps into "social, and specifically feminist, activists by 1848." She found a far more direct route—commitment to equal rights arose from egalitarian communities. The most radical reformers, asserting equality between the sexes, were primarily from rural villages: "Knowing from . . . experience that sharp differences in the roles of men and women were not ordained by nature, ultraists increasingly questioned the supposed naturalness of other divisions and distinctions." In the Burned-over District, "no city proved as strong in abolition sentiment as rural areas." Jensen also urged historians to grapple with the activism of rural women, believing they "may provide an important key to understanding the emergence of the women's rights movement. . . . The breeding grounds for early feminism may well have been the back country."[28]

The rural setting prized by Seventh Day Baptists not only provided a foundation for the school's egalitarian spirit and the Allens' vision of equal rights, it also set a model for the later work life of the alumnae. In this region, women's economic contribution was visible, necessary, and respected; it was only a quantitative change, not a qualitative one, to enhance that contribution through education. Whether motivated by personal drive or economic need, a high proportion of alumnae worked, many side by side with their husbands. "Over half of the Alfred alumnae married to classmates worked after marriage, and nearly all worked with their husbands. If we add in farm wives, minister's wives, and the woman who studied law with her husband, the figure goes up to nearly two-thirds." Of five Western New York colleges studied by Kerns, "Alfred's alumnae experienced the most continuity of experience in gender relations," beginning on their childhood farms, amplified during their education, and perpetuated in their adult lives. By contrast, farm families provided only one-third of nearby Elmira Female Colleges students in the years from its 1855 founding to 1861.[29]

Pioneer families were often closely related. Marriages among the younger generation bound these families even more tightly. To some extent, family history and denominational history were shared. These common values inevitably influenced Alfred's character, shaping attitudes toward education, women's education, and relations between men and women. Many contemporary schools assured parents that relations were like a family—in men's schools, of course, a family of fathers and sons. Alfred's family model was based on true kinship, giving the ideal a particularly intense reality.

Chapter Three

Origins
The Select School,
1836–1843

All the students seemed anxious to return.

—Mary Sheldon (Powell), "A Few Reminiscences"

A s increasing numbers of settlers established farms throughout the valleys around Alfred, schools were soon needed. Nancy Teater's first school was established by 1814, if not earlier. By 1825, Alfred had common schools in every settlement. The schoolmistress might be a young girl briefly employed by a cluster of families to teach reading, writing, spelling, and very basic mathematics. Schoolmasters were frequently drawn from a pool of itinerants who taught for a few months, soon moving on or returning to their own schooling. New York, the most progressive state in making improvements to its school system, created town school committees and districts in 1795 legislation and established a statewide system with state aid in 1812. Common schools—created by a community or group of farm families who built the schoolhouse, hired the teacher, and chose the curriculum—multiplied across the state as its population grew, from 2,756 school districts in 1815 to 10,769 in 1843.[1]

By 1835 Alfred's population was 1,903, most living on farms widely scattered around the villages of Alfred Centre (now called Alfred) and Baker's Bridge (now called Alfred Station). Alfred Centre included about a dozen houses, mostly small and unfinished, one store, a blacksmith shop, a cabinet shop, a tannery, and an ashery. The post office was two miles away in Baker's Bridge; mail was brought once a week on horseback. The town surrounding these villages was divided into fifteen school districts (each schoolhouse had to be within walking distance of surrounding homes or farms); 518 young people were enrolled by 1838.

Like many frontier schools, the school that became Alfred University began as a local enterprise; unlike most, it began at student initiative. Amos West Coon, age eighteen, wanted to continue his education. During an 1835 visit to his grandparents in Rensselaer County, he met Bethuel Church, a convert to Seventh Day Baptism, and they became friends. Church was relatively well educated, having studied at Cortland Academy (Homer, New York) and the Oneida Conference Seminary (Cazenovia, New York). Coon suggested Church might come to Alfred to start a "select school," offering advanced education, supported by tuition charges and open to those qualified by prior study in common schools. When Church attended the September 1836 Seventh Day Baptist General Conference, held in Alfred, the two formed plans for Church to return in the winter. Coon promised he would find a location and enlist twenty students at $3 per person.

Community support, critical to the school's development, was immediately available. "Too poor to send their children away to school, and equally determined to give them advantages to obtain a higher education," Alfred's families prepared a schoolroom. Mrs. Orson Sheldon, sister of Dr. John R. Hartshorn (who later taught anatomy and physiology at the Academy, and became a trustee of the Academy and University) and of Charles Hartshorn (teacher at a nearby district school), offered an unfinished upstairs chamber in her house. The chamber was lathed and plastered by townsmen and fitted up for a schoolroom. The "fittings" were modest indeed. "A small blackboard was made and placed on the wall, which was quite an innovation in those days; and each pupil brought his own chair, and held slate and books on his lap until rough boards could be put up for desks." Church did return as promised and found nineteen students ready to pay their tuition. He toured the region, going from "house to house, and from farm to farm" to find additional aspiring scholars.[2]

On a nearby farm, Church found Jonathan Allen, a boy of thirteen. "In the fall of 1836, while chopping with his father and brothers near the home, a gentleman came to the woods. After a pleasant 'good-morning' he said, 'I have come into town to start a select school, and would like to have you send this boy,' designating Jonathan. 'I can't afford it,' said the father. Bethuel Church . . . thought a moment: 'We shall need wood, and I will take that for the tuition.' How the boy's heart bounded when the father said, 'If he will chop it, he can go.'. . . But that evening when parents noted the lack of suitable clothes, again it was felt that the boy must give it up. Argument was not thought of in that New England household, but Jonathan could not press back the tears of disappointment. 'If he feels like that,' said his father, 'he must go.' His mother put his clothes in the best possible repair, and go Jonathan did."[3]

This rustic scene was repeated throughout the village environs and more than the requisite twenty students, with Allen the youngest, arrived at the schoolroom on December 5, 1836, each carrying his or her own chair and cold johnnycake for lunch. The students roomed with the Sheldons and in other village homes, establishing a close community connection that continued for decades. Church introduced "novel" instructional methods, including composition, rhetorical practice, and work at the blackboard, embarrassing those singled out to perform. The cost was $2.50 per quarter for the common branches or $3 for philosophy. By the end of the term, thirty-seven had enrolled; thirty-four from Alfred, two from Little Genesee (twenty miles away), and one from Rhode Island. Twenty-two of the first thirty-seven were young women; nearly all became teachers. Of the young men, four became ministers; four doctors; three high school principals; two teachers; one a justice of the peace; and one, Jonathan Allen, a college president.[4]

The familial, egalitarian character of the school proved a durable trait, persisting in recollections sixty years later: "The select school held in the upper room . . . was attended by about thirty young men and women, who were mainly brothers and sisters of about half that number of families, the sisters being in the majority. From that day to this the sister has not only known upon what intellectual food her brother was nourished but by a never questioned right she has shared his daily fare upon absolutely equal terms, so far as she has chosen to do so. That she has as fully shared his honors is a matter of historical record."[5] Alfred became notable for its vision that the sexes naturally shared an educational mission, reform values, and life work.

Church's term as teacher energized the town's cultural life: in school, church, and private company, he stimulated talk of an academy. "He preached at the church, as well as taught the school, during the winter, and his constant theme was education. His private talks to both old and young were of the needs in this community for a high school or academy."[6] Schoolteacher Charles Hartshorn helped Church set up the Alfred Debating Society, a literary group that met for essays, orations, debating, and reading a handwritten newspaper. This was the ancestor of the four literary societies that dominated students' extracurricular life at the university for eighty years. People came from miles around to hear these sessions, foreshadowing the importance of the school in the region's cultural life. In 1845 women were invited to serve as the jury when women's suffrage was debated. Even that level of participation in a public event was unusual for women of the time.

At the end of the term, Church left, studying for several years at DeRuyter Institute, a Seventh Day Baptist school that opened in the fall of 1837. Later he alternated teaching with preaching, organizing a black church in Texas. John Nelson Norwood described him as restless and a "rover," not unlike many early itinerant teachers. Still, however brief his stay, Church had traits that came to characterize Alfred's faculty: he was a Seventh Day Baptist, a reformer, and an advocate for education.

Although Church had departed, the first term was judged a success, and over the summer a school building was erected. Its impetus came from Maxson Stillman, builder and church chorister. A strong believer in education, he helped plan or construct nearly every building put up at Alfred Academy and University in the nineteenth century, and served as trustee until three years before his death at ninety-eight in 1896.

Stillman had opened a small singing-school in 1835, holding its lessons in the church. Some objected and "the feeling of sacrilege was greatly heightened one evening during an intermission, when a thoughtless young man as to rules of propriety, took the liberty to kiss a young lady in the meeting-house, in the presence of other young people. This act, in a dedicated meeting house, could not be attoned [*sic*], and the school was closed."[7] Stillman soon nailed to the door of Luke Greene's store a call for a meeting of "all persons interested in having a place in which we can hold a singing-school, and for other purposes." Eighteen townspeople met in the evening after church, the store interior dimly lit by one oil lamp. Stillman argued that the young people should learn to sing and, since the church could not be used, a new building was needed for a singing school, select school, and other gatherings. After debate, his motion was approved.

The townspeople pledged more than $600 and a board of trustees was selected for what was already called an "academy." As Sizer noted, for early schools "the trustees' task was to find building, teacher, and students; all were difficult to locate." Construction began on a lot in the village center (donated by another interested townsman, Maxson Greene). The building was about 28 feet by 38 feet, with high arched rooms and a small second-story area used as bell room, office, and principal's sleeping area, surmounted by a belfry. School furniture and "a small set of apparatus" completed the arrangements. Officially called the Cadmus, the little building with its odd cupola was soon dubbed the "Horned Bug."[8]

Halsey H. Baker, who came to Alfred in March 1837 as pastor for a season, was invited to become principal. Already engaged elsewhere, Baker proposed that an acquaintance, James Read Irish, a student at Union College, be invited.[9] David Stillman traveled to Schenectady and notified Maxson Greene that he had engaged Irish:

> I have contracted with James Irish to teach a school for 25 dollars per month, 24 days for a month.
> He must be boarded at one place at our expense and this is the best I think that we could do. He would come for 20 dollars if we would pay his expense there and back and I think that we had better have the amount in the start.
> The school to commence the first Monday in December.[10]

James Irish was born in North Stonington, Connecticut, on December 18, 1811. As a boy he worked summers, attended school each winter for three or four months, and at seventeen began teaching at nine dollars a month, "sometimes taking a few weeks before opening my schools to brush up, at some country academy or select school, and thus to add a little to my scanty stock of learning."[11] In 1834 he went to Phillips Academy to prepare for the ministry, working for his tuition and eating at a boarding club for 75 to 90 cents a week.

At that time, Seventh Day Baptists had neither academy nor college; those who sought higher education were vulnerable to the draw of other faiths. Irish received much-appreciated financial support from Phillips Academy when none was forthcoming from his own denomination: "This aid might have proved a snare to me, especially as I was receiving so little sympathy from my own people, had it not been for the agitation of the slavery question." Irish was strongly antislavery and left Phillips after leading a student protest against the school's policy opposing expression of antislavery views. "The trustees and the faculty of the institution undertook, as I thought, a course which crushed out the manhood of the students, as really as American slavery had done in the poor African. I demurred, and withdrew from the school, having, with my own hand, drawn up the resolution on the subject which was subsequently discussed and subscribed to by fifty other young men, asking also for their dismissal from the academy."[12]

"Wearing a homespun suit, boarding himself and working," still obliged to practice the strictest economy, in 1836 Irish entered Union College (founded in 1795). There he roomed with another impoverished young man who had struggled to prepare himself for college, William C. Kenyon. Irish was a twenty-six-year-old sophomore when the teaching offer came from Alfred. "Called away by poverty and then by the pressure of accumulating duties," Irish could return to Union for only one more term and completed his studies on his own, receiving the M.A. in 1848.[13]

Irish's religious fervor and antislavery views were congenial to his new employers. Pioneering in an isolated region, Alfred's families were nevertheless on the fringes of New York's Burned-over District, which stirred with religious excitement. The Great Revival, which swept across New England and then into New York, culminated with the conversions produced by Charles Grandison Finney in his campaigns of 1826 and 1831. For six months of 1831, Finney preached every night and three times on Sunday in Rochester; church membership doubled. His revival techniques were much admired; a crowd of young converts, nicknamed the "Holy Band," spread his influence and the new creed. "Within a few years free agency, perfectionism, and millennialism were middle-class orthodoxy."[14]

The Burned-over District, so called because revivalist spiritual fires scorched the entire area, was located in upstate New York. With the fires came a multitude of benevolent activities and a "regional ethos that encouraged radical religious and social experimentation, which contemporaries called 'ultraism.'" Calvinism faded as new religious sects such as Mormonism, the apocalyptic vision of William Miller, Seventh Day Adventism, and Shaker colonies sprang up; communal societies, manual labor institutions, and utopian experiments commenced. This turbulent period gave birth to the moral crusades of antislavery and temperance.

The Finney converts, Theodore Weld (who married Angelina Grimké) and his friend Henry Stanton (husband of Elizabeth Cady), were two upstate New Yorkers who early linked revivalism with abolition. Their wives linked both to women's rights.[15]

Alfred's students were vigorously interested in these movements. While maintaining staunch adherence to Seventh Day Baptism, religious enthusiasm was high, revivals flourished, and social reform was embraced: temperance, antislavery, and soon the issue of women's rights were of continuing interest to faculty and students. "Seventh-day Baptists have always been in the front rank as Reformers in political, social, moral, and religious movements," wrote one denominational historian. "Independence in thought and action is an essential element in their existence. While this sometimes gives excessive individualism, it also gives radical tendencies and fixed purposes, which are indispensable in all reformatory movements." Both men and women were expected to work toward a more perfect world. "At the 1850 anniversary dinner a local minister gave the following (non-alcoholic) toast: to the "Ladies of our Literary Institutions—May they ever spurn the rule of fashion, and be true and zealous reformers."[16]

Antislavery feelings developed early among Seventh Day Baptists. At the 1836 Seventh Day Baptist General Conference, held in Alfred, delegates adopted the following resolutions:

> 1. *Resolved,* That we consider the practice of holding human beings as mere goods and chattels . . . is a practice forbidden by the law of God, at variance with the Gospel of Jesus Christ, which no human legislation can render morally right—which no worldly considerations can justify—and which ought to be immediately abandoned.
>
> 2. *Resolved,* That the condition of more than two millions of native Americans, unrighteously held in such bondage, demands the sympathies and prayers of citizens, who are commanded to "remember them that are in bonds, as bound with them."[17]

Opposition was firm, but the remedies offered in 1836 were sympathy and prayer, in keeping with contemporary belief in the power of moral suasion to induce change. Many remained reluctant to speak out, for mob violence was frequently the response. Antislavery speakers were stoned in Boston, and in 1837 Elijah Lovejoy was murdered defending his press in Illinois. At the 1843 General Conference, the delegates reiterated their 1836 resolutions and added another, declaring slavery a sin and urging that all Seventh Day Baptists immediately abandon slave-holding.[18]

It was always easier to generate opposition to slavery among persons with no direct economic interest in the practice, and northern distaste grew as its slave-holding declined. With New England origins and mostly northern habitats, few Seventh Day Baptists owned slaves; their antislavery stand did not affect coreligionists. Eventually the issue of slave holding tore apart the larger Baptist, Methodist, and Presbyterian churches as they split along sectional lines in the decades preceding the Civil War.

The student dispute with Phillips Academy led by James Irish was far from unique; several colleges and seminaries expelled students with abolitionist beliefs. Nearby Madison University (later Colgate University) expelled a freshman for publishing an antislavery paper. At Western Reserve College, Amherst, Hamilton, Hanover, Marietta, and Denison, antislavery societies were shut down and abolitionist faculty dismissed. Into the 1850s faculty were dismissed from Harvard, Yale, and Michigan for similar offenses.[19]

A few schools did support antislavery or abolitionist sentiment.[20] The Oneida Institute spawned several, including Olivet, Knox, and Oberlin, which became famous as an abolitionist college and town (after the influx of the "Lane rebels" led by Theodore Weld when Oberlin officials were desperate for funds for the faltering new enterprise).[21] From its first days, Alfred's students and faculty were committed to the antislavery movement and some were abolitionists. Yet only at Alfred did reformers extend the egalitarian vision to develop radical views on women's rights.

When James Irish reached Alfred in late November 1837, he found "the shavings and the mortar were still in the new building, and men were at work putting up temporary seats." School opened on the first Monday in December with dedication of the new building. "The whole town assembled to meet him outside, and inside such a roomful of eager and expectant pupils as he had never before seen its like." Eight of the first term's students returned, and new ones came as well, including fifteen men and twenty-one women. The townspeople "threw open their doors, and gave up every available space to the incomers, and when the houses were full to overflowing, rooms in wood sheds and even barns were fitted up and occupied."[22]

Wishing to provide academy-level instruction, the trustees established a more advanced curriculum, adding natural philosophy, astronomy, Latin, and Greek. Irish acknowledged later that he was poorly prepared for his new responsibilities: "I had not yet completed the Sophomore Year at Union College, and felt the awkwardness of my situation, as study after study, to which I was a stranger, was set down in the programme." He prepared enough each evening to guide his pupils' recitations but found his mind became a sieve, in which "very little or nothing was retained, while it transmitted knowledge to others."[23]

Finding "in most of the studies I was able to keep well ahead of my classes," Irish taught sixteen classes daily, gave occasional evening talks on intellectual and moral issues, and held a weekly review for parents. He also preached on occasional Sabbaths, as the church had no regular pastor. At the end of the four-month term, public examinations were held. "Many of the young people went beyond all faith they had in their own powers; and, though the addresses were not Ciceronian, nor the colloquies Shakespearean, they were such as met the approval of the best-informed of the patrons, and were the wonder of the crowded house."[24]

Irish proved to be a popular teacher with a genial unpretentious nature and an earnest preacher. Student initiative had started the school; now the students formed a group to demand his return. "Pending negotiations for my return to teach the following year, and fearing a disagreement between the trustees and myself, the young people organized and marched *en masse* to the office of the trustees, and insisted on my re-engagement." He went back to college in the spring of 1838, trying to catch up but finding he was far behind in his classes. His work was further interrupted by his roommate's falling ill with smallpox, his missing Friday night lyceums and Saturday lessons each week because of Sabbath observance, and then his deep involvement in a revival sweeping Union. "I was specially requested by Dr. Nott, the President of the College, to converse and pray with the inquiring students, and to assist in their religious meetings" by providing religious instruction.[25]

Returning to Alfred in August, Irish taught a sparsely attended session, averaging less than thirty students, since the harvest was not yet gathered and young people were needed on the farms. Fresh from Union's revival, he prayed over the unconverted or indifferent. After Christmas, winter term opened with seventy-two students. Interest in religion exploded in the winter of 1838–1839, as an extensive revival broke out, centered on the young people at Irish's school. "New-born souls almost daily reinforced the happy company" and 206 new members were added to the First Alfred Church alone. Irish helped conduct local revival meetings, "held every evening somewhere in the society, and on the Seventh and First-days at the church. That was especially a praying revival. The forests were vocal with prayer. Family altars were erected [for worship in the home], social visits were largely seasons of prayer." On one memorable day, forty persons were baptized in a millpond below the village. It was so cold that thick ice had to be broken through for immersion of new members, as the audience stood in a circle on the ice.[26]

Irish's revival work led to the community prevailing upon him to become their first permanent pastor and, concluding that this step was consistent with divine will, Irish was ordained April 3, 1839, serving as pastor of the Alfred Seventh Day Baptist Church until 1845. Irish's Union College roommate, William C. Kenyon, observed the ceremony: "This day, Brother Irish, according to previous appointment, was, after examination, ordained the gospel ministry, in the presence of a crowded audience. . . . He is now the Rev. J. R. Irish. The Church over which he has been set numbers between five and six hundred."[27]

But Kenyon was there for another purpose. Irish's ordination meant a new teacher must be found, and Irish suggested that his roommate be appointed. Like Stillman before him, George Coon (father of Amos Coon, who had initiated the select school) visited Schenectady to make final arrangements, and Kenyon arrived on March 30, 1839, the last day of winter term.

Fig. 3.1. William C. Kenyon in 1839, his first year as Select School teacher.

Traveling into this rather remote region was still difficult when Kenyon made his trip to Alfred: to Utica by rail; to Syracuse by stage, traveling the fifty miles in eighteen miserable hours, often stuck in the mud, breaking down twice; to Auburn by rail; thence to Geneva and Bath by stage, arriving at midnight "after a long and comfortable shaking"; from Bath to Alfred (thirty miles) on foot, "over hill and down dale, through mud and snow, seeing for the first half of the distance, nothing but a wilderness and log houses." He arrived in time to view end-of-term exercises and meet the students.[28]

Mary A. Sheldon long remembered that day. She was thirteen and still in a common school when her teacher said, "There is to be an exhibition at the Corners in Alfred Academy tomorrow; I wish some of you could attend." Mary walked four miles to view the school's final exercises and watched while "James R. Irish, the pleasant-voiced teacher, called the names of the eldest and more advanced students, who came forward and spoke from the platform, either original or otherwise. The younger ones read their compositions standing by their seats. I well remember Clark Burdick read a composition, subject, 'spring.' He said it was pleasant to see the squirrels skipping from branch to branch upon the trees and to breathe the pure air and to see the flowers; and pleasant sunshine and to him it was the most pleasant season."[29]

Irish bade his students goodbye and introduced his friend, who had just arrived after trudging through the snow. Kenyon's first words excited the students.

> [Kenyon] arose and with a quick impulsive movement, addressed the students upon the advantages of education, preparatory to meeting the great responsibilities of life. He said he did not know that he could fill the place of their beloved teacher, but with God's help, he would do the best he could. His words were a magnetic inspiration. All the students seemed anxious to return at the end of a three weeks' vacation. I too wished to be one of them.
>
> My parents had six children to care for, how could they let me go? Finally my mother said she thought she could spare enough butter to pay my $1.50 tuition for thirteen weeks and my father thought he could sell enough grain to pay my other expenses. So at the end of three weeks my father drove to the door, loaded in feather bed, bedding, a chair and a box of provisions. Arriving at the Academy and supposing I could find a place almost anywhere, I found every room was more than filled. Uncle Amos Burdick came along and said to my father, "Go home with me to dinner and perhaps ma will take your little girl." She did, and when I went in said: "You are to be my little girl this term are you?" To me she was a true mother for the year, at the close of which I had engaged to teach a district school three months at 75 cents per week and board. At the end of that time I was engaged to teach a month longer at $1.00 per week, for which I was the proud possessor of $13. My father

needed $10 of it to pay taxes, leaving me with $3.00, and never afterwards when receiving $1.00 per day was I better satisfied.[30]

Like other young women who flocked to Alfred, Mary was eager to learn and eager to study. Although financial support was limited, she had her family's emotional support to attend, but needed to earn her own way. She began teaching at fourteen and, continuing to alternate study with teaching, graduated in 1849. Another early student, Cordelia Hartshorn, wrote in 1837 of her "burning desire to continue her education" but feared her hopes would be disappointed because her parents were moving away from Alfred. To Cordelia's delight, her parents sent her and her sister Minerva to Alfred from 1838 to 1840. In later years, her son remembered how she often paged through her album, "living over again the two years of intellectual and spiritual bloom. She told of the wonderful revival and her baptism in the dead of winter" and spoke fondly of "the most congenial friends she had ever known." These characteristics— a deep drive to become educated, family support for their ambitious daughters working their way through school, economic independence— came to typify the female students.[31]

Alfred's archives are replete with accounts of the poverty of its founders, faculty, and students. James Irish, William Kenyon, Jonathan Allen, Abigail Maxson, and Boothe Davis struggled to earn their way through school, then accepted very low salaries to reduce costs for the young people who followed them. "Tuition was placed very low that no hungry mind might go unfed"; as late as 1914, Alfred's $60 tuition and fees were reported as lowest in the state. Low cost became an ideology, spoken of as a Christian ideal. In Jonathan Allen's description, Alfred "has ever been the school of the poor. Not many sons and daughters of the rich have entered its portals. Beginning its mission in a small upper room or chamber, it has ever since been able to give a proof of its divine work similar to that given by Christ of the divinity of his mission. . . . May it ever continue thus."[32]

Kenyon's remarkable energy drove him up from poverty, and that energy was an inspiration to his students. Jonathan Allen (who like Kenyon taught to earn money for college and in 1867 succeeded Kenyon as president of Alfred) also vividly remembered Kenyon's first words that wintry day in 1839: "One of those slender, compact, nervous, magnetic men— a man very earnest, very incisive, somewhat radical, even eccentric, if you please, yet very genuine—the first sight of him, on his arrival here to take charge of the school, stirred one young life to the core. The first address that we heard him deliver roused and thrilled us as no other, and we worked for days in a dream; and his teaching was suggestive, electric, inspiring. We students in those early days, in our little gatherings, voted him, save in a few points, the greatest man living. His whole being appeared to our youthful eyes condensed, intensified, spiritual energy, with strange fascinating power."[33]

For his part, Kenyon had a very favorable impression of the young scholars assembled that day. "I was just in time to attend the examinations. The school assembled at 9 o'clock. I was escorted into the room and introduced to the school in due order by its Principal [his friend Irish]. It was composed of girls and boys, or rather young ladies and gentlemen, about forty in number. I surveyed them very closely, I can assure you, and discovered many intelligent countenances. The examinations occupied the entire day. I was pleased by the promptness manifested by the pupils in answering questions. . . . I was led to form an exalted idea of their attainments."[34] He married one of those students, Melissa Ward, a year and a half later.

Like Irish, Kenyon found it taxing to teach so many subjects: "My school will commence the first day of May. Eleven weeks constitute a term, and four terms a year. I do not expect it will be very large this summer, likely about thirty scholars. I have an arduous work before me. I shall have to teach Geography, Grammar, Arithmetic, Algebra, Surveying, Bookkeeping, Natural Philosophy, Chemistry, Botany, Astronomy, Zoology, Geology, Mental and Moral Philosophy, besides Latin, Greek, etc., etc., and preparing and delivering a course of lectures on Chemistry and Natural Philosophy, accompanied with experiments, in the course of next Fall and Winter Terms. Judge now of the leisure I shall have."[35]

Although the school was already described locally as the "academy" during Irish's two years, it was Kenyon who is regarded as the founder of Alfred Academy and then Alfred University. Arriving in 1839 at the age of twenty-seven, he remained until his death in 1867. By 1839, Kenyon had achieved recognition among Seventh Day Baptists as an educational leader. He received financial support from the denomination for his studies in 1837, and in 1838 was asked to join its Committee on Education, where he argued that a higher level of education should be available to Seventh Day Baptists.

Kenyon's passionate advocacy of education for both sexes developed early. When still a student at Union, he wrote in his diary, "It is worthy of a true and noble ambition to build seminaries and colleges, and fill them with young men and women who, properly trained, might go forth to exert an influence as lasting as time." He brought with him, as did all Alfred's early teachers, a high purpose, antislavery beliefs, a reformer's spirit, and strong commitment to education. Remembered by all for his insistence that any person could achieve any purpose, Kenyon urged his students to "do something," to make something of themselves. "He made all students feel that they were placed in this world for the express purpose of doing something, and that they were in school expressly to get a good ready [*sic*] to do this something." He urged active work in the world for both men and women, and encouraged both to enter reform movements.[36]

A slender, highly strung man, "active and uneasy when not strenuously engaged in his calling," Kenyon was keenly intelligent, with a very strong will, quick-tempered, and often impatient. He quickly became known as "Boss" Kenyon for his innate drive to direct. It is reported that a "rough farmer" said of Kenyon, "as a boy, he never took hold of a job that he did not *boss* before it was through." He was praised for his executive ability. A pragmatic taskmaster and drillmaster ("since training the mind to think was the chief goal, drill was used above all other means for reaching that goal" by many teachers), his scholarship was viewed by some as inferior. Not a deep thinker, not a broad scholar, he was yet a remarkable teacher.[37]

Kenyon was born in Rhode Island in 1812, "in poverty, of almost unknown parentage"; even his family name is uncertain.[38] At five years old, he was indentured to a guardian and experienced many bitter years. He was "hired out" summers to work on neighboring farms and worked through the winter, getting very little schooling, showing little aptitude for study and little pleasure in life. At thirteen, a kindly teacher came into his life, changing its course. A schoolmate remembered:

> Our winter's school was opened by a teacher who had enjoyed the advantages of an academic education. He had the reputation of being a fine scholar, and having promising abilities for teaching. *Kindness* was his power. Among some forty others, there came one, a child of misfortune, who had received many more curses and kicks than smiles and kisses. He was a boy of some thirteen summers, his form slender, slightly clothed, and his countenance care worn. He had been a member of our school, a part of the time, the two past winters, but no one had ever made him a companion, or thought of doing so. He appeared melancholy and heart-stricken; said little to any one. . . . Books had no charm for him. He could only read the easiest lessons; and as to spelling, he was often known to fail in getting a single letter to a word that belonged to it. . . . Without looking at the teacher, or any one else, he glided noiselessly to the remotest corner, and sat down in a place partly concealed from observation by the desks of the writing benches. When the teacher, in his talks with the scholars individually, finally reached him, he placed his hand lightly upon his head, and looking him fully in the face, spoke to him in words full of kindness and sympathy. He had never known his teacher to speak kindly to him before, and had never heard any one do so. . . . His face lighted up with a smile, and his eyes beamed with a sudden gleam of intelligence. After a moment's consideration, the boy was told, among other things to be done, that he must study arithmetic, and to be prepared next morning with arithmetic and slate. . . . Somehow, the example set by the teacher seemed to be contagious. All began to look upon him as one of the school. Something seemed to gladden him, and chase away his usual sadness; but the next morning he came with his accustomed appearance, and when asked by the teacher for his arithmetic and slate—"Hav'nt got any," was his response, "our folks say I shan't have any, that I must learn to read first." "Doubtless your folks will allow me to be judge of what you must do while attending school," replied the teacher; "but if they will not provide the necessary books, I

hardly know what we can do." At this, one of the scholars, feeling an interest in the effort made for him, said, "I have a small slate that I will lend him, if some one will let him have an arithmetic." The teacher said, "I will furnish the arithmetic." That day he commenced "cyphering." Before the winter closed, he proved to be the best arithmetician in the school, was a very good reader, and a tolerable speller. We next met him in college. He was a member of the Senior Class—a superior mathematician, and no mean linguist.[39]

This was the genesis of Kenyon's passionate commitment to what he called "the Power of Education," echoing such earlier advocates as Thomas Jefferson, Benjamin Rush, and Noah Webster, who urged a system of free schools that would create a "moral, intelligent, and unified citizenry." Kenyon and Irish both studied for the ministry, but Irish chose to spend his life in the ministry while Kenyon took another path. As many were converts to religious purposes in those days, Kenyon became a convert to the cause of education. "He used to admit that slavery was powerful, and he hated it, but he thought that the despotism of ignorance was worse, if possible. He regarded education as one of the great national interests. The welfare of the public is linked in with it, the safety and perpetuity of the nation depends upon it. His theory of education included three things: letters, liberty, and religion." In this trinity, religion was subsumed under education. At other colleges, education was subsumed under religious purposes.[40]

The warm influence of his teacher was reinforced by Kenyon's good fortune in joining the "refining and elevating" households of Deacons Daniel Lewis and John Langworthy in Hopkinton, Rhode Island, for the next three winters while attending school. Carrying a book as he went about his farm chores, he seized moments to read, and was always glad to be asked to build the morning fire, for it meant good light and brief quiet for reading. At nineteen he exchanged his indentured status for a promissory note to his guardian and went to work in a machine shop, trying to prepare for college at the same time. "He did much of his studying in the shop, learning his lessons while working with the lathe and file." A friend remembered him reciting "bonus, bona, bonum" as he stood at the workbench. "He entered Union College in the summer of 1836, having gone over only about half of the studies usually required for entering. Owing to this circumstance, he had to work very hard in order to keep up with his classes, standing, at first, 'medium,' rising soon to 'max' in mathematics, and 'good' in languages."[41]

Even after entering Union, Kenyon had to interrupt his studies to earn money as machinist or common school teacher. Dr. Eliphalet Nott, President of Union from 1804 to 1866, "cheered him on" and tried to obtain aid for Kenyon from the American Education Society but that Congregational society refused to help a Seventh Day Baptist. Kenyon did get help from the American Seventh-Day Baptist Education Society, a short-lived organization that began in 1835 to support young men studying for the ministry. In 1837, Kenyon and Bethuel Church each received forty dollars (the maximum authorized), but the society's aid was very limited. Only four young men were assisted and all support ceased in 1838.[42]

President Nott tried to help Kenyon in another way, for Kenyon worked as a machinist in the Novelty Iron Works, owned by Nott's sons and producing Nott-invented stoves and ship boilers. Kenyon was deeply grateful and praised Nott's nonsectarianism in helping a Seventh Day Baptist. Nevertheless Kenyon expressed his "utter aversion to dependence on any one for the supplying of temporal wants," and it is no surprise that he left Union for Alfred in 1839, his junior year. Continuing to study while teaching, Kenyon received his Union degree in 1844.[43]

Kenyon's expectations were high, his methods demanding. Neither his rhetoric nor his vision distinguished between men and women. Although Union's famous president took him under his wing, Kenyon clearly did not share Nott's view that educating men and women together would endanger "alike their virtue and happiness." Nott's dependent and shrinking women had nothing in common with Kenyon's view of the ideal woman. Kenyon's women were like Nott's men: decisive, self-reliant, independent, and brave.

Both men and women were driven hard by Kenyon; his "Theory of Thorough" was well-known to all. "How he used to scorn a sham!" remembered Professor Darius Ford. "He was always urgent to go to the bottom of things and taught his pupils to love the rugged labor of being thorough and accurate." Judge Nathaniel M. Hubbard remembered, "He was merciless to a blockhead, but all gentleness and encouragement to a student who had capacity and industry."[44]

Kenyon's own sufferings from poverty, the early loss of his family, and his subsequent loneliness were reflected in his veneration of the "self-made" man. "Everyone is the son of his own work," he reiterated. The virtue of hard work became a dogma to him, one not always tempered by kindliness; at times he forgot that he himself did not thrive, or become "self-made," until a thoughtful teacher went out of his way. Daily chapel lectures were a forum for repeatedly driving home his hard-learned lessons: "Whatever you try, go through with it." And "Be something." Edward Tomlinson (faculty member and graduate of Bucknell, Frederick William University in Berlin, and the University of Leipzig) remembered, "Patience, attention to little details and a stout heart under poverty and discouragement, was the silver thread running through his Theory of Thorough."[45]

Self-sacrifice was also a cardinal virtue to Kenyon. He preached it and he exemplified it. "Duty first, pleasure afterwards" was his maxim. If Kenyon wished to be memorialized for self-sacrifice, he was granted that wish. Borrowing money personally to fund the beginnings of a campus; proposing the "Compact" of subsistence salaries for years to build toward a college; lending money or food to impoverished students—he did without to build the school. The legend grew that he died in service to the school—he "died before his natural time through over-work" for Alfred's welfare, said one; "William C. Kenyon lived, toiled—O how incessantly, how unselfishly he toiled—and *died* for the cause of education in Western New York," said another.[46]

As in the state-sponsored normal schools that soon spread across the country, modest tuition charges and even personal loans from the principals eased the way for low-income students. Kenyon was always generous with the school's resources, and his own, to students who struggled to educate themselves. "Many of the young men and the young women who attended school at Alfred Academy in its earlier years, were so poor that their studies must frequently be interrupted to secure means to continue. It would often happen that Prof. Kenyon would say to one and another promising youth—'Go on; and when you have completed your course of study, earn money and pay up your indebtedness.'. . . He used laughingly to say that the young ladies paid up these pledges for assistance, more promptly than the young men; and altho it is true that several thousand dollars of these obligations were never paid; and Prof. Kenyon was largely the loser, yet this seemed to make not the slightest difference to his benevolence toward others."[47]

Alfred lent money, offered work, and held its costs down, so that students without means could attend:

> From the first it was a non-sectarian school. All denominations were welcome and made to feel at home. It was the poor boy's and the poor girl's university. The pupils came from the farms and villages throughout Allegany and adjoining counties. Many of them walked to Alfred for it was eight years after the academy was organized before the New York & Erie railroad grade was made through the hills of Allegany county. Many of the boys worked on the farm in summer and spent the money earned in paying their way through the university during the winter months.
>
> The teachers in this pioneer University were true to their trust and accepted gladly the scanty salaries that the University could afford to pay.[48]

One story was often repeated: "A young man in New England wrote to Professor Kenyon, asking if there were any way at Alfred by which a boy not afraid of hard work, fired with an ambition for an education, but almost penniless, could take a course of study. Professor Kenyon replied by return mail: 'Come on, young man. There is room here for lots of just such boys as you.' He came and worked his way through the entire course. That young man was Darwin E. Maxson," who became an assistant teacher in 1847 and joined the faculty in 1849.[49]

All who knew Kenyon agreed that his temper was at best uneven—and at worst, unforgivable. "His fiery temper, at times ungoverned and seemingly ungovernable . . . Though the thunderstorm of his wrath and indignation sometimes blasted and destroyed, it more often cleared the mental atmosphere of the young and enabled them to see the path of duty and honor. His readiness to make amends when he had been unjust or too severe, went far toward counteracting all unpleasant consequences and even all unpleasant feelings toward him." Not all, however. His temper and impetuous remarks probably contributed to a coolness that grew up between Kenyon and his colleagues, and between him and University trustees at a later date. "Overleaping the mere prudential values," Kenyon was also accused of financial extravagance, even recklessness, in his readiness to assume obligations for the school with no clear means of repayment. "He was a man of large plans." Accused of lack of prudence, yes, but never lack of enthusiasm.[50]

This driven, demanding, magnetic, impatient, forgiving—and often forgiven—visionary "began at once to call in students. He gave lectures about the county on the subject of education. . . . Wherever he went there was an educational revival. With his profound convictions, ardent nature and unbounded 'genius for hard work,' it could not have been otherwise. He visited families for similar purposes and with similar results. Students came to the academy, came fired with noble ambitions . . . In some cases the boys and girls were sorely needed at home to help develop the farm and support the family."[51]

His urgent proselytizing quickly increased demand for education in the region. His flock of scholars grew from 85 in 1839 to 145 in 1840; it was time to add a second teacher—his wife. Melissa Bloomfield Ward, born in Schenectady on October 13, 1823, had become a student at the select school in 1839, one of those "intelligent countenances" Kenyon surveyed when he was introduced to the school. On August 5, 1840, she and Kenyon were married. "Thenceforward," said one student, "her life was inseparably interwoven with the life of the Institution. . . . As a teacher, she was sincere, frank, and cordial, inspiring enthusiasm and a generous emulation. Quick to appreciate effort and good intention, slow to give over the dull, she was ever the friend and helper of diffident, uncultured, but earnest seekers after knowledge."[52]

In 1840, the seventeen-year-old Melissa Ward Kenyon was appointed assistant teacher in the English department. The first woman to be added to the staff, she was one of the most important influences in the school's early years. Revered for her maternal qualities, she became known as "Mother Kenyon," spending many days and nights at the bedside of sick students. "Always befriending the unfortunate, nursing the sick, and consoling the afflicted . . . Together with her husband, for weeks at a time she nearly starved in order to lend money or anything that she had to some student earnestly desiring an education." One student recalled, "Mrs. Kenyon is notable chiefly for her heart power. She was not a scholar, and did not impress herself upon the intellectual life of the school; but she was a mother to all students, and *mother* she was reverently called. The poor, the lonely, the sick, the sorrowing, always found in her a tender and sympathetic friend."[53]

Fig. 3.2. Melissa Ward Kenyon, wife of William C. Kenyon. Late 1850s.

The Kenyons, like the Allens after them, both taught at the school. From 1840 until 1892, these two marriages exemplified mutual respect, shared work, and the intertwined lives of president with wife, teacher with teacher. If Melissa Kenyon did not impress herself upon the intellectual life of the school, teaching as she did at the elementary level, women would soon be added to the faculty who did leave such an impress, women who were intellectual models as well as "mothers": Caroline Maxson and Abigail A. Maxson (no relation to each other).

A vision of men and women studying together as sister and brother already permeated the young school. That vision was expressed in its earliest days by a valedictory address delivered about 1840, which Jonathan Allen, and perhaps Abigail A. Maxson, would have attended. Almost thirty-five years later, when Abigail A. Maxson Allen described the family model of coeducation, she used the same image as this early speaker:

> Schoolmates! . . . We have been reared in the same community, aye, even some of us have been nourished under the same roof, as brothers and sisters. Oh! how sacred the ties which bind us together now as one: if not one in mind: one in purpose. . . .
>
> By associations we are brothers and sisters although a common blood circulates not in our veins yet be it well known that oftimes varied scenes bind us closer then the ties of consanguinity. . . . Here are born the noblest asperations of the young mind: here "the young idea" first finds that there is a world beyond the visable horison [sic].

The speaker then expressed the high purpose to which these young people had been taught to aspire:

> When the time comes for you to leave school let not your desire for learning be in the least abated: grasp every thing fit for your consideration, overcome every obstacle, mount to the summit of your profession: be no mean aspirant for distinction, be energetic, be manly, be conscientiously defiant in the face of the world . . . Never let obstacles overcome your philanthropic labors. . . . the world is calling for true men and women.[54]

In addition to shared aspirations for men and women, other factors helped form a liberal environment. The Kenyons' marriage set a model for the student body: both husband and wife worked as teachers and both influenced their students' lives and expectations. A woman of impressive intellect, Caroline Maxson, joined the faculty in 1842. Commitment to the reform movements of antislavery and temperance was strong. Although faculty and students were chiefly from one denomination, the school was not evangelical in purpose: its mission would not be training of ministers, an exclusively male profession. In fact, Kenyon's belief in the value of education would set its purpose—training of teachers, an occupation that uniquely opened opportunities for women.

The next step was not far off. In 1846, Abigail Maxson joined the faculty and in 1849 Jonathan Allen did the same. Their marriage brought explicit advocacy for women's rights and the Enlightenment values of natural rights. Under their influence, a notably supportive environment became a unique environment.

Chapter Four

Alfred Academy
Educational Reform

I am more anxious to have a move made for a College as soon as practicable. . . . On this object I am bent; for it my life is pledged.

—William Kenyon to Jonathan Allen, May 1849

O nly five years after its first class, the nascent school's mission was defined as teacher education. Traveling among local common schools, Kenyon saw a real need to improve the quality of teacher training. Such a mission was best adapted to providing opportunities for women (as teaching was being redefined to a profession admirably suited for women) and that mission predominated even after Alfred was chosen to provide theological instruction for the Seventh Day Baptist denomination.

In 1841, New York began a series of educational reforms, becoming the first state to provide a system for training common school teachers, improving standards, increasing pay, and creating county-level supervision of schools. Kenyon was appointed Superintendent of Common Schools for Allegany County's Southern District that year and asked James Irish to return to teaching with the assistance of Olive B. Forbes and Asa C. Burdick, so Kenyon could spend several months visiting the county's common schools. His excitement and energy were soon felt by many. "The stir and rush and enthusiasm attending his visits to the schools made a powerful impression and many of the teachers with others followed him to Alfred to place themselves for a longer time under his instruction and inspiration."[1]

Kenyon returned convinced he could do the greatest good by focusing on improved teacher training, a much needed reform; instructional methods, particularly at the elementary level, ranged from haphazard to horrific. "The pioneer teachers were many of them very ingenious in the contrivance of original modes of punishment, which from their novelty and their untried terrors were a by no means inoperative agency in maintaining the authority which was regarded as so essential to the well-being of the school." Teachers were untrained, poorly paid, transient, occasionally dissolute. "Sometimes, so uncertain and unreliable were they, three or four changes would occur in a single year, the first going away and giving place to another and he, in turn, making a place for a new comer." Memorization was the pedagogy and beatings induced cooperation; given the conditions, terms were mercifully short.[2]

New York's Superintendent of Common Schools reported in 1843, "some district schools had not been inspected in twenty years and that some local communities had certified teachers who could not even add. Some teachers, he said, were not only ignorant but intemperate." Benches were log slabs, desks rare, textbooks few, blackboards unknown, "and the entire stock of apparatus consisted of a half-dozen well-seasoned switches, and a substantial ruler, and no opportunity was neglected to make use of these appliances for the general advancement of the causes of education and good manners." In her campaign to improve educational conditions, Catharine Beecher cited "unhung doors, broken sashes, absent panes, stilted benches, yawning roofs, and muddy, moldering floors," as well as "low, vulgar, obscene, intemperate, and utterly incompetent" teachers. As a result, "thousands of the young . . . contract a durable horror for books."[3]

Kenyon's own experience in school was sorry enough, yet it was reinforced by his roommate's tales of terror. When James Irish was three, he accompanied an older sister and brother to school. The whole class was put to work braiding straw for hats:

> All passed off tolerably well with me, until the "school-ma'am" found it in her heart to assume the authority to flagellate a little urchin, in whose safety I was interested. When she could not otherwise bring him to terms she shut him in a box, by the mental picture of which I now compare it to a tea-chest. Here for a long time he bawled lustily, but finally subsided by fainter and fainter ones, until all was still. Filled with anxiety I seized the first moment when all eyes were turned to their braiding, and slipped down from the high bench on which I was perched and stealthily raised the cover, and saw my friend curled up in the bottom of the box and great drops of sweat rolling from his face. . . . but a sharp yelp called my attention to a flash of wrath darting from a pair of black eyes, which palsied my hand so that the cover dropped, and I returned, mounting as fast as possible to the bench from which I had gone on my errand. Whether my meddling saved Dr. Paul Clarke to the world, and freed the teacher from the charge of suffocating her pupil, I have, in later years, had but little doubt. . . . I deemed caution the better part of valor; and as soon as all eyes were again turned from me I slid along on my bench to the door, dropped on all fours, moved backwards, keeping my eyes on the presiding genius of the room, until the door-post hid her from my sight, and then ran for home. Thus ended my schooling at that place.[4]

Clearly Beecher did not have this schoolmistress in mind when she argued that women's gentle, loving natures made them the best teachers.

Women began to flow into teaching in the early nineteenth century as men moved into more remunerative employment. By replacing male teachers with females who had some teacher education, school districts were able to correct the evils of poor training, occasional dissolution, and brutality (in most cases), while continuing low pay. Teaching served women well: it gave them the cash to attend schools such as Alfred and then gave them a profession after graduation. One Alfred student remembered that a large proportion of students paid their own way and perhaps half supported themselves by teaching. As Joan Jensen asserted, "the new prescription to teach the children of others provided the rationale for a new public place for young single women . . . and provided an important link to the feminist movement that emerged in the 1840s." Alfred's young women were proud of their ability to earn money, live an independent life, and contribute to their family's maintenance.[5]

As Alfred became noted for training teachers, the number of students grew and better-educated teachers with improved methods were furnished to the area. New textbooks were adopted, including Kenyon's *Grammar*, "which contained an excellent system of analysis . . . all of which combined to give our schools an impetus heretofore unknown. Compensation of teachers advanced from $12 to $18 per month for gentlemen and from $1 to $3 per week for ladies, and board with the scholars. New schoolhouses were built, the dunce block was exchanged for blackboards, and the fools' cap gave place to chalk and maps."[6]

Kenyon's students were convinced they were preparing for a noble, inspiring vocation, "one of the most important occupations within the round of the varied vocations of man." For a number of years, Alfred sent out more teachers (and better prepared ones, according to state reports) than any similar institution in the state. In 1841, attendance reached 171; that summer, a two-story building was added, at a cost of about $2,500, providing chapel, classrooms, and student rooms. By 1844, Academy officials boasted that 150 teachers had been provided in each of the last two years. Not only were many women prepared for a teaching career, they comprised nearly half Alfred's student body (now nearly 250 in size), and one-third to one-half the faculty (in 1844, seven).[7]

Alfred's emphasis on preparing teachers, its "special work," in Abigail Allen's words, was central to shaping its egalitarian environment. Because the Seventh Day Baptist denomination, like other antiformalist religions, resisted higher education for its ministers and supported literacy for all, Kenyon was under no constraints to favor ministerial training over teacher education. This led to a mission quite distinct from Oberlin's, for instance, which was founded to train men for the ministry, or from St. Lawrence University, an early coeducational school established primarily as a theological seminary. St. Lawrence's charter gave the Universalist denomination control over appointment of trustees and officers until 1910. Women first entered when a preparatory department was established and later admitted to the College of Letters and Sciences. However, that college was regarded as "an afterthought," according to St. Lawrence president Alpheus Hervey.[8]

Most early college faculties were made up entirely or predominantly of ministers, who were after all "the largest pool of trained intellectuals" but who frequently held very conservative views on women's proper role. Antioch was considered to have a low ratio of ministers, with only three of its seven faculty ministers. Alfred was very unusual in that there were no ministers on its faculty until the theology department was established in 1864. The academy's secular mission thus gave women an occupational status and nourished a more liberal attitude toward gender relations.[9]

With the school's growth, it seemed essential to add a preceptress for the young women. In 1842, twenty-year-old Caroline B. Maxson was hired and also assigned to teach modern languages and assist in mathematics. She quickly won the students' hearts and proved to be a very important intellectual influence during her four years of employment. Later she was credited with being one of the individuals who formed Alfred's distinctive character:

> ... she became a living force in the school. With a high range of mental power and sweep, with a comprehension of the subjects to be taught clear and direct as light, with a self-poise that no rudeness could jostle, with a gentleness that won its way to the hearts of the roughest, with an equi-poise which no provocation could unsettle, but mild, calm, serene, she taught her pupils to be so. Never scolding nor fretting, nor fault-finding, she gave her helpful hand to the diffident and trembling and the weary, and with winsome words led them on.[10]

Caroline Maxson was born in Homer, New York, in 1822. She came to Alfred after teaching at DeRuyter Institute, which her father, editor of an early Seventh Day Baptist paper, had founded. She was "a genial lady-like woman, lovely in spirit, keen in intellect, beautiful in person, beloved by all who knew her." For decades, people remembered her intellectual brilliance and warm dedication to teaching and helping students. Maxson's intellect, joined with her warmth, offered a model that challenged gender stereotypes and supported students' intellectual ambitions. Forty years later, an alumna gathered recollections: "One fellow student says of her: 'She was the nicest, prettiest woman I ever knew.' Another says: 'She had one of the most logical, philosophical minds I ever knew *in a woman.*'" Crossed out in the manuscript copy of these recollections prepared for the semi-centennial anniversary of 1886 is the pungent observation—"A man said that of course."[11]

Adored by students, she balanced Kenyon's passionate, demanding nature, meeting with the young women Wednesday afternoons for an hour, giving advice and letting them ask any questions they wished. Mary Sheldon, the eager thirteen-year-old who came to school in 1839, long treasured the admonitions written into her album from "Carrie" Maxson, her favorite teacher:

> Life is but a link in the chain of endless years, a leaf from the tree of immortality. Brief as it is, it is allotted for noble purposes.
>
> Each day should be a record of holy aims, high resolves, and lofty accomplishments.
>
> An eternity is before us and the duties of life are too pressing to allow time for indolence and inactivity, too important to give place to frivolous amusements and visionary schemes.[12]

Maxson left Alfred in 1846, shortly before her marriage to Dr. Jacob D. B. Stillman, who had been principal of DeRuyter. She died at thirty, a few weeks after childbirth; her son eventually taught chemistry at Stanford.[13]

The addition of a preceptress came as the trustees sought recognition for the school as an academy. On the strength of its expanded facilities, increased number of faculty, large enrollment, and broad scope of instruction, the trustees requested an academy charter from the Board of Regents (which had supervised the state's academies since 1784) in August 1842, and on January 31, 1843, Alfred Academy received that charter, joining the ranks of thousands of academies that flourished in the early nineteenth century. That fall enrollment reached more than 200—137 men and 80 women.

Chartered in the academies' "period of most rapid growth" in New York State (101 were incorporated from 1836 to 1845; by 1855, Henry Barnard counted 887), Alfred Academy was in many ways typical of this amazing expansion of educational opportunity. Cherished as "a community enterprise and fostered by the state," these new academies brought secondary education to thousands of young people. Most were coeducational; often more women than men enrolled. New York had recognized the importance of academies early, establishing them as quasi-public institutions in the first state legislative session (1784) and permitting incorporation to those with a "proper building," permanent (if modest) funding, and a high standard of instruction. Incorporated academies gained legal status and prestige, were managed by a self-perpetuating board of trustees, and could draw on various revenue sources. A combination of state support with some local funding, community support, a little endowment, and tuition charges gave academies relative financial stability. They received state aid (at various times and under varying formulas) from the "literature fund" for their college preparatory programs and, in return, observed the Regents' ordinances, reported annually on finances, enrollment, faculty, and instruction, and were forbidden to require a religious test of their teachers. Alfred received a $200 grant immediately after gaining the charter. Kenyon probably also hoped to draw state funds for teacher training, but that appropriation was dropped the year Alfred received academy status, as the state established its first normal school (six years later, support for academies was reinstated since they clearly were needed for teacher training).[14]

In only four years, Kenyon had defined the school's focus, added women to its faculty, and achieved academy status. This entrepreneurial principal then took over the school's management, "in fact, for years it was not easy to say whether the Academy was a personal or a corporate enterprise." In most academies, the trustees were the dominant force, providing continuity and guidance; teachers "were generally short-term hired hands with little power" who stayed only a year or two.[15] Usually, if the board failed, the school failed. Kenyon was one of the few teachers, like Mount Holyoke's Mary Lyon, Hartford Female Seminary's Catharine Beecher, and Union's Eliphalet Nott, who almost single-handedly shaped a successful institution. He took over most financial matters, sometimes to the trustees' discomfort, paying all expenses and trying to clear up debts.

Most early academies and colleges struggled to remain solvent, often running deficits, stripping themselves of revenues through shortsighted "scholarship" schemes, or taking on crushing debt. Some drew on denominational support or sent their presidents on fund-raising expeditions to New England philanthropists or even overseas. Knox College and Oberlin College counted on their abolitionist connections and evangelical roots for funds before the Civil War. Later in the century, Williams, Wesleyan, Amherst, and Dartmouth reoriented from their rural origins, drawing both funding and new campus values from the growing cities.[16]

In contrast, despite strong antislavery sentiments, there is no record of Alfred's seeking support from abolitionist philanthropists. With the exception of Gerrit Smith, who gave Alfred only a few hundred dollars, Alfred had no wealthy patrons and no organized denominational support until receiving its university charter in 1857. In fact, it is not clear that Alfred ever sought wealthy patrons. Because most Seventh Day Baptists remained in small rural communities sharing the Saturday Sabbath, they were excluded from economic opportunities in the fast-growing cities. In addition, Alfred's many alumni who became teachers would never become wealthy benefactors. Alfred survived through modest community support, intermittent state assistance, its teachers' dedication, and Kenyon's adventurous financing.

Kenyon's financial strategy seems to have been to undertake projects personally—running ahead of trustee support, borrowing in his own name. The academy charter was granted just as the country began to recover from a lengthy depression dating from 1837, adding to the stress of financing even though the student body increased each year. In the winter of 1843, Dr. John Collins wrote that his son's employment at the academy teaching Latin, mathematics, and natural science was dependent on enrollment, and in general, "Times are growing easier, money is more plenty, but still property is very low."[17]

Immediately after receiving the charter, a three-year Teachers' Course, including practice teaching, was developed. The catalog noted, "Ladies recite in classes with gentlemen as far as they are pursuing the same branches. All needful facilities for acquiring a knowledge of the polite and ornamental branches of education will be furnished."[18] Despite this statement, Kenyon's attitude toward the "polite and ornamental branches" was clear: Alfred's curriculum was to be thorough and practical. He sharply criticized ordinary female education in his 1845 annual report to the New York State Regents:

> Our colleges, academies, and especially our female seminaries, are too much engrossed in putting on a mere gloss, an ill-advised varnish, calculated only to captivate the unthinking, rather than benefit the individual or society. The management of these female seminaries, in too many instances, we believe to be a curse to all under their influence, a miserable farce, calculated to bring into disrepute all really solid, really worthy education, their whole tendency being to send forth into society, swarms of drones and leeches, rather than good and wholesome members. . . .
>
> Here must the remedy begin to be applied. . . . Let academies and their sister seminaries cease to labor for mere outside show. Let them labor to send out teachers thoroughly imbued . . . in short, good and efficient teachers. Let them do their duty to the teachers they furnish society, and, in due time, the evil will vanish.[19]

Kenyon assumed that women would be active workers in society, as much as men, and should obtain a well-grounded education to prepare for that role. In fact, a high proportion of Alfred's alumnae did work, both before and after marriage. The Academy's first graduating class, in 1844, included eight women and thirteen men. Several returned to teach at the Academy: Jonathan Allen; John Collins (physiology and anatomy); Gurdon Evans (mathematics); Daniel Pickett, who went on to Union College (modern languages and mathematics); Ira Sayles (languages); Olive Forbes (assistant teacher); Melissa Ward Kenyon (Primary Department); Abigail Maxson (preceptress); and Serena White (assistant teacher).

More than three hundred students (174 men, 153 women) enrolled in 1845 and the Cadmus seemed outgrown, even with its 1841 addition. Trustees were unwilling to fund new buildings, but with their approval, Kenyon and Ira Sayles (who in 1845 joined Kenyon as associate principal) charged ahead to secure the funds themselves. They borrowed $10,000 from Sayles's father-in-law, Samuel White of Whitesville (husband of Nancy Teater, the town's first teacher), to purchase six and a half acres (the heart of the current campus) on the wooded hillside facing the village and began construction of three buildings. The community pitched in again, as villagers contributed labor, materials, or a little money.

In 1846, with enrollment nearing four hundred, the Academy moved from the village center to the new acreage across the creek with completion of "North Hall," "Middle Building," and "South Hall," all three-story wooden buildings. Forests still covered the hill and the new halls were built in narrow clearings in these woods; development of a "campus" with broad lawns would come much later. The buildings were described as "splendid" by a student in 1847: "they are placed on a rise of ground in a fine grove, and I think it will be an enticing place when the yard is fenced and dressed out with a taste corresponding to that displayed in the buildings." Eight years later, the grounds were still "little better than a sheep pasture, with foot paths leading here and there through the brush to the several buildings." Even at the end of the century, although the area had been cleared, many trees planted by Allen and students, and numerous flower beds tended by "Frau Kenyon" (William Kenyon's second wife), the grass was scythed only once a year, just before Commencement. As a result, the lawns were decorated with haystacks for Commencement celebrations.[20]

North Hall contained a few classrooms and housed male students, who were supervised by Professor and Mrs. Pickett at one time, Jonathan Allen at another. "Mrs. Pickett, with pencil and blank book, patrolled the precincts every study hour of the day, looked in at the rooms and carefully noted down all absentees who were not properly elsewhere engaged. At quarter past nine P. M., the professor came around to see if all lights were out and the occupants of the respective rooms at home and in bed. The rattling of the doors below as the Professor commenced his rounds, would frequently call forth some desperate efforts and exercises in grand and lofty tumbling on the part of residents of the upper floors in order that the lights might be extinguished and their forms in a position of serene repose before their doors were reached."[21]

South Hall housed women and was supervised first by the preceptress, later by Professor Ford and his wife. The upper story was used for a chapel (with an outside stairway for the men's entrance) and recitation rooms, and later for music rooms and the Ladies' Literary Society. Men were not permitted into South Hall, known to the classically minded as "home of the nymphs," except to perform a few coveted tasks. The work of keeping the women's wood-boxes filled was viewed as a very "enviable position": "It was considered a post of great honor and trust, but was not very remunerative in a pecuniary sense, as on account of the numerous applications for the position the faculty took advantage of the situation to cut down the salary to a very modest figure."[22]

Middle Building housed more classrooms, some faculty (Kenyon and Sayles for a while) with their families, and the kitchen with its mammoth bake ovens. The dining hall was also here, serving more than one hundred people at two long tables. "The gents entrance was under the front flight of steps. And for ladies there was one at the south end of the hall. The ladies and gentlemen were seated vis-à-vis up and down the long tables."[23] The school building left behind in the village, renamed West Hall, housed students who boarded themselves with supervision.

The year 1846 was also notable for an addition to the faculty: Abigail Maxson returned to the Academy, following Caroline Maxson's resignation. Preceptress from 1846 to 1850, and 1856 to 1861, Abigail also taught languages, mathematics, botany, metaphysics, painting, drawing, and art history. A strong-minded woman, dedicated teacher, and reformer who became an early suffragist, she was crucial in shaping the school's development and intensifying its liberal environment. Numerous women must have inspired young female students: Melissa Kenyon was beloved by students as their teacher, guide, and nurse; Carrie Maxson was an early model of intelligence and dedication. But Abigail Maxson Allen, that "strong, true character," teacher from 1846 and wife of Jonathan Allen from 1849, made the strongest connection between educational ideals and social reform. Ambitious, intelligent, and hardworking, she pressed for social justice, a public role for women, broader employment opportunities, and egalitarian gender relations. In concert with her husband, she defined a uniquely liberal educational environment.

While Jonathan Allen's biography was written by his wife after his death, her life must be understood from scattered sources: a memorial volume, institutional histories, her own writings. Born on February 4, 1824, in Friendship, New York, Abigail Ann Maxson was the daughter of Abel and Abigail Lull Maxson. She entered Alfred at fifteen, in 1839, beginning a connection that lasted more than sixty years. After three years of study, Kenyon encouraged her to attend LeRoy Female Seminary (later Ingham University) for advanced work.[24] She was particularly eager to study painting, not then taught at Alfred, and must have been grateful for her teacher's encouragement, as there were several children in her family and she cared for the younger ones:

> . . . there had to be the greatest effort made and much self-denial, in order that one or more of the children might be allowed the time to pursue a higher education. This privilege [she] longed to have. . . . At length, however, after she had graduated at Alfred Academy, the day arrived when she could be spared to go to LeRoy Seminary, then the best school for young women in that section of the country. Sixty miles was a long drive to take in those days of bad roads and poor conveyances, and meant much to a young girl leaving home for many months, but this daughter, filled with the highest purposes, was glad to make any sacrifice that might lead her in the way of gaining knowledge. For she had an ardent hope of becoming a successful teacher, and of leading the younger members of her family to broader culture.[25]

Emily Ingham, founder and Principal of LeRoy, also encouraged Abigail, who wrote to Ingham in 1844, perhaps expressing doubts (the letter is lost). Ingham responded, "come as you propose and come without delay. We love to have those dear children here of whom we have so much hope. The voice I believe will direct you and He will do it by

Fig. 4.1. Abigail Maxson Allen. About 1860.

trying your faith. That you may be a vessel fitted for His use.—Do trust him my child."[26]

Abigail Maxson taught at LeRoy while she studied. Ingham tried to convince her to stay on as teacher after her graduation but Abigail chose a district school instead. Like most district teachers, she taught a wide range of subjects and twelve to thirteen classes a day. Unlike most, she demanded pay equal to a man's: "Mrs. Abigail A. (Maxson) Allen was the first woman in this [Allegany] county that demanded and received adequate pay for teaching. In 1844 she demanded $20 per month and received it. Jonathan Allen, afterwards her husband, received at the same time $15 per month." In contrast, Tolley and Beadie report that female teachers earned an average $7 per month in New York's common schools at that time, $12.50 in Massachusetts.[27]

A few years later, Abigail listened, transfixed, when Susan B. Anthony rose to her feet at the 1853 State Teachers' Convention—the first time a woman spoke at that annual event even though they formed the majority of delegates—and demanded equitable salaries for women, just as Abigail herself had done. Abigail praised Anthony for keeping the state teachers "in hot water till some acknowledgement was made for women's work."[28] Throughout her life, Abigail remained deeply concerned about inequities in women's opportunities and pay. She employed and boarded female students in her home, planned to construct a glove factory to employ female students, urged others to employ women so they might earn enough to continue their education, and befriended Caroline Dall, a feminist journalist who wrote on labor issues. Abigail saw that the achievement of women's rights inevitably required reforms in both education and labor.

A stronger public voice for women was the second component of her vision. Immediately after being hired at Alfred Academy in 1846, Abigail Maxson took an important and unusual step—she started Alfred's first literary society for women, the Alphadelphian Society. This was one of the earliest women's literary societies in the country, a crucial forum for debate, development of self-confidence, and encouragement to take an active, public role in society. From its first years, the Alphadelphian kept the issues of women's work and needs at the fore and sponsored Alfred's first female lecturer in 1854. After Abigail's death in 1902, the women's literary societies published a tribute because she "had always labored for their success and advancement."[29] Liberty of conscience and the freedom to speak out were prized by Abigail and her husband equally, as divine intent and essential to political action.

Abigail counted feminists Caroline Dall, Julia Ward Howe, and Elizabeth Cady Stanton among her friends and invited them to campus when other coeducational schools discouraged such visits. She herself was invited by Julia Ward Howe to speak on coeducation at an 1873 women's rights convention. Abigail advocated women's suffrage and led a locally famous voting incident in 1887, some years after Susan B. Anthony had made her notorious attempt to vote. A few months before Abigail's death in 1902, her sight nearly lost, she drove through the muddy, flood-damaged roads of the Allegany hills, persuading women to exercise their privilege of voting in school elections. In recognition of her work on behalf of women's rights, Abigail was invited to the gala 1900 reception in honor of Anthony's eightieth birthday held in Washington, D.C., and at her death, she was heralded as "one of the pioneers in this state for the advancement of the political rights of woman."[30]

Like her husband, Abigail was opposed to slavery. "The stories of slavery were among her first childhood recollections, and even then her blood rose hot and fast over the injustice of man to man. Hence it was not strange that through all the later years of national turmoil and tribulation she entered with her whole life into the anti-slavery movement." She also worked actively for the temperance cause, though her strongest contribution was to women's rights. One student testified that many owed Abigail Allen a debt "for the things she made possible to woman when co-education was in its infancy."[31]

Everyone who knew Abigail and Jonathan Allen saw them as a team, united in their commitment to education, antislavery, temperance, and women's rights. From 1849 until 1892, the marriage of the Allens, like that of the Kenyons before them, exemplified mutual respect, shared work, and the intertwined lives of president with wife, teacher with teacher. In this partnership, the Allens mirrored the marriages of numerous contemporary feminist leaders. Hersh noted that twenty-eight of thirty-seven early feminists married men who were also feminists: "In these unions, they achieved a notable degree of equality and sharing. The models of egalitarian marriage they created represented a pivotal reform in the nineteenth-century women's movement which has gone unnoticed by historians."[32]

The Allens believed that education itself was a deeply reformatory enterprise; they instilled a faith that education led individual minds and, collectively, civilization to increasingly progressive stages. Historians have argued that women's participation in reform movements, particularly antislavery agitation, was a crucial foundation for the rise of the women's rights movement; ironically, women's educators failed to make the leap. Several colleges notable for radical reform agitation remained conservative on the role of women, and most educators did not embrace women's rights. The Allens were unique among early educators in their conviction that intellectual capacity and development were independent of sex. Thus the Allens aligned themselves with such leaders as Elizabeth Cady Stanton, Lucy Stone, and the Grimké sisters, who drew on natural rights arguments to press their case for women's rights.

Remembered as "a friend to all and generous to a fault," Abigail maintained close ties with students after they left school. She kept in touch with many, writing letters full of encouragement and sympathy. At her death, one wrote: "She had a gift, a very genius, for friendship. . . . There was one noticeable thing about Mrs. Allen's friendship for young people—she always treated them as capable of great and noble things. That was because she felt that we are all God's children. She spoke directly to the best that is in us. She assumed that we had high aims. She believed in us, and that made us believe in ourselves."[33]

Strong-minded and confident, although naturally retiring in her manner, she was a person with large, deep views of life and a serious demeanor. Sincerity, tender sympathy, courage—these were traits remarked by her friends. She was never idle—"nothing less than active, constant employment could bring out for her life's fullest and completest meaning."[34] To the end of her life she sought new knowledge—studying art at Cooper Union and summer schools around the country, for example—and engaged in new projects: anthropology and natural history, local school boards, fund-raising for university scholarships, freedmen's schools, suffrage activities.

With the employment of Abigail Maxson, two of the three people who shaped the school throughout the nineteenth century were in place. In 1849, the third, Jonathan Allen, finished college at Oberlin and joined his wife-to-be, Abigail Maxson, and his teacher, William Kenyon, on the faculty.

His eye always on the future, Kenyon bought eighty acres from Maxson Greene in May 1846, months before completing the move to the new six-acre campus. His ambitious plans were certainly justified by surging enrollments. Growth was so fast that "in one term in 1847, only four academies of the 150 in New York State had enrollments exceeding Alfred's." Rarely did Kenyon allow his ambitions to be limited by any prudent reckoning of resources. His entrepreneurial drive culminated in 1849 when he added several more men to the faculty and convinced these six associates to restrict their income in a common effort to expand the academy to college status. The result was the pivotal "Compact." One remembered the excitement of their planning: "With exalted hopes and enthusiasm at fever heat, we entered upon our new career. The school increased rapidly; new buildings were planned and erected, more land secured, the farm opened up, and the question of assuming collegiate rank and honor was gravely discussed in our counsels. We were preparing many young men and women to enter with advanced standing in other colleges. The State reports gave us the credit of sending out more and a higher grade of teachers than any other similar Institution in the State. Why should we not have the credit of the work done?"[35]

Kenyon had long nurtured the desire to found a college: "The world is demanding better educated men and women, and let no one suppose that qualifications which may render him a successful and acceptable laborer in the world's vineyard this year, will render him such ten years hence." It is notable that his vision included women equally with men. Most colleges, however, were established with denominational support, and Kenyon's aspirations were incompatible with the Seventh Day Baptist belief in the "priesthood of all believers." James Irish remembered the pastor he had as a boy, who was "a good man, but he was wonderfully prejudiced against 'man-made, college-bred ministers.'" As a result, Seventh Day Baptists had no college.[36]

Presbyterians, Congregationalists, and Episcopalians had long favored an educated clergy and therefore founded colleges earlier than did antiformalist churches. Methodists and Baptists nurtured an "active prejudice" against collegiate training, and it was "not until late in the period before the Civil War that they began to appreciate the necessity of higher standards for the ministry and to establish colleges designed to accomplish this purpose." Some Seventh Day Baptists became concerned about their sect's aversion to clerical education. To remove the reproach that its clergy were illiterate, Alexander Campbell founded DeRuyter Institute. Jonathan Allen was also nettled by criticism: "When President Allen and other Alfred young men were in school at Oberlin they were challenged to a debate on the Sabbath question; and one of their opponents, failing in argument, resorted to ridicule, twitting them for belonging to a denomination, 'not even able to train its own theological students.' There then entered into the mind of Mr. Allen the determination to supply this lack in the near future. This was in 1848."[37]

These feelings culminated in Kenyon and Allen's drive to build Alfred Academy into a college. After decades of intermittent debate, consensus was forming within the denomination that both college and theological seminary were desirable. At other schools, accommodations were not always satisfactory for Seventh Day Baptists, as Irish discovered, and the pull of other faiths endangered their small sect's future. The denomination was an obvious source, probably the only source, for the funds to expand. But while they wished to serve their denomination, they would not permit it to dominate. Because Alfred's character was set—resolutely coeducational, its mission to educate teachers—development of the theological department proved slow, frustrating denominational supporters who, in contributing toward the college, expected to gain control of curriculum.

In late winter of 1849, Kenyon wrote to Ambrose Spicer (who enrolled at Alfred Academy in 1840 and later went to Oberlin with Jonathan Allen) describing his fatigue and perplexed state of mind:

> What the best course will be for establishing a college I will not now pretend to say. Nor am I confident that I know. Of one thing I am perfectly convinced, we are behind the times in point of education, something must be done, done soon, done efficiently. My own health is very poor, my days are numbered, I am well-nigh worn out, though not yet arrived at the prime of life. I must abandon teaching for a time at least, perhaps forever. The thought has saddened my heart, but I am not now sad. I am in good spirits, and never felt more determined to spend my allotted time in working with all my might for the cause of education, primarily among our people, and for the world.[38]

His discouragement did not last long. By spring, Kenyon had decided not to abandon teaching but instead to enlist colleagues to join him in building a college. In May 1849, he wrote a letter, probably to Jonathan Allen, who after his 1844 graduation from the Academy became an assistant teacher there before leaving for college work at Oberlin: "No letter that I have ever received was more welcome, or ever rejoiced my heart more, than yours in reply to my last. . . . Your resolutions, expressed in your last, have given me more of hope than I have been accustomed to indulge in. . . . Right glad am I to hear you say, that you are consecrated. I am more anxious to have a move made for a College as soon as practicable, since it will necessarily take a long time to mature plans, and secure the necessary funds to carry it into operation; yet I do not wish to have anything crowded unnecessarily. On this object I am bent; for it my life is pledged."[39]

Abigail Allen relates that Kenyon wrote "often and freely" to Jonathan Allen while he was at Oberlin "of his hopes in reference to building up the school in a higher plane, even to the establishment of a college. Mr. Allen entered warmly into his plans, and pledged his whole energies to the work. In answering his last letter, Professor Kenyon said: 'Nothing has so cheered me as the words in your letter. It will take time, and it may be a long, hard struggle, but it can be done.'"[40]

The Compact brought together a talented group of seven faculty: Kenyon and Ira Sayles, who had already worked together for several years, Jonathan Allen, Darwin Maxson (Brown University and Union Theological Seminary graduate), Darius Ford (also a Brown graduate), Daniel Pickett, and James Marvin (later Chancellor of the University of Kansas). Several were already employed as assistant teachers at the Academy while they advanced in their studies.[41] Jonathan Allen was recruited to return to Alfred as soon as he finished at Oberlin in the spring of 1849. The year of the Compact was also the year of the Allens' marriage, forming the partnership that dominated the institution after the Civil War.

Recollections vary about the terms of the July 4, 1849 Compact, "this strange pledge," as Abigail Allen called it. The most reliable sources describe an agreement that each would teach five years at a fixed salary of $300 each, giving "their entire time and all the surplus funds to the growth of the school," the seven sharing governance, teaching, and financial management. Any additional revenues would be used to retire debt and make physical improvements. They spent their spare time, including vacations, making repairs, working on the school farm, or otherwise being useful. Over the years, differences arose among them and several left. (Thirty-six years later, students still remembered what must have been an epic clash between Kenyon and Sayles over an "oyster supper.") But the goal was achieved: the faculty positioned the Academy for its next step.[42]

Their ambitions were broad. The signers of the Compact were by choice a nonsectarian group, with three Seventh Day Baptists (Kenyon, Allen, and Maxson) and four non-Sabbatarians. Even though the trustees,

Fig.4.2. The signers of the 1849 Compact. Seated, left to right: Darwin E. Maxon, Jonathan Allen, William C. Kenyon, Daniel D. Pickett. Standing, left to right: James Marvin, Ira Sayles, Darius Ford.

most faculty, and most students were Seventh Day Baptist, the school was dominated by Kenyon and Allen, whose convictions were nonsectarian and whose interests went well beyond their denomination. Writing in 1895, when the school was mired in financial difficulties, William Place asserted, "So far as Alfred is concerned, I do not believe there is any hope for her except to go back to the ground that Pres. Kenyon first planted her on, that her work is to make men and women, not S. D. Baptists. In saying that I do not mean to say that S. D. B.s are to surrender the school, but that they are to fill it with the generous spirit that prizes most of all manhood and womanhood, and puts sect after that."[43]

We gain further insight into what Kenyon meant by "non-sectarian" by examining his alma mater's approach. Union was the second largest college in the country (only Yale was larger) when Kenyon attended. Although Kenyon clearly broke with Union's President Eliphalet Nott on women's capabilities, they agreed on the purpose of education. Nott's biographer described the 1839 Union curriculum as "uninhibited by the sectarian demands which were then seeding church dominated colleges across the nation," citing Yale's "sectarian curriculum producing those proliferators of church colleges" and Princeton "almost destroyed by Presbyterian zealots." While Hislop, echoing Hofstadter, may have exaggerated the "intellectual retrogression" of sectarian schools, Union's spirit so prized by Kenyon was one of practical education for hard-working entrepreneurs like Nott and Kenyon himself and a helping hand regardless of sect.[44]

Kenyon's original concept of a nonsectarian school was modeled on his recollections of Union's "beneficent spirit": "I was educated in an Institution where those of all classes participated equally in all the arrangements of the Institution. I witnessed its beneficent effects and drank of its benevolent spirit. I can never be a sectarian, in the ordinary sense of that term."[45] The uneasy balance between the Seventh Day Baptist denomination and Alfred's nonsectarian stance became obvious as events unfolded through the 1860s. Ironically, the independent stance typical of Baptist philosophy was used at Alfred to maintain independence from the denomination itself.

The Teachers' Course became a four-year program, extending the study of languages and adding fourth-year courses in philosophy, "Moral Sciences," and "Evidences of Christianity." Its offerings were supported by several departments: Languages, including Latin, Greek, Italian, French, German, and Hebrew; Mathematics; Natural Science; Agricultural Chemistry; Moral Science; and Instrumental and Vocal Music. (By 1854, the curriculum was altered again, providing four-year courses in both the Classical and the Teachers' departments.) Simultaneously, the student literary societies split and reformulated: three societies emerged in 1850—one female, two male. With the addition of one more female society eight years later, these literary societies defined student extracurricular life for the rest of the century.

Setting high ideals and encouraged to live up to them, Alfred's women were permitted to study any course or subject, and some happily competed with the men. Whether in the classroom, literary societies, in pranks or socializing, camaraderie with the male students was real. Myra McAlmont wrote home from Alfred Academy in 1852, "I am studying Latin, Rhetoric, Algebra, and Analytical Geometry. The reason of my taking the last study which does not come in this course, was that about ten of our best schollars in the Institution, all gentlemen[,] formed a 'crack' class. Miss L. Pickett and myself went in to show them what we can do. Thus far we have sustained ourselves with honor. You will perhaps be surprised that I should commence Latin. But I think it will do much to strengthen my mind if nothing more." McAlmont went on to show others what she could do in geometry; she became a Professor of Mathematics in the Female College of Little Rock, Arkansas.[46]

The Compactors, under the firm name of "Kenyon, Sayles, and Co.," immediately bought 150 more acres, deeding them to Alfred Academy in 1850; at the same time Kenyon deeded the 80 acres he had bought in 1846. The Compactors' sacrifice was evident. Average teacher salaries plunged from 1845's $351 to 1850's $196 (well below the median $318 for Regents academies) but there was reason for "exalted hopes." The number of faculty rose from seven to thirteen, enrollment of Regents students rose rapidly from 1845's 174 to 1850's 319 (third largest in the state) and capital assets increased from $3,341 to $22,137; debt was high, but so was the revenue surplus (nearly $3,000, highest among New York's academies in 1850). Among the debts, they borrowed $10,000 from the state and put up a new large chapel (now called "Alumni Hall") designed and built by Maxson Stillman. It contained twenty rooms for classes, library, and lyceum meetings, and an auditorium big enough to hold Commencement "anniversary" audiences of five hundred people.[47]

Daily chapel services brought the whole school together. Every morning at eight, all students filed into chapel, men on one side, women on the other, and were seated alphabetically. But unlike almost every other Christian school, Sabbath was celebrated from sundown Friday to sundown Saturday. Non-Sabbatarians invariably commented on the Saturday Sabbath, which seemed odd at first, but quickly grew familiar. "It seems strange enough to me to sit here by my window and watch load after load of sabbatarians going to church," Mary Goff wrote her first week at Alfred. When Julia Ward Howe visited the village on a Sunday, she was startled to see "a cheese factory in full operation." Tasting the curd, admiring the great store of cheeses, she noticed that the elderly man at work seemed "to have no sense of violating the Sabbath." Furthermore, shops were open and wash hung out on the lines. The rhythm of life became clear when she was told the village kept the Jewish Sabbath.[48]

Formulation of college plans and the country's tumultuous political events preoccupied faculty and students throughout the 1850s, the decade that proved to be the peak of the college founding movement in America.[49] Student-run organizations such as the "Senate of the Academy" (mimicking the U.S. Senate) and the literary societies were concerned with the increasingly tense political scene, reflecting the passionate and increasingly divisive conflict over slavery. As the struggle intensified, moderate northerners moved away from compromise positions in disgust and moderate southerners retreated in defense of their culture and economy. In 1850 the Fugitive Slave Law was forced through Congress by a southern majority. Appalled northerners passed personal liberty legislation in several states to counteract the repugnant law; widespread defiance eroded the commitment to nonviolence, and abolitionism became more popular.

The reaction in Alfred, already deeply antislavery, may be gauged from a student's 1851 letter to his sister: "Tell Father that he is right about the fugitive slave laws being the exciting topic of the day, and well may a nation of freemen become excited where such a pondrous engine of death and destruction is turned loose upon them." A few months later he reiterated, "Tell father that his views of the fugitive slave law are correct. A darker stain was never cast on our nation." A literary society paper contained an

Fig. 4.3. The Chapel, built 1851, housing classrooms,
literary societies, and school assemblies. The Gothic is on the right.

impassioned plea against slavery, describing it as a hydra, emerging from
an evil ooze: "Ye free citizens and christians of Allegany . . . dedicate your
lives and all your energies in supporting the noble sentiment, 'That all men
are created free and equal.'"[50]

In 1854, the Kansas-Nebraska Law was passed, allowing those new territories to vote whether to be slave or free. "Bleeding Kansas" became a
battleground where raids, ambushes, and massacres combined with election fraud and rival territorial governments (for and against slavery) to
create a local civil war, prelude to the Civil War of 1861–1865. Hopes for
peaceful resolution were abandoned as violence escalated. Among those
who rushed to swell Kansas's antislavery numbers were Alfred alumni
and Allegany County residents. One student, Mark Sheppard, left school
to "aid Kansas in her struggle to secure freedom from slavery" and the
town of Alfred sent a brass cannon belonging to its militia. "Two or three
hundred Allegany families had made homes in Kansas, and, under the
captaincy of old John Brown, of Osawatomie, were struggling to hold free
the soil, as against the border ruffians striving to force slavery into the territories."[51] Free-Soilers ultimately predominated by a two-to-one majority and Kansas joined as a free state in 1861. Alfred graduates were among
those who wrote the new state's constitution and joined its government.

Concern for issues of women's status became evident in the 1850s. The 1854 and 1856 catalogs listed a very unusual course: "The Legal Rights of Women." That course must have been stimulated by Abigail Allen's interest in women's employment and was probably taught by Jonathan Allen. Two other milestones were reached in 1854. First, the Ladies' Literary Society invited the first female lecturer to be heard at Alfred—Elizabeth Oakes Smith. Abigail Allen later credited her husband with the invitation: "He procured the first woman who came to Alfred as a lecturer."[52] Second, Alfred's women began giving orations at graduation—a very daring step and the earliest known orations given by female graduates in the country.

In pursuit of funds for their college, Allen and Kenyon traveled from Seventh Day Baptist town to town, scattered over a thousand miles. In 1854, Jonathan Allen was appointed as general agent to visit the entire denomination, soliciting funds. Allen soon reported numerous barriers to this project: denominational leaders were not committed; few funds were available (Allen could raise only $20,000 to $30,000 of the $100,000 goal); and no location for a college had been selected. Nineteen churches voted on their preferred location. Since most of these churches were in the Alfred area, the unsurprising result was 690 of 769 members favored Alfred, which was a logical choice: its well-developed academy was located within a large concentration of Seventh Day Baptists and the First Alfred church would soon be the largest Seventh Day Baptist church in the country. Finally, there was no plan to pay Allen as general agent or even reimburse his expenses; he received $1 toward his travel expenses of $250 and returned to teaching.[53]

Although Allen may have been discouraged, these efforts slowly generated momentum and he was praised in later years as the man who convinced the far-flung Seventh Day Baptists that they should unite in support of a college. Scant denominational support was not atypical. Princeton, Bucknell, Franklin and Marshall, and Swarthmore similarly received little denominational assistance. "Academies, theological seminaries, and foreign and home missionary societies" all competed with nascent colleges for funding. Nevertheless, the Seventh Day Baptists formed a new Education Society, authorized to "establish a Literary Institution and Theological Seminary," and a committee agreed that Alfred Academy, as a well-established school, with no nearby competitors, located in "a retired and moral district" with numerous Seventh Day Baptist churches, was indeed the best location.[54]

In September 1856, Kenyon pressed his point at the Education Society's first meeting, lobbying the group to establish a well-endowed college: Harvard, Yale, "Princeton, Columbia, Brown, Dartmouth, Union, Amherst, and some hundred and forty other American Colleges, have all been founded and endowed in the faith and prayers of God's people." Kenyon went on to list denominations, including even those "that a few years ago affected to despise collegiate learning," that had recently started colleges all across the country. Antiformalist groups such as "Episcopal

Methodists . . . have founded some twenty Colleges" since 1821, while "the Baptists are founding Colleges in nearly every State in the Union." Interestingly, Kenyon did not note that of twenty or more Baptist colleges founded before the Civil War, none was coeducational. Only Free Will Baptist Hillsdale and Seventh Day Baptist Alfred were founded as coeducational colleges. The fact that only two splinter Baptist groups sponsored coeducation at the advanced level supports the notion that reformers were drawn from the ranks of religious independents.

The faculty continued to construct a collegiate curriculum and the 1856 catalog included Greek, Latin, Hebrew, French, German, and Italian, with expanded study of chemistry and astronomy. Among the faculty were several women: Abigail Allen; Susan Larkin, who taught music, French, Geometry, and English; Amanda Crandall, who taught music; and Ellen Ford, who taught natural sciences. Although most of the male teachers held college degrees, none of the women did. In years to come, several would earn their degrees at Alfred. Given the dearth of a college-educated population, many early schools educated their own faculty in this fashion, hiring their graduates.[55]

A preliminary college faculty was formed of Kenyon, Pickett, and Ethan Larkin. The trustees then approached the state, applying for a college charter and permission to operate a seminary. State officials advised the trustees to draw up a university charter instead, under which they could operate the academy, a college, and a seminary. On January 8, 1857, Jonathan Allen was appointed to go to Albany and lobby for the bill's passage. He stayed several months, during which time he studied at the Albany Law School and was admitted to the bar.

The institution was chartered by special act of the legislature, signed by the Governor on March 28, 1857, as Alfred University, which "by that name shall have perpetual succession for the purpose of promoting education by cultivating art, literature, and science." The legislation established a thirty-three person Board of Trustees with power to create an academic department: "They shall organize a college department with separate departments or courses of study for males and females; both departments possessing equal privileges and powers." On April 15, 1857, the College department was organized.

Alfred University thus became the first coeducational college in New York State and New England, one of the earliest coeducational colleges in the nation. Many antebellum colleges, like Alfred, began as local efforts in rural or frontier settings. Dependent on community support for their success, residents provided land, helped put up the buildings, and sent their children to be educated. Community ties were crucial. As Leslie points out, "the phrase 'denominational college' obscures the complex nature of support." In Alfred's case, the denomination furnished paltry funding, the founders were consciously nonsectarian, and instruction was not doctrinal.[56]

In one arena, Alfred was surely not typical. While early coeducational colleges were often ambivalent about their inclusion of women, Alfred's faculty appears never to have entertained doubts. Kenyon was certainly supportive of women's education and helped create Alfred's model of co-education. Young women were as excited and inspired by his words as young men. He criticized superficial women's education and worked hard to found a coeducational college at a time when women's higher education was still controversial and coeducation rare. He encouraged numerous women, including Abigail Allen, to pursue further study, often lending them money. An egalitarian attitude is evident in the school's teaching mission as well. There is no evidence that Kenyon or other faculty saw women, because of their ascribed domestic virtues, as better suited for teaching than men; they instilled in both sexes the belief that teaching was a noble profession.

At Alfred women were not an afterthought. Kenyon's attitude was liberal for his time, drawing from Republican Motherhood tenets but going beyond them to urge women to become active in society. In an 1851 address to the graduating class, Kenyon used images of Republican Motherhood: "And as you have surveyed the moral world, you have learned that men are needed who have the spirit to 'beard the lion in his den,' to scale the Alps, to swim the Rubicon, and smite the Goliaths single handed; and that women too are needed who have the spirit and the heart, the firmness and the intelligence, to be the trainers of youth who shall become such men." Yet in the same speech he urged both women and men to independence and self-reliance:

> men and women are demanded of great intellects, of disinterested philanthropy, of devoted patriotism, and of unconquerable habits of industry. . . . Our highest ambition has been that your education should constantly contribute to make you plain, matter-of-fact, common sense, independent thinkers and actors, who could give a reason for your faith and your practice, on all subjects. . . . We have not treated you as babes, but as men and women soon to assume the mighty trusts of a great empire, civil, political, and religious. . . . In your reliance upon yourselves—upon your reasonings and upon your judgments—you have become independent thinkers and actors, and not servile co-priests.
>
> To you, as students, our best counsels are given—our benedictions attend you. We have done.[57]

Women were called to the same aspirations and virtues as men; Kenyon never suggested they should be educated for domesticity. By contrast, LeeAnna Michelle Lawrence found at Oberlin, "independence and assertion were encouraged of men, but not of women. . . . A woman's methods had to remain womanly; otherwise, Oberlinites would have to redefine the whole concept of the spheres, and that would precipitate spiritual crisis—something that in the end they could not avoid." An Oberlin student, Maria Cowles, wrote in her diary in 1849 that she must work to suppress her weaknesses of assertiveness and self-confident speech: "Have learned to-day that some ladies whom I much respect, think I have not improved in manners latterly; that I have rather an air of independence and self-confidence, and speak as one having authority; that I say 'It is' so-and-so, instead of 'I think it is' so-and-so . . . I must overcome it." Similarly, Mount Holyoke faculty disbanded a debating society formed by Olympia and Oella Brown in 1854 because it made the women "too independent."[58]

Alfred alone extended egalitarian principles from antislavery to women's rights. It is perplexing that such a challenge should have been so rare. It appears that the dominance of conventional evangelical Protestantism at Oberlin, Olivet, Antioch, and Mount Holyoke may have contributed to their conservatism. The contrast with Oberlin's environment is quite striking. Oberlin and Alfred were similar in several ways: migrant New Englanders predominated among faculty and students; their students, mostly quite poor, came primarily from farm families; commitment to the antislavery movement was widespread; and religion was an important foundation for both schools. Yet the two colleges had very different views toward women's public role and the women's rights movement.

Oberlin was a "queer mixture of liberality and conservatism." From its first days, it had an intensely religious atmosphere. Its founders viewed it as a college for missionary training within a communal, Christian settlement. While many of its graduates became teachers, evangelical values were uppermost for forty years: "learning was always looked upon as the handmaid of religion." Charles Grandison Finney, charismatic revivalist, teacher and Oberlin president from 1851 to 1867, tried to dissuade students from abolition lecturing, preferring that they devote themselves to revivalism; in 1864, nearly thirty years after joining the faculty, Finney was still insisting that conversion of sinners should be paramount. In this effort, a woman's role was to work quietly at her husband's side. He opposed women preaching or speaking in public. The "advanced woman" was seen as a "troublesome creature" by Oberlin's Ladies' Board of Managers, a group of faculty wives who, in the absence of female administrators and faculty, supervised the women students.[59]

That the first coeducational school should be opposed to the women's rights movement is one among many ironies in the history of women's education. In fact, most Oberlin faculty were opposed. Lucy Stone's famous protest was accurate: "They hate Garrison, and women's rights. I love both, and often find myself at swords' points with them." While Oberlinites were firmly antislavery, the Boston abolitionist William Lloyd Garrison, with his rejection of organized religion and political institutions, was seen as too radical and women's rights adherents as "ultra-radical."[60]

Finney's own wife, Lydia Andrews Finney, was helpless to alter his opposition; in fact, her views were stifled by his. In 1856, Susan B. Anthony dined with the Finneys and later described the event to Elizabeth Cady

Stanton: "After her husband denounced women's rights, 'Mrs. Finney took me to another seat and with much earnestness inquired all about what we were doing and the growth of our movement. . . . Said she you have the sympathy of a large proportion of the educated women with you. In my circle I hear the movement much talked of and earnest hopes for its spread expressed—but these women dare not speak out their sympathy.'" The most famous evangelist of his time, Finney thus exemplified Cott's assertion that for most ministers "evangelical Christianity confined women to pious self-expression, sex-specific duties, and subjection to men."[61]

By contrast, Alfred's women *were* encouraged to speak out their sympathy. Ambitious for herself, Abigail Allen was also ambitious for others. Students remembered her saying over and over: "You must improve your time better, do not let your talents rust out, but go to work at something good,—always the nearest duty—*keeping your mind centered* there. Then you will be of use, and the weaknesses and failings you grieve over will lose themselves and disappear."[62]

Opposition to women's rights by Finney at Oberlin; advocacy of women's rights by Jonathan and Abigail Allen at Alfred—each school was dominated for decades by a dynamic president, but with such a difference. One a marriage of wifely subordination, the famed evangelist a one-man show, his wife whispering her support to Anthony; the other marriage a partnership, the wife addressing a national convention for women's rights at the invitation of Julia Ward Howe. In a sense, the societal, regional, and ideological factors affecting Alfred University resolved themselves into the careers and personal beliefs of the Allens. Together the Allens embodied all these: farm origins, poverty, early commitment to reform, shared work as teachers. Together they created a vision of mutuality at Alfred University that was unique in nineteenth-century education.

Chapter Five

Kenyon's
University Years

All too soon the high-minded, noble-hearted Bacon was gone, not further South but to the great beyond and my splendid soldier was a dead soldier.

—Mary Taylor Burdick, "Fifty Years Ago"

With its university charter in 1857, Alfred joined a small group of pre-Civil War coeducational colleges, including Oberlin (founded in 1833), Knox (1837), Lawrence (1847), Genesee (1832), and Antioch (1853). Yet at the others, the public role of women was discouraged. Knox separated female and male students in the classroom and did not permit women into its college courses until 1870. Ironically, Lawrence's founder was opposed to coeducation, indeed opposed to higher education of any sort for women, but he lived in Massachusetts and the school's managers in Wisconsin admitted women, perhaps for economic reasons. At Genesee College, as at many early coeducational schools, women were a small minority of the student body, making little impact. The faculty apparently took care to keep the sexes separate.[1]

Alfred, then, enjoyed a distinctive environment. As Minnie Reynolds put it when she enrolled in 1858, choosing Alfred over Genesee College: "At that time ladies were not admitted [to Genesee College] on an equality with the gentlemen and I would not go. Through an Alfred graduate, I had formed an opinion that Alfred offered the best opportunities to ladies, better than any other school at that time." Women came with a "burning desire" to be better educated and were deliberate in their approach. When Vandelia Varnum graduated from Alfred and wrote Harvard's President Charles Eliot to ask if she could study languages there, she was skeptical that Harvard could provide the right environment: "Are the distinctions and restrictions arising from sex, of such a nature or in such a degree as to mar the advantages of Harvard? . . . Is Harvard with all its surrounding influences of culture—with all its antagonistic bearing toward woman—the best place for me to secure the best result?"[2]

The newly chartered university required reorganization of faculty and curriculum. The trustees asked Jonathan Allen to accept the university presidency. Surviving records offer no explanation for this choice; in fact, Kenyon had been the driving force behind the school's rise to academy status, then university. Yet Allen was tapped to raise funds from the denomination and to lobby in Albany for the charter, perhaps because the trustees feared Kenyon's fiery temper might sabotage the effort. An instance of that temper was recorded a few years later, when Kenyon was brought up for church discipline. A committee was asked to investigate the charge that, in a University trustee meeting, he railed at a trustee and fellow church member, calling him "scoundrel, you villain, you dastardly coward, you consummate rascal!!" The committee reported back that Kenyon maintained "the circumstances justified the language."[3]

Perhaps the trustees also sought someone whose financial approach was less risky than Kenyon's. In any case, Allen declined the presidency and instead was elected professor of history, moral science, and Hebrew. The presidency was then offered to Kenyon, who accepted and led the school for eight years until illness overtook him in 1865. If the process of selecting the first president caused any difficulty between Kenyon and Allen, the Allens never referred to it; they always praised Kenyon as the school's founder and guiding spirit.

Women were admitted immediately, moving into college courses as naturally—and unquestioned—as they once had into the select school and academy courses. In fall 1857 two women (Elvira Kenyon and Ida Sallan) and sixteen men enrolled in the "college course," while thirty-one women and seventy-three men enrolled in the "preparatory college course." With the "teachers' course" (which drew the majority of students) and the "preparatory teachers' course," 266 men and 212 women enrolled at the University, including the Academy, which continued to provide regional secondary education until 1915 when it was absorbed into the public school system. This was a typical distribution of students at a time when most colleges needed to provide secondary-level preparation. Beloit College (all male) had fifty-six preparatory students, thirty-four "normal and English" students, and thirty collegiate students in 1854–1855, for example. Knox College's academy enrolled more students than its college until the 1880s.[4]

As at most schools of the period, very few non-whites attended. A few blacks came to Alfred, including a Haitian woman (perhaps encouraged by Seventh Day Baptist missionaries), some freedmen, and a Bermudan. Just before the Civil War, a Seneca chieftain sent fifteen young Seneca women to live in village homes and study at the school. A Christian himself, he wanted them to "learn all those things that go to make Christian homes." Some of these women became teachers or missionaries.[5]

Four college courses were offered, three four-year programs—Classical, Scientific, Ladies'—and a three-year Teachers' course. The curriculum was typical for its time, utilizing "parallel courses" (Ladies', Scientific, Teachers') to meet modern demands, while protecting the prestigious classical course. In the nineteenth-century struggle over curriculum, proponents of the traditional curriculum fended off both women and new areas of knowledge—modern languages, modern literature, science—by arguing that intellectual standards would be lost. To defend the sanctity of the B.A. (awarded after completion of the classical course), many colleges added parallel courses with B.S. or B.Phil. degrees and degreeless "partial courses." Wesleyan introduced the B.S. in 1838 for the scientific course and Harvard picked it up in 1851 for its Lawrence Scientific School. Brown introduced the B.Phil. in 1850. These two, and the B.Litt., became the most common degrees for innovative curricula featuring modern languages, science, and English literature. By 1850 nearly a third of the men in sixteen Baptist colleges were in nonclassical parallel courses, preparing for teaching or business.[6]

Like the education of women itself, the Ladies' Course was, in Anne Firor Scott's phrase, an ambiguous reform—"lesser" and easier, yet revolutionary, introducing the humanities that would soon overwhelm the classics. These courses (be they literary or scientific, in men's or coeducational colleges) were reformers' initial attacks on the traditional curriculum. One can argue that liberal education was reshaped for women, not unlike the reshaping of the liberal arts to meet new purposes that occurred in previous eras. As Renaissance humanists once added Greek literature to their Latin core, the nineteenth century reached back to the Renaissance for appreciation of literature and humanist studies, substituting modern languages that, like the earlier addition of Greek, gave access to previously untaught literatures. Women's ascribed nonrational, emotional qualities were seen as well adapted to the study of literature. The "Ladies' Course" at Alfred and elsewhere also brought art and art history into the curriculum. At first rejected as "feminine" (Veysey notes that "the study of modern literature and the arts was practically unknown" at men's colleges in the 1860s), later these joined the "legitimate" liberal arts, as did philosophy and history.[7]

Not only were new degrees needed for new courses of study, they were needed for a new category of student—women. Although Oberlin used "bachelor of arts" for its female graduates, the use of "bachelor" for women was considered odd in this very gender-conscious society. Wheaton used "sister of arts," Waco "maid of arts." Alfred invented a gender-neutral term, "Laureate of Arts." Women were also awarded the Mistress of Arts, comparable to the Master of Arts. Alfred University therefore awarded the B.A. for the classical course and the L.A., its equivalent, for women completing the Classical, Scientific, or most commonly, Ladies' course.[8]

Women were required to take the same entrance exam as men (grammar, geography, Latin including Cicero and Virgil, history, algebra—only Greek was elective) and shared all classes with men. Unlike Genesee and Oberlin, which placed their Ladies' Courses at the seminary level, awarding diplomas rather than degrees, Alfred's Ladies' Course was part of its college offerings and almost identical to the Scientific Course. Only a few women joined the Classical Course, but about half Alfred's women studied Latin and some studied Greek, even though these were elective in the Ladies' Course.[9] There was a great deal of flexibility in class selection and most classes contained both men and women.

The Scientific Course and the Ladies' Course had identical first years: algebra, geometry, French, physiology, astronomy, and botany. Sophomore and junior years diverged somewhat. While both courses included trigonometry, German, chemistry, rhetoric, geology, ancient history and modern history, the Scientific Course added zoology, geography, calculus, and analytical chemistry and the Ladies' Course Italian or Anglo-Saxon, painting, and Milton. In the senior year both included logic, moral philosophy, government, theology, constitutional law, and Christianity.

Alfred's faculty contained both men and women. In contrast, there were no women on Oberlin's faculty until the 1880s, none on Cornell's until 1897, and none on St. Lawrence's until 1902. Between 1836 and 1866, eighteen men and eleven women were "Professors" at Alfred; twenty-five men and fifteen women were listed in the catalogs as "Teachers." Professorial rank was granted to those who earned college degrees; Elvira Kenyon, Ida Sallan Long Kenyon, and Abigail Allen were among those awarded the M.A. Women's salaries were comparable to those of men with the same training.[10] Although women generally taught such subjects as music, painting, and modern languages, some taught Latin, mathematics, and natural sciences. In the years after 1857 women taught French, German, Latin, history, botany, rhetoric, elocution, painting, drawing, music, geography, and reading.

The faculty of the new university (comprising academy and college) included five members of the original Compact (Kenyon, Pickett, Maxson, Allen, and Ford) and two women who had taught for many years, Melissa Kenyon (Assistant Teacher) and Abigail Allen (Preceptress and Teacher of Oil Painting and Pencilling). Newer to the school were Ethan Larkin (Latin), William A. Rogers (Languages and Mathematics), Elvira Kenyon (Assistant Teacher), Mrs. Ethan Larkin (Vocal and Instrumental Music), and two male assistant teachers.

Elvira Kenyon (who was not related to President Kenyon) joined the college course in 1857; she was appointed adjunct Latin teacher, then preceptress in 1861 for the new boarding hall, and in 1862 began teaching German as well. "Of a thoroughly inquisitive mind, gentle and winning ways, disposed to pursue every question to its logical consequences, restricted by no creeds nor conventionalities, and regardless where the truth might lead, she was satisfied with no result of her teaching, that did not arouse the dormant energies, and awaken the best powers and susceptibilities of the student."[11] She was also an accomplished speaker; in 1857 she delivered a Latin oration, "Dissertatio de Romanis," when other schools did not permit women to deliver orations in any language. An 1860 "Anniversary Exercises" program records her talk on "Heroic Lives" and includes a listener's marginal notation: "Perhaps more eloquent than any of the preceding." Kenyon left Alfred in 1866, becoming head of the Seminary for Young Ladies in Plainfield, New Jersey. Alfred awarded her an honorary degree in 1875.

Faculty were expected to cover a wide range of studies, as at most colleges; specialization did not become common until near the end of the century. William A. Rogers was hired to teach French, but when the mathematics position unexpectedly became vacant, he was asked to take that instead.[12] He soon developed astronomy as his specialty, beginning construction of an observatory in 1863.

Students, faculty, curriculum, and a president were in place, but where was the promised theological school? With this question, the university's relationship to the denomination quickly became an issue. The charter established two controlling bodies with overlapping membership: the Board of Trustees and the Seventh Day Baptist Education Society, made up of "subscribers" to the university. Immediately and inevitably, the question arose as to which body would be preeminent. This brief tussle resulted in the Board of Trustees winning control, establishing an institution that received some financial support from the denomination but was not controlled by it. The Education Society was restricted to an advisory role.

Alfred's avoidance of external control was most clearly demonstrated by its delay in establishing the theological department. In 1857, the Education Society requested that a theology department be opened "at the earliest practicable opportunity," but no action was taken. The next year the Education Society proclaimed more forcefully: "we instruct our committee to establish that department immediately."[13] They then attempted to appoint a professor to the nonexistent department, but the university trustees did not ratify this "appointment."

Forging ahead, the Education Society tried to appoint Jonathan Allen Professor of Theology in 1858, but he declined to serve since he had never been a pastor. Lacking funds to hire anyone else, the post remained vacant. In 1860 Allen studied briefly at Andover Theological Seminary (but, betraying his deep interest in public speaking, he concentrated on elocution, not theology) and in 1861 the General Conference again asked that he be appointed theology professor.[14] Only a few theology courses were offered until 1864, when Allen was ordained by the General Conference.

Slowly the theology faculty increased and the Theological Department separated from the liberal arts college in 1871, becoming a school with power to grant the Bachelor of Divinity degree, but remaining very small. Only twenty-eight B.D. degrees were granted from 1874 to 1893 and the Department lacked a dean until 1901, when the "Alfred Theological Seminary" became an independent entity within the university (ironically, after Seventh Day Baptists had become a minority of the student body).

The theology school's weak position was a natural consequence of Alfred's liberal environment. The theology school itself was branded as liberal in its early years because of Jonathan Allen's devotion to natural history and geological discoveries, as well as elocution and philosophy. Allen's God had created the world as an organic unity, in which all persons were equal; distinctions based on sex or race cramped individuals' natural development. His deep religious faith was expressed in pantheistic terms; through the eyes of his student, Boothe Colwell Davis, we see "the ponderous, lofty, deliberate, thoughtful Allen, with whom the rocks, the trees, the stars, and the up-reachings of the human mind all alike pointed to cosmic order, infinite wisdom, and infinite love."[15] Allen rationalized science as evidence of an ordered, divinely inspired universe, but that view was anathema to more fundamentalist co-religionists. His fellow faculty member Darwin Maxson was an early champion of Charles Darwin's theory of evolution and aroused much opposition by publishing numerous articles on the subject in *The Sabbath Recorder*. In later years, Arthur E. Main (theology dean from 1901 to 1933) was labeled a modernist.

Seventh Day Baptists did not make equality a tenet. Women were excluded from church governance until late in the nineteenth century, and then it was Alfred faculty who pushed for their inclusion. Darwin Maxson and Jonathan Allen fought for decades to include women in governance and allow their appointment as deaconesses. One has to assume that Nathan Hull, pastor of First Alfred from 1846 to 1881 and notably conservative, resisted the inclusion of women. His powerful position in the church would have swayed many members, despite Maxson's and Allen's urging. No woman was ordained until 1885, when Asa Burdick "Went in Co. with Elder L. M. Cottrell to Hornellsville and attended the Ordination services of Miss Experience F. Randolph—the first woman ever ordained to that office in our Denomination." At that time about two hundred women had been ordained by various denominations throughout the country.[16]

The Allens' stance thus parallels the religious experience of other early feminists. "What precipitated some women and not others to cross the boundaries from 'woman's sphere' to 'woman's rights' is not certain; but it seems that variation on or escape from the containment of conventional evangelical Protestantism—whether through Quakerism, Unitarianism, radical sectarianism, or 'de-conversion'—often led the way." Most radical feminists arose from dissident religions: "During the 1840s, reformers began to organize their own independent churches and societies. . . . As spiritual equals, and as 'co-equals' before God, men and women related to one another as kindred spirits, reciprocal and mutual partners." The Allens clearly shared these beliefs, but remained within their church, while he worked to reform its governance.[17]

In his history of the Seventh Day Baptist people, Don Sanford related, "Most of the spokesmen for the modernist or liberal theological views were connected with the denominational colleges at Alfred, Milton, and Salem. . . . The fear that students might be exposed to the teaching of evolution and the critical study of the Bible or other nonfundamentalist positions caused some students to enroll in more evangelical schools which had been established by other denominations." Allen's opposition to dogmatic theology and his liberal views hastened the day Alfred could no longer be considered a Seventh Day Baptist school. Clearly, Alfred's early history does not support the view of antebellum colleges as narrow, sectarian institutions. As noted in Potts's investigation of several Baptist colleges, local purpose and conditions were prominent influences, shaping a diverse array of institutions responsive to regional needs and impressed with their founders' stamps.[18]

The new college soon faced a crisis: South Hall, supervised by the Allens and housing the women, burned on February 14, 1858. Abigail Allen had gone to breakfast in Middle Hall; when she returned to South Hall to care for her daughter, she found the building on fire. Its residents were ordered out, some fleeing in stocking feet from their bedrooms to the Chapel. Adjoining Middle and North Halls were saved by faculty and students who climbed onto their roofs and kept the buildings wet, extinguishing sparks and small blazes.

The fire energized loyal village supporters, who rallied once more to protect their school. One local couple on this "cold February morning were driving to the Center and as they topped the Five Corners hill they saw that South Hall was in flames. 'There,' exclaimed the wife, 'I see where I'll have to wear my old dress another year.'"[19] Plans for a new building were drawn up and construction began on Ladies Hall, soon dubbed "The Brick" as it was the school's first brick building (brick was thought to be more fire-resistant than wood). Funds for the $20,000 building ran out before the roof was on. The community pitched in again and a hundred local men worked to finish the roof, while women provided table after table of "roof-raising" food. Designed and built by Maxson Stillman, "The Brick" was five stories high, housing one hundred women and a dining hall for two hundred persons.

In 1859 the first college degrees were awarded. Elvira Kenyon, Abigail Allen, and Susan Spicer received the Laureate of Arts in the Ladies' Course; Miranda Fisher received the Laureate of Philosophy in the Teachers' Course; and William H. Rogers received the Bachelor of Arts in the Classical Course. Alumnae soon reported ambitious careers. Eliza Jennie Chapin (Minard) and Ellen Frances Swinney graduated in 1861 and went on to earn their M.D. degrees and practice medicine (Swinney as a missionary in China). Earlier Academy graduates such as Jerusha Maria Maxson McCray '50 (Abigail Allen's sister), Cynthia A. Babcock (Allis) '55, Sarah A. Blakeslee (Chase Hookey) '58, and Phebe Jane Babcock (Waite)

'60 also earned M.D. degrees. Other graduates, male and female, became volunteer nurses during the Civil War.[20]

Just as support for women's public role was conspicuous, so the commitment to reform activity was notable. At this time of ferment, students participated in the multiple movements that disturbed and transformed their society. Many of these sprang up in western New York and Alfred's community of learning took an early stand on temperance, slavery, women's education, the public role of women, and the most radical demand—suffrage. Far from fearing, as Antioch's Horace Mann did, that "coeducation produced women bound to challenge their place in society," Alfred's faculty, led by the Allens, encouraged their women to issue just such a challenge.

Preoccupation with the slaves' plight deepened in the four years between the college chartering and the Civil War. Darwin Maxson checked Horace Greeley's *Tribune* each morning to "see how the slaves were coming." Frederick Douglass and Thomas K. Beecher spoke at the 1852 Commencement and both were invited back repeatedly.[21] War was an event long feared but mostly supported in this strongly antislavery school. Abigail Allen recalled, "All sides of the great questions then agitating the public mind were represented in the school. Sharp and often angry debates on these questions formed continually a part of the program of not only the gentlemen's but frequently of the ladies' literary societies." Nevertheless, radical opinions predominated and "students who were conservative on these points received little sympathy in their ideas."[22] In 1856 the Ladies' Literary Society debated the resolution "that civil war is preferable to the north yielding to the south." That year the Alleghanian Lyceum invited Frederick Douglass and another abolitionist, Gerrit Smith, as speakers. In 1859 the Ladies' Literary Society debated "That the negro has suffered more from the hand of the white man than the indian. Decided in affirmative" and "That a person is justified in not obeying a law of his country that he feels to be morally wrong."

Community ties were strong in antebellum colleges. Alfred diarists record frequent attendance at events, walking or riding into "the Center" to hear musical performances, literary society exhibitions, and speakers. Like other area residents, Maria Whitford and her husband were clearly interested in abolition and other issues: "June 29th [1857] we went to the Center to the Alleghanian session together with the Ladies Literary Society. They had 2 speakers, the Rev. Thomas K. Beecher and Elihu Burritt. 30th. The Orophillian held their session. Their speaker was Frederick Douglass a colored man from Rochester, it was very good. We only went in the afternoon of the first day and afternoon and eve the 2nd day. Sam'l came home and done the chores and came back in eve and staid to hear Music Class perform. We got home about midnight." They went to other lectures by Beecher, Douglass, and J. W. Loguen, a black preacher and member of the underground railroad whom Kenyon had admired decades earlier, and heard an ex-slave preach at their church.

Antislavery sentiment felt by faculty, students, and residents was supported by the Seventh Day Baptist General Conference. Their opposition in 1836 became a preoccupation as national events became more tumultuous. In 1852 the Conference passed a resolution against the "inhuman 'Fugitive Slave Law'"; in 1855 they engaged in prayer "for the emancipation of slaves." As war broke out they passed eight resolutions naming slavery as the cause and its overthrow as the desired result of the Civil War. In 1864, support was reaffirmed: "No compromise with, no surrender to, rebels, let the war be three years or thirty; . . . we are fighting in the interest of a holy cause, for which no suffering or sacrifices are too great."[23]

Sympathy for civil disobedience was becoming widespread. The Fugitive Slave Law and Kansas atrocities destroyed the belief that moral persuasion would eliminate slavery; many previously committed to nonviolence concluded that only forcible resistance would succeed. The clearest indication of these altered attitudes was the veneration accorded John Brown's doomed expedition to establish a mountain republic of liberated, armed slaves.

Brown became obsessed with a vision that it was his mission to free the slaves. He commanded a small band that in 1856 massacred five proslavery Kansas men and in 1857 Brown first met with the "Secret Six," a group of backers including well-known reformers—Gerrit Smith (philanthropist of great wealth, cousin of Elizabeth Cady Stanton, and later a member of Alfred University's Board of Trustees), Samuel Gridley Howe, who fought for Greece's independence and was Julia Ward Howe's husband, and their friend Thomas W. Higginson (who convinced Julia Ward Howe to attend her first women's rights meeting). The six eagerly provided guns, ammunition, and money for antislavery raids in Missouri.[24]

Brown then conceived a plan to foment a slave uprising in Virginia with a small band of guerrilla warriors, drawing clandestine support from the "Secret Six." Julia Ward Howe (soon to become a friend of Abigail Allen) recalled, "This man, Dr. Howe said, seemed to intend to devote his life to the redemption of the colored race from slavery, even as Christ had willingly offered his life for the salvation of mankind. . . . I confess that the whole scheme appeared to me wild and chimerical."[25] Brown solicited assistance from Frederick Douglass, who refused to join him, warning that Harper's Ferry was a "perfect steel-trap" and the mission suicidal. In October 1859, Brown led a raid on the Harper's Ferry armory that quickly failed; he was captured and tried. His eloquent, dignified defense was widely published and many northerners came to view him as a saint; his execution on December 2, 1859, was seen by the devoted as a martyrdom. Across the northern section of the nation, abolitionists organized ceremonial tributes to Brown.

These events were closely watched at Alfred. Gerrit Smith was an admired guest lecturer, who spoke several times on campus while deep in plans with Brown. In 1868, Smith was invited to join Alfred's Board of Trustees and given a "non-resident professorship." Like Smith, Jonathan

Allen fervently admired Brown and said after Lincoln's assassination, "I deem it one of the peculiar privileges of my life that I had the honor of taking by the hand the two great martyrs of liberty, John Brown and Abraham Lincoln."[26]

Interest in women's rights also deepened in this period. As early as 1852, a few students adopted the controversial dress reform named after Amelia Bloomer. Myra McAlmont wrote her mother, "We have only about 200 students yet, but expect more. There are 12 from Richburg Seminary, 7 gentlemen, five ladies, who occupy the castle [a residence]. The ladies wear the bloomer costume." Scattered references to the Bloomer dress occurred in later years, as diarists record making the outfit for themselves. In 1859 and 1860, Maria Whitford made herself Bloomer outfits. Abandoned by leading reformers under public pressure, many women continued to wear them, particularly in rural areas, because they were much easier to work in.[27]

William Brown recalled that women's rights were a hot topic by 1859: "Women's rights . . . were even then a theme of sore discussion." Student literary societies debated such topics as women's intelligence, their proper course of study, coeducation, and suffrage. In 1857 the Ladies' Literary Society debated these: "Resolved that the exclusion of women from our higher institutions of learning is an instance of unparalleled tyrany. Decided in the affirmative" and "Resolved that every young lady should study Latin." Topics in 1859 and 1860 included "human suffrage should be universal," "woman is more capable of speaking in public than man," and "women should study the Professions . . . question decided in the affirm." This just a few years after Mann declared he would leave Antioch if he thought its education would lead women to enter professions. The men's literary societies also sympathized, discussing "Resolved that the right of suffrage should be equally enjoyed by both sexes" and "Resolved, that the civil and political rights which are accorded to man should be accorded to women."[28]

Schools were caught up in the wartime excitement with varying levels of commitment. At Mount Union, fifteen students enlisted after Lincoln's call for volunteers, encouraged by several stirring resolutions from their literary society and by their college president, who said, "If you feel it your duty, go." Genesee was more negative. Only some senior men joined the army, and faculty were markedly less supportive: they voted not to grant the men their degrees.[29] Given Alfred's intense preoccupation with the antislavery movement, it is not surprising that idealism became action: every male senior enlisted after President Lincoln's call on April 15 for 75,000 volunteers to join the militia "for ninety days." Chapel on April 26, 1861, was extremely emotional as students and townspeople jammed the hall and each enlisting senior spoke of his reasons for volunteering. One, more radical than most (who were antislavery, not abolitionist), reportedly startled the audience by predicting the war would abolish slavery. Lincoln then was taking a more moderate stand, pledging his goal was to preserve the union, not to eradicate slavery, and that he had no intention of interfering with slavery in the South.

Mary A. Taylor (Burdick), who matriculated in 1855 and graduated in 1861, attended the chapel ceremony. Her narrative conveys the passionate emotions as the long-dreaded war broke out:

> the political world was stirred to its foundations. Ever since Mr. Lincoln's nomination in the summer of '60, the political situation had been growing tense, and before the 4th of March 1861, President Lincoln was obliged to steal into Washington. Rumors of secession and war were common. Mutterings of the storm were heard, but we felt confident it would somehow be averted. Till suddenly, Fort Sumter—then the call for 75,000 volunteers. A great wave of patriotism swept over the north, firing our boys, and before we realized what had happened, we were summoned to Chapel to hear the farewell speeches of our schoolmates who had volunteered. . . . On this never-to-be-forgotten morning, Asher Williams rose in his seat and said, "I see in large letters the writing on the wall calling me to the defense of Union. And, Mr President, I also see the end of human slavery." It was considered a very radical speech. Even President Lincoln, whose inaugural was barely cold, had said, 'I have no purpose directly or indirectly to interfere with the institution of slavery as it exists.'
>
> Impossible as it may seem, Williams was hissed. At this parting of the ways, the light-hearted school girls were suddenly transformed into dignified women and bade their lovers go to the rescue of the country with a courage born of the highest patriotism. Indeed, it seemed as if it took more courage to stay than to go. The boys went to Elmira to enlist but returned to Commencement.[30]

Abigail Allen also attended that dramatic session: "The morning meeting in the chapel, the day that our boys were to leave, can never be forgotten by any who were present. It was crowded to overflowing by citizens and students, so that there was hardly standing room. The eleven gentlemen of the graduating class were called upon in turn to state their reasons for leaving their studies and all peaceful pursuits for the turmoil and uncertainty of war. Every heart was stirred, especially when two of them said, 'we give our all—our lives—and never expect to return.' And so it proved, for these two came back only in their coffins."[31]

Although Mary Taylor felt Asher Williams's prediction was "very radical," she probably overstated the case. Abolitionist sentiments were common at Alfred; Kenyon had been considered abolitionist for thirty years and many local families left for Kansas to join the Free Soil movement. The Ladies' Literary Society was soon preoccupied with abolition. In September 1861 the members resolved "the war should continue until slavery is abolished." January 1862 they resolved "That the immediate and unconditional emancipation of slavery is the only thing that in the present state of affairs, will save the Republic" and in February 1862 offered this brave resolution: "That the Ladies should forego all of the superfluities of life. For our country's sake. And if necessary, to take the field." In 1863 they resolved "that we make no compromise with the South."

Alfred students joined the 23rd New York Volunteer Infantry, organized at Elmira on May 16, 1861. They returned to campus for June Anniversary ceremonies. A student known only as "Hattie" wrote on her program from a joint session of the Orophilian Lyceum and Ladies' Athenaeum held on June 25: "The boys that formed the army came up the Sabbath evening before the Anniversary and staid till Thursday. They all came but Edmund Edgar Maxson. They were all dressed in uniform. They did not any of them speak on the stage. It was very sad to think that perhaps that it would be the last time that all of them would meet on such an ocation. Proff Kenion addres to the graduating class was very affecting. . . . Proff Allen has gone to Washington and he said if he was needed as nurse he should stay. Mrs. Allen and children are here."[32]

The regiment left the state on July 5. Jonathan Allen visited the troops in Washington and in contrast to Genesee College's denying degrees to its volunteers, Allen granted degrees to his soldiers: "When the boys were settled in camp, Professor Allen went to Washington to visit and encourage them. He witnessed the first part of Bull Run fight, leaving the field when a Union victory seemed certain. Later he visited those of 'his boys' who were in hospitals at the front, and on all who left the university for the battle field he conferred the diplomas they would have received had they finished the prescribed course of study."[33]

When Allen returned from the first Battle of Bull Run, he gave the community a sobering account. Daniel Lewis recalled the event: "There was no heralding of his coming, but by a common impulse of grief and dismay, the people from all the surrounding hillsides came to the village. No bell called them together, but some one lighted the lamps in the chapel and all crowded within its historic walls and listened with bated breath to his graphic account of the proud advance of the army, the heroic effort, the final repulse, the fearful story of the dead and dying who fell."[34]

Casualties soon were reported back to the anxious community. One volunteering student was accidentally shot by a patrolling guard as the student returned from a "jaunt," having gone out beyond the camp lines without permission. Another student was accidentally shot by the son of his captain. Then Mary Taylor's very close friend was reported dead. Her feelings reflect the real affection that developed between male and female students:

> A student, L. L. Bacon, with whom I had a friendly, intimate acquaintance, never marred for a moment, was the next fatality. I called him my soldier. When he went away I gave him a diary with the request that it be returned when filled. Its final pages read, "I have slept on the damp ground and have chills and headache. Kenyon lies sick in his tent and I wish I could care for him." At the close he added, "'Tis greatly wise to

talk with our past hours, and ask them what report they bore to heaven, and how they might have borne more welcome news." All too soon the high-minded, noble-hearted Bacon was gone, not further South but to the great beyond and my splendid soldier was a dead soldier. As our boys began to succumb to camp life, there came to us a realizing sense of what we might expect. Not till Grant and Lee had arranged terms of surrender at Appomatox in '65, did the survivors come marching home.[35]

The war took its toll on many families. Three of Abigail Allen's brothers fought; one was wounded, and Darwin Maxson (who left his teaching post to go to war as a pastor) sat with him while Abigail traveled to be at his side. Another brother, J. Edmund B. Maxson, was among the first to be killed. His death was "a thrilling one for this college community. Amid the gloom of that funeral occasion there was born a higher resolve that the dead should not have died in vain, and from that day Alfred became a veritable nursery of patriotism."[36] Abigail canceled her talk on "Our Country's Need—Woman's Duty," scheduled for a March 8, 1862, public session of the Ladies Athenaeum. Penciled onto a program is the note, "The address was not delivered on the account of Edmund's death." On June 30, 1862, Abigail undertook the lecture again and spoke on "Woman, Her Duties in Times of War."

No wonder Northern victories were eagerly awaited. At "the first great victory," Fort Donelson's surrender to General Grant on February 16, 1862, "President Allen was as enthusiastic as a boy in the task of illuminating every window pane in the 'Brick Hall,' which was a fitting expression of the bright hopes which had finally broken the long night of our country's discontent." Although student and faculty support continued, as the "irrepressible conflict" dragged on and three months became three years, enthusiasm for war service slackened. In his 1864 diary, Abram Burt recorded Professor Williams' chapel sermon, "Watchman tell us of the night & the dawning of the day": "he brought to notice our own distracted country, which for the last three years has been enclosed in a darker night than ever enveloped the Polar regions." Burt admired his "brother Oros" (fellow members of the Orophilian Lyceum) who joined the fight—"many of their forms lie bleeding on Southern soil nobly sacrificed in defense of their country, and the right of freedom throughout the world." Yet the extent of the sacrifice was now clear, and although mass meetings to support the Union were frequent, volunteers were fewer. Burt notes in his diary the day after Williams' sermon, "Several students left to enlist in the Navy, great many enlisting for fear of the draft." A few weeks later more went to New York City "to see what the chances are for more of the students in the Navy."[37]

After emancipation and the war's end, reformers turned to concern for the freedmen's education and health. Asa Burdick "packed a barrel of clothing for the freedmen at Elder K's" (Kenyon's) in 1866. In March

1868 he "attended a lecture by a Mr. Remond—colored gentlemen from Boston—subject—What more is to be done for the colored man in America" and in October took the train to Wellsville (fifteen miles distant) to hear Gerrit Smith. Sojourner Truth visited in 1871 and dictated into a student's autograph book, "Trying for to git dese people free and out west . . . Startin for Kansas. Bless de Lord." Thirty years later, Abigail Allen was still sending barrels of books south to freedmen, and in her seventies made plans to move there herself and open a small school for "the neglected children of the South."[38]

As the nation prepared to award suffrage rights to black males (the 15th Amendment was ratified in 1870), women placed renewed emphasis on their own position. In September 1865, the Ladies' Literary Society discussed the resolution "that women should exercise the right of suffrage." Though this was hardly the first time that women's suffrage was debated at Alfred (the first recorded debate occurred in the 1840s), the frequency and intensity of these demands increased in the next decades. Soon Abigail and Jonathan Allen were publicly advocating women's suffrage.

The war years were difficult for all concerned, making institutional expansion almost impossible as finances continued to be problematic. Enrollment reached a high point the year the university charter was obtained, but this brief period of relative prosperity faded as first the Panic of 1857 and then the war reduced student numbers: enrollment of 478 in 1857 fell to 287 by 1861. Faculty took lower pay, then reduced their numbers. Building and facilities improvements were deferred. "In 1862 there were 400 outstanding claims listed against the School and no funds to meet them." A shortsighted "perpetual scholarship" scheme drained funds at Alfred as at many other early colleges. By 1866, although enrollment was rising, debts were ruinous and $10,000 was raised by subscription from the Education Society, relieving the financial crisis.[39]

Other sorrows pressed in. The students' beloved "Mother" Kenyon, only forty years old, died in 1863. At her funeral, Pastor Hull said, "It seems to me I never knew a person that would forgive so much as this sister would." Since 1840 she had sacrificed herself time and again for students who were needy or sick. She died after a particularly wearing siege of tending a student, Mary E. Wager, who lay ill with typhoid. Wager survived to receive her master's degree, travel in Europe, and become assistant editor of the *Rural New Yorker*.[40] On September 4, 1864, the widowed Kenyon married Ida Sallan Long, one of the two women who entered the college course in 1857. Abram Burt recorded the scene: "In the evening we were all surprised to learn that Prof. K. had gone off to get spliced, and would return about 9 PM, with the bride. The Boys immediately made arrangements for their reception. Anvils and Powder brought out. A pole tied across the bridge; with boys in the bush to hear the compliments. The Bell and other musical instruments in readiness . . . When they commenced their salute on the arrival of the Bride & Groom, went out and viewed proceedings for a short time; They rung the Bell till they broke the clapper and fired salutes (or I dreamed them) through the night."[41]

A native of Germany whose family moved to the United States in 1852, Ida Sallan entered Alfred Academy in 1854, graduated in 1856, entered the college course, and went on to teach in Pennsylvania and at Milton Academy in Wisconsin. She was married in 1862 and widowed within a year, then married Kenyon and began teaching Latin at Alfred, adding German when Elvira Kenyon left. She remained on Alfred's faculty as Professor of Modern Languages and Literature until 1894. After her death on March 18, 1904, she was remembered as "strong, scholarly, energetic, and deeply spiritual." She was also remembered by generations of students for her love of flowers: "She always had interesting bouquets in her windows. *She* could pick posies from the triangular flower beds on the campus because *she* was the gardener. *Students* who touched them were in bad repute. It was a reward for early rising to see Frau Kenyon working among her flowers in her regimentals, trousers with skirt only to her knees."[42]

Kenyon continued to be active statewide in teacher education and was offered a position leading the state's normal school project, but he refused due to ill health. He had become increasingly incapacitated by heart disease. In 1865, worn down by illness and fatigue, Kenyon yielded his duties to Jonathan Allen, who reluctantly became acting president (the trustees elected him president, probably fearing that Kenyon could never return, but Allen refused the appointment). Kenyon wrote to Rev. Hiram Burdick, pastor of the Hartsville church in which Kenyon often preached, "The toils of the last five years, the severest of my life, and my labors in closing up at Alfred, had reduced me much more than I was aware of till I had left Alfred."[43]

Extant letters suggest his last few years were difficult indeed. Not only was Kenyon ill but he and Allen had begun to disagree over the school's direction. Although both Kenyon's and Allen's interests reached well beyond their denomination, it is possible they clashed over the character of the theological school. Kenyon's strong will and flaring temper may have caused more frequent conflicts with university trustees and co-workers as the years passed. Hiram Burdick, who knew Kenyon well, said, "He could see an intended snub as far away, and through as dark a place, as any man."[44]

Evidence of these clashes is found in correspondence between Kenyon and Thomas R. Williams. A graduate of Alfred, Brown, and Union Theological Seminary who joined the theology faculty in 1866, Williams was critical of his fellow faculty members Nathan Hull and Jonathan Allen. Williams wrote Kenyon (then in Prussia with his wife in search of relief through rest) an acid letter attacking both men and lamenting Allen's neglect of theology for natural history:

We have been to hear Eld[er] Hull Preach today. I cannot discover any very decided improvement in his efforts; the same repetition of his sage remarks & observations. I hope our young ministers will not be moulded altogether by his stile. On the whole Alfred never had so few charms for me. . . .

. . . Prof. Allen has just made quite an addition to the Library, mostly of books on Natural History. I fear that Natural History receives more attention than Theology. There is a real need of better facilities for the study of Theology among our people. We are pretending to have what we do not have, a Theol. Seminary & what we never shall have until other men than Prof. Allen & Eld Hull, are enlisted in the work. . . . Now is it not possible to endow three Professorships for such a purpose & locate the school [elsewhere than Alfred] where these advantages can be enjoyed?

Williams and Kenyon must have commiserated previously about Allen's interests for Williams to write so pointedly. Williams' next comment reinforces the perception of conflict:

I hope our denomination will profit by your journey. But I am unwilling that you should wear out your life, imparting the results of your studies & travels, under such treatment as you have endured at Alfred. I myself recoil at the thought of ever again being subject to such treatment & much more must you shudder at the thought of being the object of false criticisms & malicious ridicule by those who ought to have the deepest respect. But those memories are not pleasant. Let us hope for better days. I trust better days are coming for you & for me.[45]

A. H. Lewis, a graduate of Alfred and Union Theological Seminary who was appointed Professor of Church History in 1868, was also bitter about the lack of support for the theological seminary: "In failing to build up that department the University had lost its chance to gain a hold on the denomination."[46] Frustrated though some may have been, the theology school remained subordinate. Kenyon, to some extent, and Allen, to a greater extent, resisted expanding ministerial education. While the university may have "lost its chance to gain a hold on the denomination," this stance also meant the denomination did not gain a hold on the university. Conservative forces remained secondary, and Allen's liberal views only intensified over the next three decades that he led the school.

Records are insufficient to trace the nature of the clash, but an 1895 rumor also reported conflict. W. F. Place, an alumnus, had extensive correspondence with Ida Kenyon, as Place hoped to write a biography of Kenyon, whom he greatly admired. Place asked Mrs. Kenyon: "There are two items that I would like to know more about, if it would not be painful, too painful I mean, to speak of them. One is the opposition of Rev. N. V. Hull to Pres. Kenyon's ordination; a matter that I remember dimly: and the truthfulness or untruthfulness of reports that I often heard that Prof. Allen was a thorn in his flesh and finally drove him to resign. Of course all that is not for the public, but I feel that the fuller knowledge I have of Pres. Kenyon's trials as well as triumphs the more perfectly shall I make him felt by others. I do not know that there is any truth to the repeated reports I have heard. Do not answer this if it seems best not to do so."[47]

Her response was destroyed and Place never finished the Kenyon biography, in part because Ida Kenyon objected at nearly every step. She ferociously defended William Kenyon's memory, her intensity enhanced by the fact that his strong will and ambitions were frustrated by illness in their few years together. She must have shared his fears for the school and bitterness at being forced to give over his duties.

William Rogers' memories reinforce the sense that Kenyon was discouraged and troubled: "I knew of no one more thoroughly honest with himself than was President Kenyon. Towards the end of his life he sometimes became doubtful of the reality of his apparent success in the prosecution of his educational work. He would sometimes say; I think I have been fairly successful as the Principal of Alfred Academy, but I have fallen a good deal below my ideal as the President of Alfred University. I think he had a feeling something like this to the close of his life. His ideal was high. . . . he sometimes became doubtful of his power to reach the goal at which he aimed."[48]

Lydia Langworthy Palmer, a student in 1857, offered a balanced view of Kenyon, even as she described arguments between them: "In the little incidents I have given, I was most at fault. But he, losing his temper, also lost his dignity; and, temporarily, my respect. But in after years, I could comprehend how ill health and so many worries, and his constant overwork, must have rendered his naturally hasty temper much more so. And as he was more exacting to us, seeming to begrudge us any pleasure, we loved him less than any other teacher." But she adds, "I had a great respect for him, knowing him to be a noble and good man, and one who had made great sacrifices for the University."[49]

Even when ill, nearing the end of his life, Kenyon continued to push himself. "Few men ever possessed so powerful a will and such tenacity of purpose. Prostrated with heart disease, I have known him time and again, to continue to hear his classes, when he could neither go to the class room without assistance, nor sit up when there. His enthusiasm was unbounded and of the catching order. Hundreds owe their success in life to new powers awakened, and new impulses received from contact with this remarkable man."[50]

Frail, plagued by tension and doubts, Kenyon rallied for a while on his European sojourn; then his heart weakened again. Fearful of the outcome, he jotted instructions in his diary for his wife should he die abroad. Eager to return home, he wrote his brother in a trembling hand from London on

Fig. 5.1. Alfred University campus, looking east from the village. "White House" (the Allens' home), observatory, Chapel, "The Gothic," and "The Brick," left to right. Pine Hill is in the background. About 1875.

May 22, 1867, "We had intended takeing steamer on the 29th at Liverpool for New York. But are delayed a few days." His health was uncertain: "I am not much but a shadow, but I am as hopeful as I can be."[51] He did not survive to make that return trip, dying in London on June 7, 1867, at the age of fifty-four.

Although Kenyon may have questioned his achievement, others did not. He "found the Institution with 74 students and under him it reached its 19th century peak with 478," historian John Norwood reflected. "He found it with one small building and left it with five. As a select school he found it, as a University he left it." Most importantly, thousands of students found inspiration in his idealism and enthusiasm.[52]

Chapter Six

"No More Thought
of Changing"
Women's Equality

Be radical, radical to the core.

—Abigail Allen, "Co-education"

In the presence of rights, race, sex, or color distinctions disappear. The
humblest and feeblest being has the same rights as the most powerful
and gifted.

—Jonathan Allen, "Suffrage"

Attention to women's issues became evident during the early university years, intensifying after the Civil War as the Allens took charge. While Kenyon drew on the language of Republican Motherhood, that ideology mutated directly into the Allens' adherence to the unfulfilled Revolutionary promise—natural rights and equality. Intellectually allied with numerous early feminists whom they befriended, the Allens very clearly staked out the territory of equal rights. Their strong advocacy of women's right to speak publicly, receive equal education, work, and vote was unique among higher education institutions.

Boothe Colwell Davis (student and later President of Alfred, 1895–1933) asserted, "There appears to have been few, if any, controversies at Alfred in the early days over prohibition, antislavery, woman's rights, etc., for the reason that Alfred University was a pioneer and ardent promoter of all these reforms. Led by President and Mrs. Allen and a sympathetic faculty, Alfred University was a center of reform in the matters of prohibition, antislavery and woman's rights. Any faculty member, student, or citizen, who disagreed with these principles of radical reform, found an uncongenial atmosphere in Alfred. Public lecturers, writers, and politicians advocating these principles, found a warm welcome and ardent allies here."[1]

Although opinion was not as fully uniform as Davis described, he was not far wrong. However, the outspoken Allens occasionally outran their trustees and male students. "The conservative and radical elements of the school did not always harmonize"; two notorious flaps arose over invitations to Julia Ward Howe and Caroline Dall.[2] But the Allens prevailed, shaping a progressive climate. Throughout their lives, they were proud to be called "radical."

Jonathan Allen, serving as acting President for two years, was elected President in 1867, leading the school until his death (like Kenyon, of heart disease) on September 21, 1892. His humanistic approach, belief in the importance of "character," love of natural history and philosophy, liberal religious faith, and joint commitment with his wife to women's rights were his chief gifts to Alfred University.

One of six children, Jonathan Allen was born January 26, 1823, in a log house in the woods, the son of Abram and Dorcas Burdick Allen, who arrived in Alfred about 1817. His father was a farmer, surveyor, and teacher, opening a Sabbath School in his home and becoming a member of the Milton (Wisconsin) Academy Board of Trustees in later years. Jonathan's busy mother placed the younger sisters and brothers in his care before he was seven: "As soon as they were old enough to walk, all the bright, sunny days were spent in the fields and woods around the home. The little girls placed in the center, and the twin brothers one on each side, with the older brothers each taking a hand of these, made quite a string of babies, the eldest being less than seven years old." He proved a watchful, loving older brother. Jonathan's brother remembered, "He was ever our peacemaker, and the champion and protector of the little twin sisters, always called 'the babies.'" Abigail felt her husband's life-long concern for women may have stemmed from this fraternal trust: "Perhaps, more than he himself knew, we owe his lifelong heroic defense of woman to the tender care of these little sisters. Rich or poor, black or white, he believed with all his soul that woman, as a child of God, had a right to live her own independent life, and work out her own soul's destiny."[3] Jonathan joined the Seventh Day Baptist church at twelve, and at thirteen, not yet able to read, joined the first select school class.

Like Abigail, Jonathan Allen hated slavery and at eighteen, in 1841, he wrote a play that was long remembered as prophetic. "The house was crowded," wrote Mrs. Susan Spicer. Inspired by a recent incident of slave recapture, "with more than the usual atrocities," Allen played the Quaker who had aided the fugitives and was himself captured, tarred, and feathered. Addressing his captors, "Allen was entirely submissive, but talked to them plainly of the cruel inhumanity of their system of slavery, sharply denouncing their brutal practices, then, finally raising his voice in cutting rebuke, he reached a climax unanticipated even by himself. In impassioned, eloquent terms he told them that their acts would react against them. . . . 'The days of slavery are already numbered, though it will die only after a hard struggle. It will die only after a baptism of our whole country in blood. Twenty years from now an antislavery President will be elected. You of the South will rebel and endeavor to establish a slaveholder's oligarchy. The North will not submit to the dissolution of these States, and a fearful carnage will follow. Slavery will be abolished, and God will preserve the nation.'" Twenty years later, Allen regarded that impromptu forecast as "inexplicable except as it was born of faith."[4]

He began teaching in a district school at seventeen and was successful in disciplining the "big boys." "This was in a neighborhood where it was the pride of the 'toughs' to have two or three successive teachers each winter. They had but *one* that winter."[5] In 1842, accompanying his parents as they followed other Alfred families west, he moved to the new Seventh Day Baptist settlement of Milton, Wisconsin, where he taught school in the winters and worked as a surveyor and on his father's farm in the summers. At twenty-one he had earned enough either to purchase a quarter-section of land near his parents' farm in Wisconsin, as they wished, or return to Alfred to continue his education. He chose to return, becoming a tutor while studying himself, replenishing his funds by teaching winter term in a district school. He graduated from the Academy in 1844 (the same year as his future wife, Abigail Maxson) and for three years taught in district schools or at the Academy as an assistant teacher.

In 1847 Allen went to Oberlin, admiring the strong religious influences there, with two other "Alfred boys," Ambrose Spicer and Ethan Larkin. The Burned-over District sent a relatively high number of young men to college; many of these schools were strongly evangelical. After Oberlin was established (and dominated after 1835 by the Burned-over District's leading revivalist, Charles Finney) "to bring eastern piety to the great 'valley of dry bones,' a substantial portion of men and a few women elected this more intensely religious education. More than two hundred students from western New York attended Oberlin College during the five years following 1835, about a third for college work and the others for preparatory or theological courses."[6]

Allen arrived at Oberlin committed to women's rights and antislavery. He was able to act on his principles when he helped slaves to freedom: "there came on the sharp run sixteen adult negroes, hatless, coatless, shoeless, and almost breathless, crying in terror: 'Oh, take care of us quick! Our masters are coming! Masters are coming!' At the same time a man from another point came on a running horse calling out, 'Take care of those men; their masters are in hot pursuit!'" Allen helped conceal the escapees on campus, while a mass of students and citizens surrounded the hotel where the slave owners were staying. A standoff ensued until the owners withdrew to a nearby town. Two days later plans to move the sixteen to Cleveland and then to a boat for Canada were complete: "the fugitives were guarded by such a force that they were not molested, and Mr. Allen and other members of the escort saw them safely on board the boat that was to land them in Canada."[7]

While Allen was at Oberlin, "a close correspondence was kept up with Professor Kenyon regarding plans for the future development of the incipient University. Indeed, Mr. Allen fully pledged himself to HELP WORK OUT these plans." Allen surely did not realize that redemption of this pledge would absorb his entire life. In the winter of 1848–1849 he taught and was principal for one term at Milton Academy, assisted by Amos Coon, who had himself invited Bethuel Church to start Alfred's select school in 1836. Allen was offered a permanent position there but, feeling committed to Kenyon and Alfred Academy, he turned it down. In 1849 he left Oberlin, returning to Alfred to marry Abigail Maxson and join the Compact. According to Oberlin records, he received his A.B. degree in 1852, providing a graduation oration on "Ultraism and Christianity," and his A.M. degree in 1855. Allen later studied at Harvard as well.[8]

To students attending Alfred in the generations after Kenyon's death, Jonathan Allen was a most distinguished and striking faculty member. He was an imposing figure, described by some as a giant: tall and broad shouldered, he weighed well over two hundred pounds. In later years his flowing white beard gave him the appearance of an Old Testament prophet. He was a strict disciplinarian but very human, with a cordial, easy manner and gentle humor. "He was dignified in his walk and general carriage, impressing all who saw or met him. As a public speaker, he was clear, logical, convincing, eloquent. His gestures were graceful and appropriate to his thought. His education was broad, and included Theology and Law in addition to College."[9]

Allen's faith, while profound, was somewhat unorthodox, pantheistic in scope, and regarded as dangerously liberal by some. His interests were so broad, his spirit so generous, that narrow dogma would have been anathema to him. Curiously, though they seem to have been at odds over the theology school's direction, it was Allen whom the denomination repeatedly chose as Professor of Theology, not Kenyon. With none of Kenyon's impetuous, fiery temperament, Allen prevailed by a more subtle influence: "There was an air of invincible intellectual energy about him which was a very inspiration." Boothe Colwell Davis remembered, "He was a man of slow movement and speech, but was graceful, dignified, and ponderous in the impressions which he made. He was a wide reader and was a master thinker in many fields. His knowledge of natural history was a marvel of scholarship for his day, of which his Steinheim collections were ample proof. His teaching of psychology, philosophy, and ethics was by the Socratic method, richly supplied with humor, sometimes with keen sarcasm."[10]

While Kenyon stressed the virtues of drill and hard work, Allen tried to develop his students' reflective abilities, appreciation for a complex natural order, and strength of character. Davis summarized, "He sought

Fig. 6.1. Jonathan Allen. About 1870.

to develop all sides of the student, the physical, the moral and the religious as well as the intellectual. He strove to make it the postulate of human personality, that it should lead all men to become not only politically free, but educated and also religious." Mary Taylor Burdick remembered, "President Allen taught us the good, the true, and emphasized the fact that towering above everything was attainment of Christian character." Allen himself wrote, "The highest end of education is, therefore, not to make scholars, simply, nor skilled workmen, but, rather, to develop characters, strong, noble and beautiful."[11]

Allen taught nearly every subject offered: mathematics, history, civics, the natural sciences, natural history, literature, rhetoric, elocution, Latin, Hebrew, metaphysics, and theology. He flung himself into field after field, learning mathematics, English philology, Hebrew, history, and particularly elocution. He studied theology, law, and even medicine for a while, hoping, after the sudden death of their two-year-old son Willie (named for William Kenyon), to be better prepared to care for his family and deal with typhoid epidemics that periodically swept the school.

Lewis remembered well the onset of Allen's passion for natural history and geology: "Away back in the sixties he returned from a trip to New York City with an exhaustive treatise—a score of volumes—on the subject of zoology, which, as far as the students were concerned, was a disaster, for we were at once required to take up that study in the regular course, and in our efforts to follow him in his exhaustive study of the subject, most of us were so hopelessly entangled in the meshes of its technicalities, that to this day we have not forgotten our ignominious discomfiture."[12]

Natural history became a joint passion with his wife and they spent a great deal of time "geologizing," gathering specimens for what became a very large collection. For more than thirty-five years, they tramped the countryside with students, sometimes camping, sometimes staying with friends, gathering plants, rocks, and fossils. They shipped back a ton of samples from a single field trip. Jonathan Allen took over the geology classes and Abigail taught botany, her students collecting and arranging up to three hundred specimens each term. "During the long vacations many a summer day was spent with hammer, basket, and botany box, in creek beds and ravines, or over the hills, for something new. In a few years the collection represented many miles of the adjacent territory traveled over in that manner, stretching out as far as Buffalo on the west, Rochester on the north, on the east to the Atlantic, and as far south as the Natural Bridge in Virginia."[13]

As Kenyon had bought the land and put up the buildings, Allen took pleasure in improving the grounds. For more than twenty years he spent his leisure hours planting and transplanting. His son, Alfred, remembered helping his father:

> He [President Allen] also took upon himself to make the grounds less unsightly. They had been calloused and bare like the palm of a peasant.

Fig. 6.2. Jonathan Allen standing among the trees he planted on campus. The Chapel is in the background. 1880s.

He gave a public park, then changed the wooden bridges to his designs in stone. Personally he drove willow stakes in the gash between the two [bridges]. . . .

Later, came purchase of trees. These came with roots wrapped in burlap. Students responded nobly, buying at cost, but there were always many left over to be paid for from his salary, never a hundred a month and already gnawed to the bone.

I was big enough to carry the smaller stones that went into the bottom of the holes, the larger on top to preserve moisture. Then I would hold the little evergreens erect while his stronger arms filled in and packed the earth. Later, it was one of my chores to carry water to keep them moist.[14]

In the last days of Jonathan Allen's life, sitting up to ease his breathing, he asked that his chair be moved to the window so that he could watch students crossing the grounds, now beautiful, that he had spent so many decades planting.

The Allen house was always open to students, as guests, boarders, or workers. Leona Burdick Merrill remembered "President Allen, the tall, white-haired figure that was every where present, the great veranda of the Allen house with its big, rustic rocking chair—every cranny of the house not occupied by the family was given over to students and their families." Their son recalled the onslaught at commencement: "Like an Arab Sheikh it was the duty of the President to feed visiting ex-students. At commencement they came in caravans. Chicken seemed their favorite. Why, I had worn out my second pair of long pants before I knew by taste a hen had white meat."[15]

Allen's accession to the presidency meant the values held jointly with his wife dominated the school for the rest of the century. Abigail described them as "co-workers," sharing interest in education, natural history, and reform movements, sharing the belief that true education was "radical," "reformatory." "President Allen was a born radical," she wrote. "In the societies, in the church, and in secular work he was a leader in all the reform questions of the day." As one speaker attested at Allen's memorial service, "He gallantly maintained woman's equal privilege with man to win in the common struggle for maintenance, for place and power." Another said, "He was among the first to believe in woman's equality with man. He believed that she had the right to an education outside of the old established domestic lines. He believed she had the right to think, to act, to vote. He espoused these principles in the face of centuries of prejudice. He demanded for woman the right to fill positions of trust; to become lawyers, doctors, ministers of the gospel, and at a time when it was but little less than martyrdom to promulgate such doctrine. He builded better than he knew."[16]

In the 1870s, Abigail and Jonathan Allen's views on women's equity, developed over forty years, reached their fullest expression. Coeducation was still controversial, particularly in the Northeast, where women's enrollment was sparse: "The number of woman undergraduates in fall 1872 at institutions of higher education in New England was fifteen (eight at

Vermont, four at Wesleyan, and one each at Bates, Colby, and Maine)." There, "from the vantage of the established male colleges," gender integration associated with coeducation was viewed as more threatening than the segregation of women's colleges. In 1870, when about 3,000 women were studying in baccalaureate programs nationally, 2,200 of them were in women's colleges. Only 800 were in coeducational colleges, and at many of these, particularly those not founded as coeducational, hostility to women was marked. This hostility only worsened as time passed.[17]

The Alfred Student quoted the Cornell Era on its disparaging attitude toward the few women who enrolled in 1872, four years after men first enrolled:

> Co-education is the siren that has lured the votary of science from his laboratory, and the literary *recluse* from his book to indulge in the frivolous amusement of hopping about to slow music; and co-education has much to answer for. During the past two years we have noticed with regret, the gradual decline of the sturdy manhood of our student yeomanry. There has been a subtle force at work, sapping and undermining its manly independence; and ere long we shall have nothing but a race of simpering, pirouetting, Frenchified coxcombs, the height of whose ambition will be to doff a stylish hat in a stylish manner to the lady acquaintances they chance to meet.[18]

Cornell's environment continued to be restrictive and "by unwritten law, the women of Cornell were definitely out of place." Campus organizations discouraged their participation and fraternities completely excluded them; they would "not allow their members to speak to women students on the campus, to invite them to parties, or to consider giving a Cornell woman a fraternity pin. . . . Ellen Coit Brown '82 reported that 'we never talked to the men in the halls or the classrooms when coming and going, nor walked anywhere with them—on the campus. In the large lecture halls and the small classrooms, filled mostly with our brothers and cousins and future husbands, we walked demurely, as inconspicuously as we could manage, and took seats, always at the front.'" Not until 1897 did any woman teach in a Cornell classroom, no woman was appointed to faculty rank until 1912, and the university maintained separate male and female alumni/ae organizations until 1960.[19]

General resistance came to a head in 1873, when Dr. Edward Clarke published *Sex in Education.* He first articulated his theories at a December 1872 meeting of the New England Woman's Club, of which Julia Ward Howe was a member. Feminists such as Howe and Caroline Dall immediately counterattacked, Howe retorting that the reason Clarke found disease in American women "is simply this, some of them wish to enter Harvard College." Harvard adamantly resisted women, even after its Annex (Radcliffe) was established. One student remembered her own brother would not deign to recognize her within Harvard Yard.

In 1871 Howe made a celebrated and controversial visit to speak at Alfred. Two years later, the first annual Woman's Congress (of the nascent Association for the Advancement of Women) was held in New York City and Howe invited Abigail Allen to speak there on coeducation. Allen's views must have been welcome to the four hundred women crowding the meeting hall. To her, coeducation was the natural order. Such a model could allay fears stirred up by Clarke's terrifying scenario of sickly undergraduates and withered wombs. If women's education was harmonious with natural family roles, then it could not be threatening or "de-sexing." Allen's argument provided a reassuringly conservative model of gender relations, preserving traditional values and societal stability; yet this was a family with a difference—one that incorporated natural rights philosophy and defined a public role for women. Like other feminists studied by Hersh, Allen "accepted the assigned feminine attributes only insofar as they were compatible with their own perspective": the family that Allen knew shared labor, responsibility for reform, and an education.[20]

Abigail Allen opened her Woman's Congress address by stating her conviction that reform was the noblest pursuit. Education itself should be radical and reforming: "Any culture to be noblest must not only have its inspiration in harmony with the great human and divine influences, but it must move on the high tide of human progress, keep abreast of the world's advance movements; in one word, be radical, radical to the core."[21] Humanity carried conservative thinkers "reluctantly as dead weights, and feels very much relieved when it shakes them off into their soon-forgotten graves, over which it weeps no tears but takes a long breath of relief, straightens up and moves on more lightly than before in its upward course." Colleges must be active in advancing human thought: "Institutions . . . must sail well ahead of the great human flotilla, not waiting to be wafted along by the breeze of public opinion, but starting currents in the spiritual atmosphere that shall waft others." Every reform has been opposed by "an immense noise," but history enforces its own "all-conquering logic," bringing reformers through the wilderness to "victorious possession of the promised land."

For Abigail, women's status was a marker of civilization: "every stage of progress in [woman's] development as a human being has been met by grave prophecies of evil that it could not be done without a general wreck of all good. Yet the simplest historian knows that he can mark the degree and the quality of the civilization of any period or people by the position of woman among that people or in that time. Social and political ethics has no more important problems to solve than those coming from this false position of one-half of the human family."

Recognition of women's economic and educational needs was essential: "The needle plied by hand is fast becoming a thing of the past, and woman, having learned the alphabet, is substituting the pen for the needle. The time has come when the higher education of woman is no longer treated lightly." Echoing Kenyon, Abigail declared, "All of the thoughtful and the observant, both of men and women, are unsatisfied with the old form boarding-school style and the institutions termed Ladies' Seminaries. . . . They have too often had it for their aim to finish women's education just at that point and period of life when the solid parts of the young man's education begins."

Yet most colleges barred women, or at best admitted them in a carefully rationed, condescending fashion. Women "have been recently knocking at the doors of most of our colleges. While some have slammed the door in the faces of the intruders, and double bolted them, others have left their doors ajar, with a coy invitation to knock again, and a little louder than before, and we may arise and let you in. Or, it may be in the style that Col. Higginson represents Harvard as replying, 'Go around to the side door, my daughters, and we will see what can be done for you. . . . but so long as you persist in knocking at the front door you must remain outside of it.'"[22]

Allen then went on to describe coeducation as practiced at Alfred University:

> Co-education means a common faculty, a common curriculum, a common examination. I can do no better, perhaps, than to relate in this connection, some of the effects of co-education, as thus defined in the institution at Alfred, in this State, with which I have been connected, first as student, then as teacher, for over a third of a century. The work of this school has been a hard and pioneer one, as must ever be the founding and building of a school without endowment, in a region without wealth. . . . In this time, it has had some 6,600 matriculates, of whom 3,600 have been males and 3,000 females. The provisions of the charter grant equal right and privileges to both sexes.

Economy was a chief advantage of coeducation, economies for the institution and also for the many students working their way through college. Recalling the sacrifices she and others had made to gain their education, she believed women were particularly in need of assistance:

> The following are some of the results: First, economy. It enables the institution to nearly double the number of students with the same means, as far as to buildings, library, apparatus and teachers as would be required for either sex alone. It enables brothers and sisters to mutually help each other. . . . Sometimes a brother sends himself and sister, and occasionally a sister a younger brother; yet there are sad features connected with these good ones. Parents are more apt to help their sons than their daughters, and society helps the young men by giving them plenty of work and good pay, whilst the work for young women is precarious, and mostly poorly paid.

Allen described other advantages. At Alfred the academic performance of women was slightly higher than that of men. Furthermore, "In the comparatively high degree of order, and moral tone of the institution, woman's presence and influence has been an important factor."

"Barbarisms" found at all-male schools were avoided: "in our vocabulary there are no such words as 'haze' and 'rush' and 'smoke.'" Such order and respect for women, she observed, was lacking at some of the "best of Eastern colleges," which were all male and overrun by a "swarming brood" of secret fraternities. By contrast, "Women at Oberlin, as in most Western colleges, work side by side with men. Instead of westward, eastward, must this civilizing influence take its way."

Character development was also enhanced in a community of young men and women sharing mutually inspiring enthusiasm. In that setting alone did men develop the finest masculine virtues, "keeping in check the animal, the trifling, the effeminate," and women the finest feminine virtues: "The highest and best development, other things being equal, is given in the family where there are both sons and daughters. . . . Our highest ideal of the school is that it should approach as near as possible the family in its general tone."

Some feared that coeducation would encourage imprudent marriages. Allen evinced no concern, based on her experience: "All of the known inter-marriages of Alfred students consequent upon their school life is *three per cent.* of the whole number. . . . it may be confidently asked under what other arrangements could more than six thousand young men and women . . . be brought into daily association . . . with less per cent. of marriages." In fact, she argued, matches that do result are "more likely to be based upon the mutual attractions that come from genuine, enduring mental and spiritual qualifications, than can be those based upon the flash acquaintances of the ball room, or the sea side." Allen's report of the "known inter-marriages" was somewhat disingenuous: the Kenyons, the Allens, the Sayles, the Davises, these marriages all were "consequent upon their school life" at Alfred.

Allen concluded:

> This Institution [Alfred], having been organized on the plan of co-education for thirty-seven years, has no more thought of changing, than parents who find in their families boys and girls, would think of organizing two households in which to train them.
>
> Again, life work means co-work of the sexes. The post-graduate course imposed by life's discipline unites the sexes. This discipline, this culture, is imperfect, one-sided, without this union. Therefore, that preparatory training is best which conforms to this great school of life.

She closed by offering the following resolution: "*Resolved*, That it is the duty of this Congress to labor earnestly and perseveringly for the opening of all of our colleges to our daughters, as to our sons, with equal rights and privileges for both." This was unanimously adopted.

Allen's address was a compelling defense of equality and coeducation. Yet her spirited words represent more than her own beliefs, more

than her husband's. First articulated in the 1840 "Valedictory" by a select
school student, the analogy to family was made frequently over the years,
perhaps most forcefully by Jonathan Allen in an 1876 article called
"Mixed Schools." With his famed sarcasm, he delivered this wholesale
indictment of woman's condition:

> Educationally ostracised, industrially an inferior, matrimonially a serf or
> appendage, politically nonexistent, civilly a child—such hitherto has
> largely been the history of woman.
>
> Notwithstanding, having learned the alphabet, she is already knock-
> ing at college doors for admission. Some have arisen and let her in,
> others are trying to compromise by throwing to her such crumbs as fall
> from her master's tables in the form of local examinations, and other,
> while many colleges have slammed their doors in her face and left her
> out in the dark and cold, to grope, and freeze, and starve. Is her demand
> a right and proper one?

Jonathan Allen saw men and women as one, working together by
divine intent. This partnership extended to all their relationships—
educational, occupational, legal, political, civil, religious. All human attempts to segregate were mistaken: "Humanity, the offspring of Divinity,
is an organic unity, with a nature, prerogatives, privileges, needs, and destiny, conformable to its origin and nature. It is not made up of individuals, segregated like a sand heap, but wrought into organic unity. This
humanity is bi-fold, masculine and feminine, with correlate and co-equal
rights, prerogatives, and needs. . . . All isolation of individuals, all segregation of classes, on the principles of caste, birth, sex, or occupation,
becomes abnormal, dwarfing, and distorting."

Mankind, he argued, is structured primarily in families, "the stem
from which branch all legitimate human organizations, social, civil, educational, and religious . . . The family is the divine type for all training of
men and women together in this earthly preparatory school, for the larger,
higher, diviner school of heaven. . . . God united the sexes in the family,
the church, the state; man and Satan have separated them in the cloister
and the camp."

In concert with such radical thinkers as Mary Wollstonecraft, John
Stuart Mill, and Elizabeth Cady Stanton, Allen asserted that intelligence
is independent of sex: "The essential powers of the spirit are neither masculine nor feminine, but human, sexless. Thought knows no sex. A common education in family and school places worthiness above gender. . . .
All educational institutions should rest upon the same divine basis as the
family. . . . The whole action and interaction of a college thus organized
is that of a family, while a college with its prerogatives and privileges
based on sex, is a system of caste as cramping and deteriorating as any
other caste system or monkish organization."[23]

Jonathan Allen's vision was very close to that of reformers studied by Isenberg, who found that religious dissidents developed a philosophy of "co-equality of the sexes" and races: "In this feminist version of the state of nature, woman like man garnered inalienable rights from God" and was endowed with equal capabilities. For these reformers, liberty of conscience and freedom of speech were paramount. "Moreover, they applied dissent as both a principle and a narrative strategy to their feminist ideology." They affirmed that "men and women—and their rights and wrongs—could never be segregated into distinct and separate spheres, because, most early feminists concluded, both spiritual and material ties bound together all human relations." Like these feminists, the Allens proclaimed themselves radical, and while it would be an exaggeration to say that Jonathan Allen was a religious dissident, he was far from a religious conformist: his deep spirituality, distinctively his own, was "larger than his denomination" and he agitated for change—granting power to women—within his church. Like his wife, Allen believed that each individual was created with a free conscience.[24]

Reflecting the Allens' views, women's rights agitation continued in Alfred's literary societies. The intense national furor spurred by Clarke's alarming assertions was reflected when his *Sex in Education* was reviewed in the April 1874 issue of *The Alfred Student*. The reviewer summarized Clarke's treatise, which described in exquisite detail the danger posed by a woman's education occurring at the same time her uterus was being formed. Tellingly, physical labor did not seem to affect "factory girls'" uteruses, but education—*that* was dangerous, particularly coeducation.

The campus response came quickly. On April 26 the Alleghanians (a men's literary society) affirmed "that sex would not Physiologically prohibit women from coeducation." The May issue of *The Alfred Student* contained a lengthy review of Julia Ward Howe's collection of essays (written by Howe, Mrs. Horace Mann, Caroline Dall, and others) refuting the physician. Dall (who would soon become acquainted with Alfred) observed acidly that "whatever danger menaces the health of America, it cannot thus far have sprung from the overeducation of her women." The reviewer agreed with Howe that Clarke's facts were insufficient (he cited only seven cases), his inferences irrelevant, and the testimonies perverted: "Laying down Dr. Clarke's book, the feeling uppermost in our mind was, that Heaven must needs grant patience to women who read the books that men presume to write about them." With its emphasis on the importance of women's independent voice, the next sentence suggests the reviewer was either Jonathan or Abigail Allen: "The perusal of Mrs. Howe's Reply awakes a thrill of intense thankfulness that women can speak for themselves."

In 1875 the Athenaeans presented a "Colloquy on 'Woman's Rights'" at their Anniversary session and the Alfriedians, in their showpiece Jubilee session on Christmas evening, staged their famous Congressional debate, placed in the distant year 2000, over the pros and cons of *giving back*—to men—the right to vote. Alfred's students also watched events at other coeducational schools with interest. They criticized Cornell's treating women as outcasts and hostility on the Wesleyan campus, where women were first admitted in 1872, labeled as "quails," and grudgingly tolerated—"though with us, are not of us."[25] A woman was elected Wesleyan's class poet in 1876 and then forced to resign by irate male undergraduates. *The Alfred Student* mocked Wesleyan for "the latest outrage" in an article, "The 'Woman' Trouble Again," that treated prescribed gender roles with irony:

> A woman has been so bold and unwomanly as to suffer herself to be elected Class Poet of the Class of '77, Wesleyan University, and thirteen out of thirty members refuse to take their part, if she persists in delivering her poem. The unblushing audacity of these women is marvelous. In opposition to all sense of propriety they have crowded themselves into college. Now, when we come home for vacation . . . the maidens don't cling to us in wonder, admiration, and awe. They have been to college, too. . . .
>
> In behalf of womanly simplicity, and modesty, and refinement, and proper dependence upon the sterner sex, we exhort the brave and immortal thirteen to stand firm. The interests of humanity are resting on you, gentlemen, and you can not falter.[26]

Wesleyan's men did not falter; they asked for "game laws" to limit the number of "quails" and finally the Wesleyan trustees voted to eliminate women from the student body.

However ardent the allies of coeducation at Alfred, a faction resistant to the most outspoken visitors reared its head when a dispute erupted between the liberal Allens and more conservative trustees. The country's first honorary LL.D. degree granted a woman was given at Alfred in 1878, to Caroline Dall, noted feminist and author. However, controversy over that honor and cloudy records leave doubt as to whether Dall ultimately received the degree.[27]

Dall's first visit to Alfred occurred in January 1876. Well-known as author of *Women's Rights Under the Law* and *The College, the Market, and the Court* (a lecture series on women's rights), one of the faculty had written her some years previous, seeking advice on Abigail Allen's long-term concern: remunerative occupations for women. This led to intermittent correspondence on women's work culminating in Abigail Allen's visit to Dall in Boston (where Abigail studied art in the summer of 1875) and an invitation to visit Alfred. Allen told Dall that the school was planning to open a glove factory where young women could work in order to support themselves while studying. According to Dall, "The industrial plans had prospered; they were about to erect a building for the making of gloves and shirts, and they wanted me to see it."[28] (No trace of this project remains in institutional records.)

Like Allen, Caroline Dall believed that "all educational institutions should be kept open" to women and was indignant at women's meager salaries. She asked that women have "free, untrammelled access to all fields of labor; and I ask it, first, on the ground that she needs to be fed, and that the question which is at this moment before the great body of working women is 'death or dishonor': for lust is a better paymaster than the mill-owner or the tailor. . . . It is pretty and lady-like, men think, to paint and chisel: philanthropic young ladies must work for nothing, like the angels. *Let* them, when they rise to angelic spheres; but, here and now, every woman who works for nothing helps to keep her sister's wages down,—helps to keep the question of death or dishonor perpetually before the women of the slop-shop." Women labored arduously, unrecognized and uncompensated, and had done so throughout human history: "I showed you that [women] were not only working hard, but had been working at hard and unwholesome work, not merely in this century, but in all centuries since the world began. I showed you how man himself has turned them back, when they have entered a well-paid career."[29]

Dall left impressed with the spirit and commitment of the people she met at Alfred: Mrs. Allen; Reverend Hull's deep knowledge of his faith; Hull's and Allen's extensive libraries; Mark Sheppard, a trustee who had been a Kansas soldier and, like Dall and Jonathan Allen, an admirer of John Brown; Mary Coon Sheppard, an Alfred graduate (who helped found the second women's literary society) and local poet who "reads a good deal of Greek and Latin, liking Livy and Thucydides best, because each of these seems to her 'the best exponent of his own people and tongue'"; people teaching Arabic and Hebrew privately and at the University; the large number of teachers among alumni. She praised "such institutions as [Oberlin and Alfred], founded in religious enthusiasm and built up by religious self-denial [in which] a truly reverent free-inquiry is born. . . . 'Why do you care so much for these people?' my friends used to say about Oberlin; 'you who think so differently from them.' And they will now make the same inquiry about Alfred. The answer which springs first to my lips is, 'I care for these people because they believe something and do something.'"[30]

In October 1877, Dall visited again, staying with Mary Coon Sheppard, whom she had praised in the pages of *The New Era*. In November, Jonathan Allen published an essay on Dall's life and beliefs in *The Alfred Student*, admiring "her work on Woman's Rights [which] has been so exhaustive in logic and facts that it has been a golden fountain from which most of the later writers and lecturers have drawn."[31] She returned in February 1878 to give lectures on Abraham Lincoln, a sermon, and a chapel lecture.

Their shared views and admiration for Dall's publications on women's legal rights led to President Allen's nominating Dall for a honorary doctor of laws degree, initially approved by the trustees in spring 1878. But objections were raised at the last moment, a board meeting was held without Allen during commencement, and the board voted to table the matter, notifying Allen of their action just minutes before he was to announce the degree. The following October the degree was reinstated at a special board meeting. The Allens and Dall were aggrieved by this incident. Whether the objections were to Dall's published criticisms of Alfred's Sabbatarians and temperance, her Unitarianism, or another cause, her outspokenness brought her the Allens' admiration but led to the board's vacillations.[32]

President Allen's sympathies lay with the women in this debate and others like it. Both Jonathan and Abigail Allen saw that equity meant education, employment, and ultimately the ballot. So many women were in need of work. Abigail's sister, Jerusha Maria Maxson McCray, earned an M.D. at the Woman's Medical College of Philadelphia after her husband's death, "finding a large family of children depending on her for support . . . largely supporting herself and children during her studies by doing anything, everything, that would help on."[33] These were women who wanted to work, who needed to work, and knew that their earnings were valuable to their families. Convinced of the importance of their economic role, they were indignant at unequal recognition, restricted opportunities, and discriminatory pay.

Most students worked and sacrificed to gain an education. However, the "universal poverty" had an uneven effect on women for they had fewer opportunities to earn their way. Women's employment was fundamental to Abigail Allen's vision of equal rights. In her 1873 address, she decried the lack of adequate training and meaningful employment, stating that typically a woman's education ended too quickly, fitting her for no occupation: "Then she sits down to wait the coming man, and to dream and fritter away several of the most precious years of her life. A young lady of this description said a short time since, 'O, how little men know of the terrible suffering of this state. The *ennui*, the routine of little nothings that absorb like a sponge all of life's noblest aspirations.' On being asked why she did not break away from them and go to work in earnest, [she] replied, 'We are bound by the silken cords of the proprieties, cords though silken and very delicate, bind with a power more irresistible, and a pressure more galling than any felon's chain and ball.' The more earnest and capable are imploring for admission to the ranks of those seeking higher culture." For those women who did make the effort, economic barriers loomed large: "A few only can be accommodated in families to work for their board, and as they hold the book in one hand, and do a servant's full work with the other, there is danger of the task being too much. Some have failed here. The teachers' profession is constantly overcrowded with us, being often two teachers to each school."[34]

Allen's preoccupation with this issue was shared by her husband. His indignant article, "Education for Women," attacked prejudice against women's education and employment. His anger was caused by an 1876 *Atlantic* article that lamented the fact that girls outnumbered boys in St. Louis high schools and perhaps throughout the entire country. Stating the cause, "owing to the early age at which boys are expected to get their living, while their sisters are not expected to do likewise at any age," the *Atlantic* proposed a remedy: "If the daughters of the trading and working classes, from the age of eighteen, could relieve the family purse by their earnings to the extent of their board and clothing merely, it is probable that their brothers could stay a longer time at their books, and thus the American voter be better prepared for his political and social responsibilities." Shocked by the essayist's ignorance of real conditions, Allen protested that countless women augmented their families' income and sacrificed their own ambitions so that their brothers "might be plastered over with a college education." Still, Allen wrote, "according to our sapient exhorter, it is her duty to smother all ambition, to cheerfully accept this state of affairs."[35]

Allen's extraordinary sympathy for women's narrow circumstances surely grew in part from his wife's convictions, which were clearly communicated to her students. Her demand for equal pay in 1844 was echoed almost fifty years later by Phebe Babcock Waite, an 1860 graduate who became a physician and mother of seven, practiced obstetrics, taught, and became dean of the Woman's Medical College. Dr. Waite encouraged other women to become physicians because she felt it was the only profession in which they could earn "equal compensation with men."[36]

Some historians have argued that women's rights leaders were elitist and upper class in their orientation; by contrast, the Allens joined those whose convictions were firmly tied to labor issues. Like Rochester feminists of agrarian origin, Abigail Allen's life was built on relatively egalitarian families, paid labor, and public service. With Quaker reformers, Abigail Allen combined "concrete knowledge of women's economic worth with a theoretical concept of equality to demand more power in the public sphere." For more than fifty years the Allens taught their students to prize both.[37]

No wonder the cloistered world of separate spheres appeared either irrelevant or fantastical to this community. Keenly aware of his wife's and sister-in-law's experiences, Allen wrote indignantly of the many women passing through Alfred who had to support themselves and their families: "among [Alfred] graduates there are more females than males who furnish their own pecuniary resources. What recompense do these women receive who for the precious sons and brothers make themselves laundresses, tailors, waiters, and, in short, slaves? . . . But I can not see why, if woman has a mind, it was given her to be cramped and dwarfed and starved. If woman is a rational creature, it is not only her privilege, but also her duty to develop perfectly and symmetrically her God-given powers, even if it takes the ballot to do it; . . . 'the exercise of equity for one day is equal to sixty years spent in prayer.'"[38] His position that voting rights might be necessary to secure woman's God-given right to develop her talents was radical for an educator in 1876.

The first public call for women's suffrage was in the famous 1848 Declaration of Sentiments, issued by the first woman's rights convention in Seneca Falls, New York. For many decades after, suffrage was viewed as the most radical demand, challenging basic social and civil relations; profound changes in the power balance, both familial and societal, were feared. Otherwise progressive women shied away from association with such a disruptive notion, some from conviction, others fearing it would jeopardize the fight for education, employment, equal pay, or property rights. Horace Greeley, liberal on many issues, opposed suffrage on the grounds that most women did not want the vote and, expressing the most profound fear, that "female suffrage seems to me to involve the balance of the family relation as it has hitherto existed."[39] But for the Allens, the family could not be unbalanced by its members sharing civic duties and concern for national issues.

In 1875 an *Alfred Student* article addressed the question "Who Should Vote?" The author stated the "road to political progress" lay in expanding the number who could vote to all who possessed "virtue and intelligence," implicitly including women.[40] Two years later Jonathan Allen's article appeared, explicitly favoring women's suffrage and discarding the view that virtue and intelligence should be the test. Based on Enlightenment principles, he argued that all citizens should vote:

> The primary duty of a nation . . . is to secure, maintain, and enforce equal or reciprocal freedom for each and every member of the nation. This springs from the original rights of humanity, higher than national prerogative, and for which nationality came into existence. . . . Nations can not bestow rights; they can only ascertain, declare, and protect what before existed. Law does not determine rights; but rights determine law. . . .
>
> The primary generic right of every person, underlying and upholding all others, is the right of participating in the national life . . . by presence and voice . . . or by vote and proxy. . . . It is the birthright of freedom. . . . A portion of the members of a state can not, of their own will, fix the status of the remainder. It is always the infringement of equality or reciprocal freedom, hence of justice, when a portion of the citizens of a state assumes to pronounce upon the rights of the remainder. . . . In the presence of rights, race, sex, or color distinctions disappear. The humblest and feeblest being has the same rights as the most powerful and gifted.[41]

Yet, most educators continued to oppose suffrage into the twentieth century, even when women's vote in public school elections was permitted in nearly half the states and full suffrage in four. Lynn Gordon's study of the Progressive Era (1890–1920) noted, "connections between higher education and feminism remained tenuous. Administrators of both single-sex and coeducational institutions denied any connections between women's higher education and the women's rights movement; at some schools, like Vassar, officials forbade organized suffrage activities. Fear of adverse public reaction and possible diminishing enrollments as well as, in many cases, their own belief in separate spheres caused presidents and deans to insist that college women should be and would be a conservative social force." Not until 1906, at a convention arranged by M. Carey Thomas, did a group of college women first publicly endorse suffrage.

Even then, women's colleges were still resisting discussion of the issue and the Association of Collegiate Alumnae refused to support it.[42]

The Allens thus were remarkable among educators in supporting the most radical demand. Abigail Allen led a locally famous voting incident in 1887 (some years after Anthony made her notorious attempt to vote), probably spurred by Lucy Barber, an Alfred resident who voted in the November 1886 Congressional election. "The men crowded into the poll-room as soon as they saw [Barber] go into it, listened very quietly with deep interest, and treated her with entire courtesy." She was arrested but a sympathetic grand jury failed to indict her. The New York City "Ladies Suffrage Committee" celebrated Barber's vote in an evening of speeches predicting women would soon vote generally throughout the state. In 1887, ten more Alfred women, led by Abigail Allen, followed Barber's example and voted in the municipal election. The *Allegany County Reporter* defended their intentions: "It is just to remark that the ladies indicted embrace the best of Alfred citizenship and that they have got into this position from the belief that they were fully entitled to the power. Some of them have visibly weakened in this belief and we imagine all would gladly abandon the path of martyrdom for the benefit of their sex, which leads through indictment, overt trial and probable conviction." They were indeed arrested and indicted, which emboldened the District Attorney to resubmit Barber's action for indictment. Charges were brought again and Barber was tried. Following a verdict of "guilty," she was sentenced to the county jail for one day.[43]

The fate of the ten indicted women is not so clear. One town legend reports the intervention of a sympathetic judge: "the women were taken to Belmont [the county seat] to stand trial. The court was filled with excited spectators. Everyone in Alfred who could possibly arrange it took a day off to see what was going to happen to the leading ladies of the community. But as the proceedings began, the judge ruled that before they could proceed with the trial, they must first prove that they were women. This so horrified the good men of Alfred that the charges were immediately dropped." According to a 1903 account, the ten were convicted and sentenced, though the sentences were never served.[44]

At Alfred, "the exercise of equity" was indeed judged supreme to sixty years of prayer. That exercise included a public platform for women. The Allens challenged the socially constructed boundaries between public and private domains, particularly in the essential act of speaking out. Women could not press their claims for equality if they were denied a voice. For the Allens, individual liberty of conscience led ultimately to political action. Freedom of speech—enabling women to speak—linked the two. In the dim glow of kerosene lamps, arguing strenuously in weekly debates, student camaraderie and competition were most evident in the literary societies. Here also, Alfred's unusually liberal environment was most evident, as women were encouraged to train for public speaking when they were forbidden that activity nearly everywhere.

Chapter Seven

"The Exercise of Equity"
A Voice for Women

The most natural way in the world. If a young woman is capable of writing a paper, she ought to be able to read it.

—Jonathan Allen, in Abigail Allen, *Life and Sermons*

Nowhere is Alfred's egalitarian environment clearer than in the arena of public speaking. Abigail Allen founded the school's first women's literary society in 1846 when other pioneering institutions suppressed such organizations as inappropriate to the private, domestic role defined by separate spheres ideology. Early development of their literary societies led Alfred's women to break other barriers—to give orations and to invite women's rights lecturers. As the years went by, women spoke out more frequently and forcefully.

Few historians have looked closely at literary society records, yet they provide fascinating insights into student response to contemporary intellectual and political issues. Student societies were, as James McLachlan termed them, a college within a college, evoking energy and enthusiasm, providing a platform to prepare for public life. "Here students sought and shaped an education that they considered relevant to their future lives." One Yale undergraduate testified that literary societies "have done more toward making men than all the rest of college training put together. . . . They are the schools which train . . . best for the practicalities of . . . [the] world."[1]

Even fewer historians had examined women's societies until Ogren's study of coeducational normal schools' societies in the late nineteenth century and Mary Kelley's exploration of literary societies at women's academies and seminaries recently appeared.[2] Within collegiate culture, itself confused by the larger question of women's status, societies were a crucial

117

field on which profound disagreements over women's role were played out. Their development was erratic, hampered by the assumption that their public purpose excluded females. Often described as conservative or cloistered at other schools, at Alfred literary societies were vital in helping women analyze current issues, build self-confidence, prepare for public life, and speak out on controversial topics. At other schools, attempts to discuss women's rights were frequently squelched by college authorities, but the Allens encouraged the societies to serve as a forum for discussion of women's equality—intellectual, legal, educational, professional, and political.

Why was this so unusual? Public speaking and the study of rhetoric presented a significant curricular problem when women sought higher education, since they were expected to be silent in public, church, and mixed company (deemed "promiscuous assemblies" when men and women were in public together). Rhetoric and oratory were highly valued by nineteenth-century educators. Frederick Barnard, President of Columbia College, said, "Nothing can possess a higher practical value, to any man, than that which . . . gives him habits of clear, systematic, and independent thought, which . . . invigorates his powers of reasoning, teaches him to analyze, chastens and refines his taste . . . and confers upon him the priceless gift of lucid and forcible utterance."[3] The oratorical tradition, with its emphasis on "forcible utterance," was central to the liberal arts from early times but incompatible with women's assigned role.

The oratorical tradition also posed a dilemma for the extracurriculum, whose "central institution" was the literary society: "the debater, the orator, the essayist were the heroes of the extracurriculum." Literary societies first appeared at Harvard in 1728; by the nineteenth century nearly every college had at least one (usually two competing societies existed) that prepared undergraduates to become accomplished public speakers. When women became students, were they to find seats on the stage, or merely sit in their accustomed chairs among the audience? As the educational foundation for public life and civic duties, oration was associated with roles—minister, statesman, legislator, lawyer—closed to women. Priscilla Mason, a young academy graduate, declared in 1793, "They have denied women a liberal education and now if we should prove capable of speaking, where could we speak? The Church, the Bar, the Senate are closed against us. Who shut them? Man, Despotic Man."[4] She found no immediate followers. Very few women spoke publicly in the next four decades; the most notable was Fanny Wright who—foreign-born, radical, and accused of favoring free love—was hardly the proper model.

In 1837, two women irreproachable in conduct and motive broke through the barrier. Sarah and Angelina Grimké—Southern-born sisters, Quaker converts—alarmed and amazed the populace by leaving the drawing room and speaking out against slavery. The sisters' obvious piety, refinement, and dignity answered their vituperative critics, and their speaking tours marked the beginning of a new freedom as others tentatively followed their example. Development was slow; when the first women's rights meeting was called at Seneca Falls, New York, in 1848, the organizers were suddenly tongue-tied when men appeared at the gathering. They asked the husband of one organizer (Lucretia Mott) to chair the meeting. But these activist women quickly realized that they could not achieve their goals without the freedom to act in the public arena. "The investigation of the rights of the slave has led me to a better understanding of my own," concluded Angelina Grimké.[5]

Frustration with these restrictions bound together many women who achieved fame in the nineteenth century. They looked to each other as models as they struggled to break through personal and societal barricades. Julia Ward Howe described the change, "little less than miraculous," brought about by women themselves, "women who have keenly felt the disabilities imposed upon them by law and custom, and who have valorously striven to win for themselves and their fellows the outlook of a larger liberty." Those gains were impossible without a public platform.[6]

The issue of course was not just decorum or custom. Frederick Douglass, who practiced oratory secretly as a young slave, was blunt: "In the public mind, oratory was not just a demonstration of great learning, though it was sometimes that, nor was it simply entertainment, though it was decidedly that as well, and people listened for hours; oratory was power." Women who moved into the public arena threatened to unseat power in both domestic and civic relationships. When Abby Kelley rose to speak at the 1840 Connecticut Anti-Slavery Society meeting, the chairman Henry G. Ludlow, a clergyman, protested: "No woman will speak or vote where I am moderator. . . . I will not submit to PETTICOAT GOVERNMENT. No woman shall ever lord it over me. *I am Major-Domo in my own house.*"[7]

Similar struggles occurred as colleges sought to define their approach to women's education. While Oberlin has long and justly been praised as the first college to admit women and blacks, its education for women has more recently been viewed as an ambiguous reform. Women were prohibited from speaking in the classroom if men were in the class and from speaking in mixed groups outside of class. Even recitation of assigned text, the basic pedagogical technique, was barred. Furthermore, while men gave orations at graduation, women's essays were read to the audience by a male professor while the author sat demurely by. President Fairchild reflected on the college's philosophy in 1883: "co-education at Oberlin was not undertaken as a radical reform, but as a practical movement in harmony with the prevalent idea of woman's work and sphere. . . . There was no attempt to put young men and young women upon the same footing, regardless of their diverse natures and relations. . . . There has been no effort to train young women as public speakers. Declamations, orations, and extemporaneous discussions have been required of young men—not of young women. Their elocutionary training has been in the direction of reading rather than of speaking." Fairchild told the student assembly in 1849, "The woman is the natural housekeeper. . . . The claims of the household are paramount, all others are secondary. . . . [I] could not cheerfully bear a part in a system of female education which is false to nature and blots out God's handwriting."[8]

Not all Oberlin women accepted these constraints. Two famous confrontations occurred: one with Antoinette Brown (1825–1921), who attended Oberlin from 1846 to 1850, was the first woman ordained (by a church in 1853) as minister, and later became a feminist leader; the other with her close friend Lucy Stone (1818–1893), who attended from 1843 to 1847 after saving earnings from nine years of teaching and became a very well-known feminist lecturer. Although both expected to remain single, doubting they could find men sympathetic to their radical views, they eventually married brothers in the reform-oriented Blackwell family.

Stone's Oberlin years were turbulent and frustrating. She felt most faculty and students were not sufficiently reform-minded: "They hate Garrison and women's rights. I love both and often find myself at sword's point with them." She wrote her family, "I was never in a place where women are so rigidly taught that they must not speak in public." Brown intended to preach, Stone to lecture; both wanted to practice public speaking in preparation for their careers. Yet "Lucy Stone's request for a debating society was denied, as was another request from women to have a literary magazine."[9]

Jonathan Allen witnessed these confrontations, for he entered Oberlin in 1847. His wife related his experiences with these courageous young women: "Miss Antoinette Brown was a member of the theological class. When each member was asked to give the reasons for the study of theology, Mr. Allen was shocked and indignant to hear the professor [Charles Grandison Finney] say to Miss Brown, 'You will not be expected to state yours.' She immediately arose and left the room, not being able to restrain her tears." Brown wrote to Lucy Stone about this incident, which occurred after her friend's graduation: "They had all told me we should have to speak & I felt so badly at what he said that I just began to cry & was obliged to leave the room. It was the first & last time that I have cried about anything connected with this matter this spring, but it came so unexpectedly." She soon wrote a paper refuting St. Paul's edict, "Let your women keep silence in the churches."[10]

The second confrontation, Stone's refusal to participate in her own graduation, became a touchstone for feminists for decades to come. The furor began with Stone and others agitating for inclusion in the public ceremony. She wrote her family, "We are trying to get the faculty to let the ladies of our class read their own pieces when they graduate. They have never been allowed to do it, but we expect to read for ourselves, or not to write." Their petition was rejected; simultaneously, Stone was elected to prepare a paper as class representative. She refused the honor, asking her family if she had done the right thing, for "I said to President Mahan that I could not accept without a sacrifice of principle that I had no right to make, and I wished to be excused." If she consented to have her paper read by a male professor, "I would make a public acknowledgment of the rectitude of the principle which takes away from women their equal rights, and denies to them the privilege of being co-laborers with men in any sphere to which their ability makes them adequate. . . . I certainly shall not write if I cannot read for myself."[11]

Allen was drawn into the controversy at the dinner table one night:

> The Alfred students boarded at Professor Fairchild's. The discussion of "woman's rights" and other reform movements of the day were agitating public sentiment everywhere. This question was often discussed by the professor and the young men at the dinner table, the discussion sometimes waxing warm, as our boys always took the woman's side.
>
> At the close of the year Lucy Stone, of Boston (now of world-wide fame), refused to graduate because she was not allowed to read her own paper. This annoyed Professor Fairchild, and one day he asked Mr. Allen, "How do you get along with that question at Alfred?" "The most natural way in the world. If a young woman is capable of writing a paper, she ought to be able to read it," was the answer.[12]

Abigail and her husband discussed these incidents with Fairchild years later: "More than a score of years afterward, when President Allen was invited to deliver the annual address at Oberlin, we were the guests of President Fairchild. One day Mr. Allen asked him how they had finally settled the question about the young ladies reading, etc., etc. 'Oh, the girls made such a fuss that we were obliged to allow them to read their theses, but bless God they have not yet asked to deliver orations!' was his quaint reply." In 1859 women were permitted to read their essays. Not until 1874 was a woman permitted to deliver an oration, and only then after "heated discussion" among the faculty. The young orator, Fanny Rice, received anonymous threats through the mail before speaking.[13]

Years later, Lucy Stone named public speaking more important to women's progress than higher education: "The open door for higher education (Oberlin) was the gray dawn of our morning. Its sure day came when the sisters Sarah and Angelina Grimké and Abby Kelley Foster began to speak publicly in behalf of the slaves. Public speaking by women was regarded as something monstrous. All the cyclones and blizzards which prejudice, bigotry and custom could raise, were let loose on these three peerless women."[14]

The environment at two other well-known schools frustrated another student, Olympia Brown, who like Antoinette Brown yearned to become a minister. When Olympia and her sister Oella arrived at Mount Holyoke in fall 1854, "They soon found time to organize a literary society where they could debate, give readings and practice public speaking." Soon, all society members were ordered to appear before a faculty committee and told they must disband because debate was making them "too independent."

The sisters were distressed: "Did all institutions of higher learning have such narrow-minded instructors and rigid regulations?"[15]

After a year at Mount Holyoke, where the multiple regulations seemed unbearable, Olympia searched for a college that would admit her. Rejecting Oberlin because Stone and Antoinette Brown had been barred from speaking, she chose Antioch but soon found barriers remained. When her English instructor announced the next assignment—men would give orations and women would read from their manuscripts—she rebelled. When her turn came, she spoke her piece from memory, keeping the furled manuscript in her hand. The faculty reproached her, but arguing that she had done nothing wrong, she continued to give orations in class, the only woman to do so.

Antioch's faculty took pains to explain that they did not encourage such unsettling behavior. Mary Mann, the President's wife, wrote her sister that one activist alumna "had not gotten her women's rights ideas at the college": "Her coming has saved her from being a furious womens rights woman. All the influence exerted here is adverse to the thing. But as this is where women can be fully educated it brings among others that very class of women greatly to Mr. Mann's annoyance. He makes them inexpressibly uncomfortable here but he tries to modify them."[16]

A female society, with members who favored women's rights, was denied the right to hold a public session: "Mann and the other officers of the college were extremely sensitive to the charge that coeducation produced women bound to challenge their place in society." One student activist, Rebecca Rice, wrote later, "Mr. Mann and the faculty could not quite see the logical results of educating young men and women together in the same classroom. . . . They could not quite put aside the fears and prejudices of the ages."[17]

Thus, opposition to women's public role was common even among the schools that pioneered women's higher education. Mount Holyoke squelched "unwomanly" independence of thought, Antioch refused a public platform, and when Vassar opened in 1865, its prospectus announced Vassar's education would be womanly and so "no encouragement would be given to oratory and debate . . . Debating societies [are] utterly incongruous and out of taste."[18] For good reason, Lucy Stone's stand at Oberlin became legendary.

Such a stand was never necessary at Alfred. Women were permitted to read their compositions before a mixed audience from the very first end-of-term exercises. Even so, Jonathan Allen remembered with amusement the tentative nature of the young women's earliest public excursions: "the proper style was for them to appear on the rostrum, two by two, arm in arm, mutual supports, while they read. Dialogues and colloquies, then very much in vogue, furnished the only exceptions, and the only opportunity for displaying the grace of action." In 1840, young Abigail Maxson was one of these speakers. A listener wrote: "You may wish to hear something concerning our exhibition. . . . Some pieces were very good but few well spoken, though some very well. There were 12 to 14 orations, one dialogue by the gentlemen, also two from the ladies. The writers were Arminda and Lydia A. Maxson of one and Abigail Maxson and Celestia Burdick of the other. Besides there were several compositions from other ladies."[19]

Jonathan Allen began to study elocution in 1852 with several prominent practitioners and worked to improve his students' skills. He recalled their growing interest "especially as these anniversary occasions draw on, not only the chapel, but likewise each vale and wood and hill, are voiced, yea, flooded, with the great tidal wave of commencement eloquence." Allen's interest intensified and "during the forty years that followed, elocution was one of the marked features of Alfred training." In this as other fields, "young women were given the same opportunities as young men." Their daughter Eva Allen Alberti studied oratory, becoming a teacher of drama and elocution at the American Academy of Dramatic Arts. Taught by her father to project her voice (as he taught many students), thousands could hear her reading a poem at an outdoor ceremony in New York City.[20]

By 1854 Alfred's young women broke two barriers: they invited a woman to present a public lecture and they began to give graduation orations. In May the Ladies' Literary Society (founded by Abigail Allen) invited Lucretia Mott to lecture on July 1. One of the earliest feminists, Mott founded a female antislavery society, organized several conventions, and attended the World's Anti-Slavery Convention in London (1840) where she and Elizabeth Cady Stanton first met. Frustrated by that convention's refusal to recognize female delegates, they vowed jointly to promote women's rights. This led to their organizing the 1848 Seneca Falls convention. After that date the fight for women's rights occupied much of Mott's energies. She must have declined Alfred's invitation, for her talk was never scheduled.

Another respected activist became Alfred's first woman lecturer. On the evening of July 3, 1854, sponsored by the Ladies' Literary Society, Elizabeth Oakes Smith spoke on Madame Roland and the French. Abigail Allen credited her husband with the invitation to Smith, a writer, reformer, women's rights advocate, and suffragist who published a series of articles in Horace Greeley's *New York Tribune*, later printed as a book, *Woman and Her Needs* (1851). Recalling her talk, Allen wrote, "Her presence was not only an inspiration to the young women, but her eloquence left its impression upon all."[21]

The next morning, Alfred's young women took center stage. "The anniversary proper [Commencement] of the Academy commenced at ten o'clock. . . . A shower the night before had cooled the air and the day was most beautiful. A large audience assembled at an early hour, which increased until the capacious chapel capable of accommodating from one thousand to fifteen hundred persons, was well filled. . . . As a sign of the progressive tendencies of the age we noticed that several of the ladies *spoke* their pieces instead of *reading* them," reported Smith. This is the earliest known date that women gave orations at either academy or college. From then on, Alfred's women routinely gave orations, some in French, German, or Latin.[22]

These breakthroughs occasioned no controversy. It is only remarkable that Jonathan Allen considered this "the most natural way in the world" when one contemplates the vehement opposition elsewhere. Abigail Allen experienced one famous incident, which occurred as a result of Susan B. Anthony attending her first teachers' convention in 1852 in Elmira, New York, and observing that although three-quarters of the delegates were women, not a single woman spoke, voted, or was appointed to a committee. She resolved to attend future conventions and gain privileges for women. One year later, Abigail was present when Anthony galvanized the 1853 State Teachers' Convention, attended by more than five hundred persons, by rising to speak to the question, "Why the profession of teacher is not as much respected as that of lawyer, doctor or minister?" "A bombshell would not have created greater commotion. For the first time in all history a woman's voice was heard in a teachers' convention. Every neck was craned and a profound hush fell upon the assembly." Men debated for a half hour whether she should be permitted to speak, as Anthony stood in her place, "fearing to lose the floor if she sat down." She finally spoke briefly to the point. When the convention adjourned for the day, many women shunned her, saying "Did you ever see such a disgraceful performance?" and "I never was so ashamed of my sex." A few supported her stand, resenting deeply that they, "equally qualified with men, are toiling side by side with them for one-half the salary. And this solely because of our sex!"[23]

One of Anthony's supporters was Abigail Allen, who was particularly attentive and sympathetic when Anthony rose to speak. Forty years later Allen remembered how the hall buzzed and stirred as the "tall, pale girl, dressed in Quaker garb, [remained] quietly standing and waiting":

> We, at Alfred, had just invited, received enthusiastically and listened, almost entranced, to the address of Mrs. Elizabeth Oakes Smith. Our own girls spoke on Anniversary days the same as the gentlemen. We could not understand the situation. After some ten minutes' debate, "Yes, the lady could speak." She cut the Gordian knot by saying, "It seem to me, gentlemen, that none of you quite comprehend the cause of the disrespect of which you complain. Do you not see that so long as society says a woman is incompetent to be a lawyer, minister or doctor, but has ample ability to be a teacher, that every man of you who chooses this profession tacitly acknowledges that he has no more brains than a woman? And this, too, is the reason that teaching is a less lucrative profession, as here men must compete with the cheap labor of woman. Would you exalt your profession, exalt those who labor with you. Would you make it more lucrative, increase the salaries of the women engaged in the noble work of educating our future Presidents, Senators, and Congressmen."

Susan B. Anthony had made her first speech among the teachers of the State, but it was not her last. She kept them in hot water till some acknowledgement was made for woman's work.[24]

Pressure to remain silent was indeed extraordinary, sometimes excruciating. Antoinette Brown stood for an hour and a half on a conference platform in 1853, waiting quietly to speak, while male delegates argued frenziedly over her presence. "Shame on the woman!" they cried. In 1854 the New York Senate invited Elizabeth Cady Stanton, the first woman to speak in that forum, to address them on married woman's property law and other legal issues. During a very painful evening in his study, her father used tears, bribes, and threats to try dissuading her from speaking before this august male group. Stanton wrote to her good friend Anthony: "I passed through a terrible scourging when last at my father's. I cannot tell you how deep the iron entered my soul. I never felt more keenly the degradation of my sex. To think that all in me of which my father would have felt a proper pride had I been a man, is deeply mortifying to him because I am a woman. That thought has stung me to a fierce decision—to speak as soon as I can do myself credit. . . . Sometimes, Susan, I struggle in deep waters."[25]

Alfred's women were aware that the Allens' valuing rhetoric for women, coupled with their conviction of rhetoric's centrality to women's rights, was highly unusual. A female student spoke at the dedication of "The Brick" boarding hall in 1858 and a local newspaper reported, "Miss Grace L. Lyman representing the Ladies' Literary Society made a marked impression. Not only did she carry her part as well as her masculine associates, but she eulogized Alfred's share in emancipating women from all current discriminatory restrictions, putting them on a plane of equality with men, as, for example, in allowing her to read that paper. She said that Alfred University was the only collegiate institution in the country to have done so."[26]

Among the school's numerous forums for public speaking, none was grander than Commencement—the annual high point for demonstrations of oratorical skill. Final exercises were popular entertainment from the select school's first year. The townspeople "took almost as much interest in the work as the students themselves. . . . The aim was to make, not simply students, but men and women who could think accurately and speak and act promptly on their feet, with clear, level heads and dexterous hands. These examinations, consequently, created great interest, and were listened to by crowded houses, composed not only of students, but also of citizens of this and adjoining towns." This elaborate event often lasted for days, as society after society put on public sessions. Commencement itself was an all-day extravaganza with hundreds, even a thousand or more attending. In 1848, there were seventy-seven student pieces (each three to five minutes long) and twenty musical interludes, all delivered in a grove above the academy buildings. Elaborate picnic lunches were spread out during the noon recess. Susan Burdick remembered the excitement of commencement preparations in the 1870s:

> People drove in from Bath, Dansville, and other towns not too distant in those pre-auto days. Larders had to be replenished in no trifling way. My Grandmother used to spread her tables in the orchard. I recall the brick oven in the orchard . . . Father used to tell of the quantity of wood he had to make ready and of the procedure of making the oven hot. Various kinds of bread, meats and pies were put in and left to bake slowly all night.
>
> I think the Commencement exercises were usually held out of doors. The sloping hill sides above the chapel made a natural amphitheater. It was a thrilling moment when the brass band arrived. Certain alumnae made a point of returning for Commencement. The four lyceums called back their gifted members to give the lectures, a poem or some item of the especial program.[27]

Commencement orations were taken very seriously. Inherited from the medieval university, they exhibited the intellectual competence of the graduates and demonstrated their fitness for public life. It was no small thing to admit women to this two-thousand-year-old tradition. Each speaker was drilled by the President:

> President Allen's method of training commencement speakers (all seniors were required to have commencement orations) was first to have conferences with the senior in regard to the subject matter of his "oration." These productions were often severely criticized as to subject matter and not infrequently had to be rewritten before any attempt was made to commit them to memory.
>
> When the paper was accepted by the President as passable in content, then it must be committed to memory. The President then met the senior, on one or two occasions at an early morning hour, for criticism of his method of delivery. The first appointments were in the chapel auditorium where he could see and criticize the speaker's manner, dress, gestures, and enunciation. Then each senior was required to rehearse his oration once or twice from a distance. Sometimes the President required him to go on a hill back of "the Castle" [about one-half mile distant] while he sat on his front porch to listen to the oration. Sometimes the President would put the student on the front porch of Kenyon Memorial Hall and himself walk up the valley toward Jericho [Hill] to see how far he could hear his enunciation distinctly.[28]

Numerous graduates remembered those early morning rehearsals. Susan Burdick wrote: "To recall Commencement doings and not mention the rehearsals in the early morning with Pres. Allen on his porch and the would-be orator on the hill opposite, standing just in the edge of the woods back of the 'Castle' would be an important omission. 'Louder' would come the admonition across the valley from the President." Edna Bliss also remembered the dawn rehearsals: "On early spring mornings as Commencement time drew near it was not unusual for the village folk to hear faint streams of oratory floating overhead. President Allen loved the morning hours and enjoyed standing on his spacious veranda listening to some weak-voiced senior across the valley practicing for Commencement Day."[29]

Hannah Simpson began working on her presentation on June 1, 1861: "We did up the work then went up on the hill to write. Wrote a piece but it will not do." Next weekend, she "tried to get time to write some on my piece, but there was so much work." A few days later she went up on the hill to keep working on it but "accomplished very little." After planning to wear her old "purple lawn" for this important occasion, she changed her mind and bought a dress. June 20 she went to the church to rehearse her piece with Allen, then revised it again: "Wrote on my Apos. Never before worked so hard writing." On the 24th she read it to Allen again. Finally came the joint Anniversary session and Simpson presented "Apostrophe, 'Freedom,'" but not until a third rehearsal: "Read my piece before Prof. Allen who said that it was *first rate*. Worked busily as possible. Was ready for session in time. Did better on the stage than I had hoped. Had the attention of the audience. Cheers at the close. After Session Vira came and said I had done nobly. That my piece was one of the finest of our Session. It did do me good."[30]

Grace Lyman, Hannah Simpson, and their fellow students received their oratorical training in student literary societies. Oddly, since they "engrossed more of the interests and activities of the students than any other aspect of college life," literary societies (also called lyceums) have been overlooked in most studies. Self-financed through fees, fines, lecture charges, and fund-raising events, they were a significant public platform, a freewheeling intellectual forum, weekly entertainment, and the chief social outlet. Student run, each "a little democracy," they provided relief from other closely regulated activities and the classroom's monotonous drill.[31]

Building on the Alfred Debating Society, organized in the select school's first term, a more formal group was established in 1842, named "The Franklin Academic Lyceum of Alfred," with Ira Sayles (who enrolled in 1838, joined the faculty in 1845, and the Compact in 1849) as president. Women attended as well and read papers, but did not join the debates.

The first women's literary society, the Alphadelphian, was established by Abigail Allen as soon as she returned as Alfred's preceptress in 1846. This was not the first women's literary society in the nation's colleges, as one local newspaper claimed; Oberlin's "Young Ladies' Association . . . for the promotion of literature and religion" was established in 1835 but quickly fell dormant. Lucy Stone led an effort to revive it in 1846, but Oberlin's conservative Ladies Board banned the group and they were forced to meet secretly at a black woman's home on the edge of town. Alfred's Alphadelphian Society, however, is the first known to remain in continuous operation and is surely the most progressive. The group discussed "among other things many questions of woman's work and needs," invited Alfred's first female lecturer, and encouraged oration. Unfortunately its literary magazine was lost when all society files were destroyed in the 1858 South Hall fire.[32]

In January 1847, an explicitly coeducational society, the Didaskalian, or Teachers' Association, was formed "with special reference to the wants and interests of teachers." As enrollment grew, the number of societies grew, then merged into the Didaskalian which soon overshadowed the others. "The Franklin, however, did not surrender without a struggle. The unionists and anti-unionists met in many an earnest conflict, before full and excited houses." Parliamentary training was considered valuable, but preoccupation with procedure became excessive in this large society, born of several contentious mergers. Lyceums thrived on rivalry and soon the overgrown, quarrelsome Didaskalian ("a single point of order, for instance, called out seventy-two speeches, by actual count, in a single evening") proved unwieldy. So large that not all members could participate, the situation deteriorated until just a few men did most of the work, an unsatisfactory arrangement to the women. Unlike Antioch, whose faculty forbade coeducational societies, Alfred's students appear to have voluntarily abandoned theirs.[33]

By 1850, three societies emerged: two male, the Alleghanian and the Orophilian (among its founders were two of Jonathan Allen's brothers); one female, the Ladies' Literary Society, which developed from the original Alphadelphian and then took the name Alfriedian Lyceum in 1864. One more women's society, the Ladies' Athenaeum (subsequently called the Athenaean), joined these in 1858.

Just as Abigail Maxson Allen started the first women's society, her sister, LaMyra Maxson Prentice, suggested the second, believing competition, "friendly rivalry," between two women's societies would stimulate better literary work. (In fact, competition between the women's societies exceeded the men's.) May Allen (the Allens' daughter) wrote later that the Ladies' Literary Society was in a "state of depression" at the time. One April evening, "an especially stupid session suggested the idea of organizing another lyceum, to do more earnest work, and stimulate the other."[34] The women found a room, a name, members, and a motto. Their choice shows they were well schooled in Cicero's model of the orator, combining wisdom and eloquence. Since the Orophilians (their companion society) featured eloquence in their motto—"Eloquentia mundum regit"—the new society adopted the goddess of Wisdom, Athena, as its guide and "La sagesse soutient l'univers" as its motto.

They nervously began to develop their skills for their first performance. "As the public sessions drew on, how carefully we arranged that fancy edged ribbon of pure white bearing our name, Athenaean and the dainty white cord and tassel encircling each head." May Allen reported the excited neophytes' success: "The first public session was held on Lincoln's birthday, 1860, and occasioned great surprise on account of its literary merit."[35]

Originally a bit aloof, the Orophilians had viewed the two other societies as foes. Feeling they "had not quite been able to make headway against the allied forces of the 'Alleghanians' and the Ladies' Literary," the Orophilians immediately wrote a congratulatory letter when the Ladies' Athenaeum "came into the field." Remarkably welcoming, this letter explicitly offered the relationship of brother and sister consistent with the ethos so often observed in this school. Declaring themselves "sisterless and alone," the men offered "equal footing in the race for honor."[36] They remained allied until societies themselves disappeared from the University sixty years later.

These four societies structured students' extracurricular, social, and intellectual life into the twentieth century, dissolving just before World War I when eating clubs and secret fraternal societies took their place. Most students belonged to one. Joint sessions and exchange of delegates provided the school's only organized social life. Each society room contained a library of at least several hundred books—essays, histories, poetry, novels—and together comprised the largest collection at the school.

Leona Burdick Merrill, a member of the Alfriedian Lyceum in the early 1870s, recalled their activities:

> Campus activities centered in the four lyceums or literary societies. The Alfriedians and Atheneans, or ladies' societies, occupied very large, pleasant rooms in each end of the top floor of the Brick—the Alfriedians looking west over the village, and the Atheneans, east toward the Chapel. The men's lyceums, the Alleganian and Orophilean, occupied large, square rooms on the ground floor of the Chapel. These rooms were pleasantly and comfortably furnished. Programs were carefully prepared for each Saturday night throughout the thirty-nine weeks of the school year.
>
> The literary work was carried on seriously and discussions carefully prepared and carried on under strictly parliamentary rules. I venture to say that all members of those old lyceums were fitted to preside over meetings the world over wherever necessary and to preside with dignity and precision. It was itself an education. There was naturally much rivalry, sometimes friendly and sometimes not. Alleganians and Alfriedians fore-gathered—as did Orophilians and Atheneans. The girl's lyceums were not supposed to be friendly on general principles.
>
> . . . Each lyceum had a large room with platform stage, a good three-ply ingrain carpet, comfortable arm chairs, a library and a piano. Add to these a chandelier, with bright oil lamps, two student lamps, a warm wood fire and heavy curtains over the one great window and you have material for pleasant and profitable evenings. It was the duty of the Tellers to sweep and dust, build the fires and keep the lamps clean and brilliantly alight. . . .
>
> The critic, who with the secretary sat at a small table at the right on the platform, watched all procedure and made a detailed report at the end of the session. Guest programs were exchanged during the year.[37]

Fig. 7.1. Literary society event in the Athenaean Lyceum room. About 1894.

Officers included president, vice-president, corresponding secretary, critic, and tellers. The tellers' duties were somewhat romanticized in retrospect. In addition to cleaning the room and tending the lamps, they carried chairs up to the Chapel for public sessions and did other such chores. Edna Bliss, elected the Athenaeans' Second Teller in 1882, recalled the glow of lamp and intellectual fire:

> Lyceum days glow in the memories of faithful members of the societies. These organizations were certainly conceived in high and noble purposes as evidenced by their banners with their inspiring mottoes. Saturday night to village and college was lyceum night. . . . Were you ever a Teller, first, second or third? If so you can still smell the kerosene of the lamps you had to clean and feel the gloom of the dark and musty air. . . . twenty-five years after many men and women of the world give heart-felt thanks for the training and inspiration they gained in the old lyceum rooms.[38]

A typical evening started with the call to order, scripture reading, roll call, and reading of minutes. Then the literary program began. It might include an essay, a review, a biography, a declamation, a lecture, a poem, debate of a resolution, extemporaneous speaking, and music. Each item was assigned to a different member and at each session assignments for the following week or two were made. Each society presented a weekly paper, prepared by an editor and assistants, which was handwritten and read aloud. Following the literary program, a business meeting was held to deal with myriad details connected with membership, finances, fund raising, furnishings, library purchases, and planning the large public sessions. There were annual elections of officers, occasional invitations to other societies, and committees appointed to deal with every eventuality. Fund-raising suppers and festivals were carefully planned by committees on oysters, on table arrangements, on coffee and tea.

Society rooms were furnished at great expense. The Alfriedians raised $550, half through members' fees and public festivals, half contributed by the university. At further expense of $600, carpet, chairs, chandelier, lamps, and a piano were added. It took the women four years to complete this project. In 1863 the two women's societies planned a Festival to benefit the Soldiers' Aid Society as well as themselves. The program included small shops arranged in the Brick for Christmas presents, Christmas letters, and a "grab bag." After shopping and music, supper was served: "turkey, oysters, pork and beans, apple-pie, mince-pie, bread, butter, and cheese," followed by a performance and an auction. Guests did not leave until two in the morning. A few years later, the Alfriedians held a festival, charging 10 cents admission and 50 cents for supper. The event was organized by a multitude of committees: music, "soliciting cake," "Post Office," "Fish Pond," "obtaining nuts and candies," "bread and butter," supper table, tea and coffee, making molasses candy, "fancy table," posting bills, general management, among others. They raised $70 to furnish their meeting room. In 1870, the Athenaeans refurbished their room at a cost of $600; the university agreed to double all funds raised by the women.

The cycle of weekly meetings was punctuated by special public sessions held twice a year—Jubilee at Christmas, Anniversary during commencement week. These had audiences of hundreds, sometimes over a thousand. Five hundred people attended the Ladies Athenaeum Anniversary session in June of 1860. On occasion, 1,000 programs were printed.

Literary societies provided a platform for intellectual exercises and an opportunity to develop speaking talents, sharper thinking, and self-confidence in intimidating circumstances. One member recalled: "It is truly wonderful to note the change that a year's active lyceum work often makes in an individual. The self-conscious, hesitating school girl, afraid of her own voice, frequently becomes an independent speaker, confidently expressing her views on any subject, sure that if they do not meet with approval they will at least be respected."[39]

The Critic sat at the side of the stage during each session, assessing each member's performance. A critic's report was recorded in the Athenaean minutes of February 1884: "The session as a whole was good, the music especially good. The rule against cheering was violated several times. Words mispronounced: veritable, interesting, donkey."[40] Under such scrutiny, the women polished their analytical and oratorical skills each week.

Listeners also participated in the critique. Two audience members, who clearly understood that speaking required considerable art, jotted comments on their programs for the Alfriedian's Anniversary session on June 30, 1873. Hattie Stillman's Salute, "The Flying Shuttle," was "Very good. A nice figure of the loom of humanity." Sarah Saunders' Oration, "Moral Principle," was "Good. Rather deeper in thought than the above . . . nobility is essential in *public*." Susie Sinnette's Recitation, "Cobbler Keesar's Vision," was "passable," but she "laughed too much." After a musical interlude, M. A. Fisher Dean delivered her Lecture, "Culture—Our Life Work." This appears to have been a miserable failure. One listener noted, "Uninteresting because so poorly read. The production was very commonplace. Reads too fast and articulates very poorly, so much so as to spoil the effect of her best ideas." The listener wrote caustically, "A wonderful *amount* of 'culture' will be required to fit her for the platform. How some of the members drop their chins & look down! Too bad." Another listener agreed: "Excellent in sentiment but very poorly delivered." The Valedictory, "Unity in Diversity," delivered by M. E. Stillman was "*Splendid. Best of all.*"

Such scrutiny could be frightening. Lawrence describes the "first composition crisis" at Oberlin in 1839, "when President Mahan suggested that the men and women take composition classes together. Women reacted with panic. Twenty-three frantically petitioned the faculty to keep them out of the men's class, and several, less politically motivated, simply locked themselves in their rooms 'and wept at the dire necessity they supposed to be laid upon them.'" Modesty perhaps, terror certainly. "Reading before critical males who were accustomed to public discourse as warfare" was alarming. "Nor were they prepared to be judged by the same critical standards as the men were; their efforts were critiqued in a privacy of their tutor's room, in the margins of the paper, while the men's rhetorical exercises always had an obvious winner—and loser—of the 'honors.'"[41]

Not only did women gain intellectual sharpness and self-confidence, they also used the societies to explore issues excluded from the rather rigid curriculum, which relied on a few textbooks and rote recitation. Discussion, debate, provocative contemporary topics—these were notably absent from instruction at Alfred as at nearly all nineteenth-century colleges. McLachlan said of Princeton and Harvard, "No single reason why the formal curriculum could not have been made interesting to students is immediately apparent." Cortez Clawson described a typical scene in President Allen's senior classes: "[They] recited in the back part of the old chapel main floor. He would pace the floor back and forth while different ones were reciting and scarcely ever would make any comment one way or the other. Lessons were assigned by chapters or pages from some particular textbook and members of the class were called out by name with no indication as to the subject." "Frau" Ida Kenyon knitted in her language classes while students recited: "Seldom did she look up from her work during the recitation period."[42]

"With few exceptions the teaching in those days was poor," Clawson wrote. Most teachers were expected to lead up to twelve or fifteen classes a day and student memorization of text followed by recitation was standard. Kenyon was famous for drill, not scholarship. It was regarded as an innovation when Allen introduced free discussion to his classes in 1889: "Instead of giving courses of lectures by dictation on Metaphysics, Philosophy, Civilization, Religions . . . according to the old method, he now . . . requires the students to study them up thoroughly and present in class carefully-prepared papers on them; after reading, a free discussion and criticism on the papers and topics are in order by instructor and students."[43]

Not just a forum for debate on current issues, "the lyceums provided a substitute for fraternities and sororities, for organized social activities, and for formal training in English, Public Speech, and Parliamentary Law." They supported interest in belles lettres, tested leadership and imagination as recitations did not, and were "advance agents" of new fields and approaches. "Students derived from the extracurricular fabric of clubs, athletics, libraries, and fraternities a kind of instruction and experience that anticipated their needs and their futures. If much that was first extracurricular in time became curricular—English literature, American history, fine arts, music—for a considerable period the intellectual and vocational interests of students were supported by the extracurriculum." As Ogren noted, "it was in the literary societies, by far the most long-lived, popular, and far-reaching student organizations, where students worked hardest to refine themselves."[44]

Lyceum libraries were far more actively used than college libraries. For example, Princeton's library added no books in 1828, one gift book in 1829, and three books in 1830. In the 1860s the Princeton library was open only one hour per week. When Mount Union seminary received its college charter in 1858, the two literary societies' 547 volumes comprised the college's entire library.[45]

Alfred University's library contained a few hundred books and was open one-half hour each week, while the lyceum libraries owned several thousand volumes. The 1878 Alfriedian library catalog listed nearly 1,000 volumes and the Alleghanians owned 1,144 in 1881. The Alfriedians had numerous volumes on English literature, modern languages, and art, as well as women's issues: women's biographies, Margaret Fuller's memoirs, *Noble Deeds of American Women*, Dall's *The College, the Market, and the Court*. Across the country, the curriculum slowly broadened to include these interests, but not without substantial controversy and reassessment of purpose.

While commencement pieces were somewhat formulaic and gender-specific—women dealing mostly with philosophical and ethical issues while men spoke more often on political ones—topics chosen by men and women for weekly sessions did not differ significantly. Students debated and orated on capital punishment, the credit system, public education, conscience, and the modern novel, as well as "Happiness" and "Nature's Book." They debated resolutions on election of judges, states' rights, the condition of slaves and American Indians, Mormonism, the Grange, study of natural history, temperance (numerous times), and cremation, as well as history, literature, music, beauty, and moral action.

Here was certainly an outlet for students to analyze social and political events. Nathaniel Hubbard, the student who named the Orophilian paper "Radiator and Review," wrote later of "an itching I used to have to criticise most everybody. I used to think, in those days, that the world needed a great deal of overhauling, and that I had some sort of roving commission in that direction. I am glad to tell you, I think the world is going on very well now, without my assistance, and I am not in the missionary business nearly as much as I was."[46]

The societies provided a forum to assert views on women's equality. In the 1850s the Ladies' Literary Society affirmed that "the mind of woman is not inferior to that of man," "woman can attain to as high a degree of intellectual eminence as man," "the exclusion of women from our colleges and seminaries of learning is an unparalelled instance of tyranny," "women should study the professions," and "woman is more capable of speaking in public than man." Abigail Allen asked that they discuss "Resolved that every young lady should study Latin"; they also considered whether it was "the duty of American women to adopt the Bloomer Costume." The women's societies also debated education, politics, philosophy, and curricular concerns, such as "the study of the classics affords better discipline to the mind than that of mathematics."

In the 1860s and 1870s the Athenaeans affirmed their beliefs that "woman's intellectual powers are equal to those of man," "women [should] receive equal pay with men for similar work as well performed" (sharpening the argument from an earlier debate on the resolution, "woman should receive the same wages that man receives"), "more ladies should prepare themselves for Physicians," "the Sexes should have equal right in the Curch [sic]," and "women should be encouraged on public lecture courses."

Aware that coeducation was often repudiated elsewhere, students time and again reaffirmed the value of educating men and women together. In 1854 the male Orophilians "*Resolved*, That for the advancement of knowledge, the male and female *attendance* should be allowed to mingle properly together" and reportedly felt themselves bound by the decision ever after.[47] In 1855 the Ladies' Literary Society negatived that "it is improper for *Ladies* and *Gentlemen* to attend the same School" and in the following years repeatedly affirmed the advantages of coeducation. In 1872 the society discussed the resolution that "all Colleges should be open to both sexes"; there were then only about thirty coeducational colleges in the country.

Suffrage was debated numerous times and suffrage sympathies were widespread decades before culminating in Abigail Allen's activism in the 1880s. The male societies frequently supported women's right to vote. In 1858 the Alleghanians debated "the right of suffrage should be equally enjoyed by both sexes" and in 1859 "the civil and political rights which are accorded to man should be accorded to woman." After 1865, the societies affirmed time and again that suffrage should be extended to women. This was an unusually assertive stand, taken when numerous schools stifled such discussion.

Student societies also sponsored visiting speakers, who often discussed political issues. For example, in 1855 the Alleghanians brought Thomas K. Beecher (pastor of an Elmira, New York, church, brother of Harriet Beecher Stowe and Catharine Beecher) and the Orophilians brought Joshua R. Giddings, a U.S. Representative who crusaded against slavery. Beecher was invited again in 1857 by the Ladies' Literary Society and the Alleghanian Lyceum to speak with pacifist Elihu Burritt. The Alleghanians presented the first "lecture course in the history of the community" in the winters of 1858, 1859, and 1860, bringing Ralph Waldo Emerson, Horace Greeley, Henry Ward Beecher, Charles Sumner, Horace Mann, and others. Abraham Lincoln was invited by Eunice E. Howell (representing the Athenaean Lyceum) in 1860, a few months before his nomination for president. Lincoln wrote back from Springfield, "I now find it impossible that I should lecture for you this winter. Several things conspire forcing me to this conclusion."[48]

The range and number of lyceum events was remarkable. In January 1861 Hannah Simpson attended the reading of a poem on slavery, Ralph

Waldo Emerson's talk on "the Classes of Men," a lecture on the "sufferings of the citizens of Kansas," and a lecture by Frederick Douglass. Asa Burdick recorded many activities: society sessions, church events, and such lecturers as Gerrit Smith, Burritt, Thomas K. Beecher, Schuyler Colfax, and Sojourner Truth. On June 28, 1870, he went to "a lecture in the evening by Mrs. Cady Stanton" (admission was fifty cents). In November 1870, Burdick heard another feminist: "Lecture Miss Susan B. Anthony, 25 cents." Concerts, poets, and dramatic performances were also presented.[49]

Lyceums provided both solidarity and rivalry. Students identified with their society as they would decades later with fraternities and sororities. It was said, for instance, that an Athenaean could be recognized by the hang of her skirt. Membership was for life and very few strayed from their chosen affiliation. In a rare incident, on September 8, 1860, an Alleghanian, Joseph Williams, was expelled for consenting "to identify himself with a brother society, a case unparalelled in the history of either Lyceum, and contrary to the constitution of Alleghanians."[50]

Closely regimented in the classroom, supervised in the drawing room, students had a surprising amount of independence in their literary societies. Faculty did not interfere in their management or oversee their activities. On the contrary, society rooms and furnishings were used by faculty only with permission and that permission was granted with conditions, even occasionally denied. The Orophilians carried out protracted negotiations with President Allen, ultimately exchanging his use of their chandelier for their use of the chapel, and debated at length the president's request to rent their organ before telling him "no":

> March 9, 1872 . . . Moved that we send Prof Allen word that we cannot let our organ go in chapel for chapel exercises, amended to be laid on table for next session. . . .
>
> May 6, 1872—Moved and carried that the motion laid on the table about renting the organ be taken off. Moved and carried that on consideration we have decided not to let our organ go in chapel.[51]

Charges were levied for damaged property. The Alleghanians were clearly irritated by Professor Larkin's tardiness in repaying them for a broken lamp.

> September 11, 1875—On motion, voted that our Treasurer be a committee to ask Prof. E. P. Larkin to replace the lamp which was lent to him and broken before returned.
>
> November 6, 1875—Broken Lamp Committee (E. A. Witter) instructed to repair lamp and collect the amount due him for such services from the smasher—E. P. Larkin.
>
> February 19, 1876—Lamp com. reported progress.[52]

Students utilized society solidarity in occasional protests against faculty dictates, particularly the much-resented prohibition on "Unpermitted Association of ladies and gentlemen." The most famous instance of student rebellion occurred in 1853. William Kinney, an Orophilian, was expelled just before graduation when he refused to apologize for "unpermitted association" with another student, Dell Anderson, a Ladies' Literary Society member. Apparently they attended a party in the next town and returned late without an excuse. A mass of students was adamant that Kinney be reinstated and permitted to give his prepared piece at commencement. The faculty were equally adamant that order would be maintained and the rules enforced. At one point in the "great rebellion," thirty students were suspended after repeated mass meetings interfered with classes. Agreement was eventually reached and all were taken back except Kinney, who did not depart without exacting a final "sweet revenge." He telegraphed Horace Greeley, that year's commencement speaker, that the event was postponed. As a result, neither Kinney nor Greeley spoke at commencement.[53]

Gender relations among the societies were normally consistent with the school's familial ethos: respectful, affectionate, informal, sometimes teasing, gently competitive, egalitarian. Public sessions usually included exchange of delegates. Male and female societies frequently invited each other for joint sessions and mutual debate. This was unusual. At Oberlin, "No record exists of a joint meeting of the Aeolian or L. L. S. [Ladies' Literary Society] and the Men's Lyceum; men and women debaters remained in separate spheres, each with the same skills and knowledge, but removed from each other's arena of competition." At the University of Wisconsin, "one of the men's literary societies was distinguished for courtesy in inviting the young women to the meetings, while the other ignored them." Genesee College men were not permitted to invite women students to their sessions. By contrast, Ogren found that "gender segregation was less rigid in the Midwest and West," with men and women participating "on a relatively equal basis" later in the century and Radke reports suffrage activism in western land-grant universities as campaigns for state suffrage amendments occurred.[54]

There was genial repartee in Alfred's joint sessions. A particularly witty observer recorded a Ladies' Literary Society session when Mary A. Taylor was its President and a male society attended. Turning stereotypes on their heads, the women teased their guests for their silence and timidity:

8th. Discussion of the resolution [that Americans were justified in taking up arms against the British crown]. Misses Sherman and Langworthy appointed chief disputants.

. . . . 11th. There being a goodly number of gentlemen present, it was resolved that they be invited to participate in the discussion.

But alas for the faintheartedness of 1859 men.

They all declined. Some would like to be excused, as they "did not come in with the intention of speaking but solely to see & be seen." Something of the spirit which actuated the British when displaying their scarlet regalia and glittering arms to the astonished gaze of the *natives,* congregated on Bunkers Hill. Others plead inability to speak on such a momentous subject. Others timidity. Bold champions of American Freedom! Had that memorable year 1776 produced such heroic spirits, how much blood might have remained unspilled, and how short might the period of "the Revolution" have been!

12th. Decision of the House called for, after which the Committee reported as follows:

"The question being miserably supported in the negative, it was decided in the affirmative."[55]

Two years later, Hannah Simpson reported her society's triumph over the male Orophilian Lyceum: "Session of Soc. immediately after Chapel. Were soon invited to meet the Oros. Went, won the day."[56]

In 1877 Vandelia Varnum won a debate on women's legal situation with the male Alleghanians. The discussion "was opened by W. F. Place, who affirmed that all criminal laws favored woman; that all vocations were open to her; that her property rights were not only equal, but superior to the property rights granted to man, as the husband was compelled to support the family, no matter what his or her financial circumstances might be; that suffrage was not a natural right, but a privilege to be conferred on those only whom the founders of the law deemed worthy; otherwise the child might claim the ballot."

Varnum then took the negative by "claiming that law treated woman as inferior by classing her with the sloughs of society, and clothing her with no more power as a citizen than the infant, idiot, or lunatic; her property rights were in the grossest sense wrongs so long as the law granted her simply the use of only one-third of the mutual property; the husband was guardian of the wife and could exercise restraints over her freedom; and finally, the law deprives her of the rights which all citizens amenable to the law can claim—the right of suffrage." The argument swayed back and forth but proponents (male and female) of the negative prevailed. In response to the argument that only those who bear arms should vote, one woman pointed out, "only the strong male citizens between the ages of twenty one and forty-five were compelled to enter active war service, and yet they all, the weak and the old, held the ballot. Woman was too weak to slip a ballot in the box, but she was strong enough to 'swing hemp.'"[57]

These were assertive voices, yet relations were normally respectful and friendly. A unique instance of open warfare broke out over an invitation to a lecturer, Julia Ward Howe, who was well-known as a poet, author of "The Battle Hymn of the Republic," and suffragist. This memorable flap developed partially from society rivalries. As Howe recounted, "the whole romance of sending for the lecturer, and not allowing her to speak, grew out of a disagreement in the region of these lyceums." The innocent beginning can be traced in all four societies' minutes. They agreed in January 1871 to hold a joint Anniversary session of all four, in itself unusual (normally only two societies—the male/female companion groups—combined), but this was to be a special event to raise money for the broken Chapel chandelier. Each society contributed one or two members to a planning committee, which selected Howe as lecturer, and she received "a summons . . . to name her own terms, and deliver a Commencement lecture."[58] All proceeded smoothly until the April 15 society meetings. And why not? There was nothing unusual about inviting female lecturers: it was seventeen years since the first had visited; Stanton and Anthony had spoken recently.

Trouble arose when Pastor Hull dropped a bombshell by writing to the societies stating he would not read the notice of the joint session in church (a routine means of publicity). President Allen weighed in and "the gentlemen, exasperated by remarks made by President Allen in the meantime, on the subject of Equal Rights, declared the action taken illegal, and that no woman should lecture upon that stage. The ladies felt themselves pledged to Mrs. Howe, and would not yield." Bickering among the societies soon began. "The feeling became so ridiculously intense that one of the leaders of the opposition said, 'If Mrs. Howe goes upon that stage, it will be over my dead body.' President Allen's merriment, when told of this tragical declaration, can only be appreciated by those who knew how keen was his sense of the ridiculous."[59]

It is not clear, more than a century later, why the male societies did not stand behind their invitation. Caroline Dall blamed the conservative but influential Pastor Hull, asserting that he stirred up the townspeople against Howe (presumably to block her from speaking in the Chapel). On May 13, in what could not have been a coincidence, the Athenaeans retorted by debating "Question. 'Resolved that the writings of St. Paul in reference to women talking in churches referred to *that* time and *not* ours.' After ably debating it was decided in aff[irmative]."[60] On May 19 both male societies called a special session and repudiated "the action of our Committee on Anniversary Lecture, in favoring the appointment of Julia Ward Howe."

The next day the women's societies met and reaffirmed their choice. A joint committee of unprecedented size—eight members from each of the four societies—was set up to decide anew on the Anniversary lecturer. Harsh words were spoken, according to May Allen: "so much was said that the matter became personal and the discussion bitter upon the vexed question of woman's rights. . . . The school, the Faculty, the townspeople, and the community at large entered the contest, till the excitement became ridiculously intense."[61]

The women, "sure they had the right to engage" Howe, put posters up all over Alfred announcing her lecture on "Living Interest," a title proposed by Allen and accepted with delight because it was vague enough to keep their opponents anxious for a few more days. At this juncture, local men who claimed to be pondering donations to the university threatened to revoke their phantom gifts. The youthful committee then reconsidered. They had Allen's authorization to hold Howe's lecture in the Chapel, but they did not wish to harm their university's financial prospects. Ultimately the indignant women maintained their commitment to Howe but moved her lecture to a hall in Hornellsville, a nearby town.

Howe arrived at the Hornellsville train depot, expecting to travel on to Alfred (about ten miles further). Instead she was met by the "committee" of "two bright-eyed young ladies" and was told of the intense dispute. Soon a male committee showed up, trying to explain themselves to the famous visitor. The lecture, a "quiet essay" from this pragmatic reformer, occurred as scheduled and was attended, in Howe's description, by the Allen family, the "cream of Alfred" and the "upper crust of Hornellsville."[62]

The next morning Mrs. Howe visited Alfred, dining with the Allens and having tea with university and village women. She later praised the "bumptious and defiant little village" and the liberal spirit of a college where women have "the same educational opportunities as are enjoyed by the young men." The Allens spoke of their concern that, while men could find farm work or odd jobs, it was more difficult for young women to "combine remunerative occupation with competent culture." Lunch was served by a student who was working for the Allens to earn tuition money. At tea that afternoon with the women's literary societies, Howe was very impressed by an undergraduate "who had earned her own support since the age of twelve, and whose principal treasure seemed to be a shelf of Greek classics, of which the contents were familiar to her. Herodotus, Homer, Thucydides, Plato,—the young girl lived upon such diet as this, while earning her own bread, and assisting a young brother at the college."[63]

Howe wrote shortly after that she hoped "peace has been made long ere this between the youths and maidens." The Allens' daughter May was upset; she wrote in annoyance ten years later, "As a result of this controversy, the spirit of the societies was so cowed that they have not since dared to employ a woman for the Annual Lecture."[64] The male societies tried to repair relations with the President, who had aided the women time and again throughout the furor; on June 10, there was a "Joint Session of the Alleghanian's & Orophilian's in the Orophilian Session Room. Moved & carried that a committee of four be appointed to draft resolutions with respect to reconciliation with Professor Allen." Abigail Allen soon had the opportunity to make her own statement on public speaking and women's rights, for Howe invited Allen to speak on "Coeducation" at the Woman's Congress, held two years later.

The societies resumed their normal joint sessions and, perhaps to make amends, the Alleghanians visited both women's societies in the fall. In January 1872 the Athenaeans voted to invite Howe again, but there is no record of another visit. While May Allen may have felt they were cowed, the women did take revenge. The Alfriedians' 1875 Jubilee session made a real splash with its "Debating Club in the Year 2000" on male suffrage, a much-discussed spoof described as lively and amusing. The session featured a mock debate in the U.S. Senate on the resolution: "If the House concur, that, to ensure the best interests of humanity, the constitution be so amended as to extend the right of suffrage to man." Women seized the opportunity to make comical arguments that men should stay in their appointed sphere and that women would be forced to wash dishes again if men were granted suffrage.

The Virginia Senator warned, "The question is of man's fitness to hold certain positions now occupied exclusively by woman. At the present time, he is certainly not qualified. Consider the evil effect of those long ages, when he believed himself *so* superior to woman that she must not question what he did, or why he did it!" The New York Senator reminded her listeners of abuses that would eventuate: "Give them equality, and they will abuse the gift by domineering over us, and trampling us under foot. My grandmother, of whom I spoke, attended . . . Alfred University, and she remembered at one time a terrible excitement, because the gentlemen of the college refused to allow a lady to deliver a lecture in the building, giving as a reason, that it was out of woman's sphere, and a disgrace to her. But to-day the most profound, and at the same time the most brilliant speakers are ladies." The Utah Senator opined that if the resolution passed, "we should be obliged to share in the drudgery of the household, which, for my part, I am willing to let entirely alone." In spite of their reservations, the women exercised "that grand charity which works good to all mankind" and voted to permit men to share once more in ruling the nation.[65]

Thus, Alfred's women continued to sharpen their views and exert their voices on this public platform, drawing strength from peers and encouraged by faculty. McLachlan described the attitude of Princeton's faculty toward their student societies as "benign neglect" and reported that Brown did not even provide rooms for its societies when Horace Mann was a student there.[66] However, "benign neglect" would not describe the approach of Alfred's faculty. Church and Hartshorn began the first debating society; Abigail Allen founded the Ladies' Literary Society; her sister was a founder of the Athenaean; Jonathan Allen suggested the name Alleghanian for that society. The university provided meeting room space and helped pay for furnishings; faculty attended and sometimes participated in their sessions. In fact, Alfred's faculty explicitly supported student control of the societies. Unlike McLachlan, David Potts found that antebellum educators "gave their wholehearted assistance to these popular organizations," regarding them as valuable auxiliaries to the formal curriculum, and Ogren found them "a lively forum for intellectual exploration," supported by the faculty. Alfred's encouragement of student independence, allowing an arena for autonomy and experimentation, may have been more common than Princeton and Brown's neglect.[67]

Literary societies remained the predominant organizing social force at Alfred until the twentieth century, although they faded from the scene at many colleges as early as the 1850s, eclipsed by the growth of secret fraternities. At nearby Hamilton about half the students belonged to secret societies as early as 1840 and two-thirds did by the Civil War. *The Alfred Student* noted in 1874 that Northwestern's literary societies were being destroyed by encroaching fraternities, "a common complaint in all colleges." College presidents tried to suppress these groups, but by the 1880s fraternities, athletics, and other activities had captured the interest of many students. Inadvertently, colleges themselves contributed to the literary societies' slow demise by eroding their intellectual role as faculty expanded the curriculum—incorporating topics that the societies first introduced—and colleges began to build comprehensive libraries, supplanting that important contribution of the societies.[68]

Alfred's faculty and students firmly opposed secret societies throughout the nineteenth century, congratulating themselves on resisting this "blight." Abigail Allen excoriated them in her 1873 address on coeducation: "We . . . have been free of the swarming brood of secret societies which are infesting most of the male colleges, honey-combing them, producing a dry-rot throughout the entire organization, acting as nurseries, in general, of idleness, ignorance, and immorality, ruining more students than any other one cause in connection with college life, polluting like leprosy, eating like cancer into the student life." They were condemned as exclusive, jealous, narrow, and destructive of ideal college life: "Squads of young men . . . holding themselves aloof from each other" produced "warring factions," not a community.[69]

As literary societies disappeared and a backlash against coeducation developed elsewhere at the end of the century, Alfred remained steadfast. In addition to the Allens' adamant support for women's rights, the rural orientation and familial values contributed to this enduring commitment to an egalitarian environment. The camaraderie evident in Alfred's literary societies reflected the relations among students and faculty throughout the nineteenth century.

Chapter Eight

Student Ties

Are the pines there now?

—Mary Emma Darrow (Almy), to Ellis Drake, July 27, 1934

Historians have described widespread resistance to advancing women's education. Indeed there was resistance but there was also demand: two hundred women applied for Mount Holyoke's first term in 1837 and four women sought admission to Oberlin's collegiate course in the same year. Alfred's women joined in these demands and their unassuming, hardworking families appeared to find women's intellectual aspirations as natural as the Allens did, encouraging their daughters to pursue both education and economic opportunity. They did not seem disturbed by fears that their pioneering daughters would be distorted, destroyed, or rendered sterile by pursuing college degrees. Furthermore, there is no evidence they were offended or frightened by the Allens' views on women's rights. In fact, there was a surprising level of support. Time and again, families sacrificed to help their daughters.

Prejudice against women's higher education could not have been as uniform as was commonly portrayed. The "relatively friendly atmosphere" that Nash found is evident in western New York. Alfred's women came with their families' explicit backing. Other antebellum schools in the region shared this pattern: "fully half the families" in Lima and LeRoy sent their daughters to Genesee College and LeRoy Female Seminary (later Ingham University). Students' daily experiences underscore Potts' observation that antebellum colleges promoted a deep and lasting faith in education.[1]

Student voices, fresh as when first penned, tell of encouragement and of profound ties—with family, with community, with each other. Mary Goff wrote her aunt in 1859 that although Mary was teaching and "had given up all idea of coming" to Alfred University, her family made sure she could attend: "But our folks engaged me a room and made all the arrangements previous to letting me know anything about it and Blake went after me Thursday." Like many students, she roomed with a relative: "I have a very pleasant room in the village. My room mate is a cousin to Aunt Amanda Cline from Hallsport. She is a very quiet, good girl, and we are enjoying ourselves very much." Twelve students boarded in her building, "which makes quite a family when we come together."[2]

Alice Vinette Wells grew up on a small farm about thirty miles away, in Abigail Allen's home town, "and the family knew about Alfred. . . . probably the deciding factor was the persuasive word of her friend, Sarah Ayars, who was studying in Alfred at the time. . . . and when she described what fun it was to get one's own meals, study with different teachers and even offered to share her room, the family seem to have become convinced that it was possible." Alice's school clothes were made at home—"Ma cut out my bloomer dress and sewed on it. . . . I made an apron"—and her family drove her the six-hour wagon ride from Friendship. In March 1872, Alice finished her courses and began teaching school. Sarah went on to earn an M.D. and practice medicine in Los Angeles.[3]

Sisters, brothers, cousins, friends of cousins, cousins of friends attended, coming from the whole matrix of Seventh Day Baptist towns. Abigail Allen's sisters and brothers enrolled, as did Jonathan's. Preston Randolph arrived from West Virginia in 1855 with his two brothers and a sister; they "boarded themselves at a total expense of less than seventy cents a week."[4] Boothe Colwell Davis chose Alfred in 1885 because his mother's two cousins had attended, as well as two older friends from his native West Virginia, and he arrived with his younger brother, Wardner.

A father's willingness to send his daughters to school is evident in Asa Burdick's diaries: Nellie, Ida, and Dellie all went to Alfred. He recorded tuition payments in March, April, September, and December of 1868: "Ida's tuition, 10.00 . . . Ida's tuition, 10.00 . . . Ida's tuition, 7.00 . . . Ida's tuition, 10.00." These were large expenses in an account that also listed "Wire, 02 cents . . . Carpet tacks, 05 . . . Lamp cleaner, 25 . . . Cheese 9 lbs, 1.35 . . . 1 pk turnips, 18."[5]

Students' autograph books illustrate the dense family connections. Ida M. Burdick's book was signed by her cousins Orville Clark (matriculated 1865), Charles Stillman (1864), and Sarah Hamilton (1867), her sister Dellie (1868), and her brother-in-law Deloss Remington (1856). Her sister Nellie's book carried good wishes from five other cousins who attended Alfred. Lydia Allen's autograph book was signed by her cousin Carrie Langworthy (matriculated 1857), her brother John G. Allen (1852), her "friend and cousin" Walter Saunders (1861), her brother Nathan Allen (1855, killed in the war), and her cousin Sarah Saunders (1856). Non-Sabbatarians also came in family clusters: Mary Goff roomed with her aunt's cousin; Hannah Simpson, brought by her friend William W. Brown, came from Pennsylvania with her two sisters.

Daniel Maxson left Leonardsville, New York, to study at Alfred. His letters to his younger sister, Artemesia, are unusually moving: "Artemesia you are not forgotten by me although the hills of Allegany encloses the spot where I am laboring. No, that little girl whose laughing eyes, and cheerful countinance used to greet my return to the family of which I was a member can never fail to occupy a prominent place on memories page." Daniel was as concerned for his sister's education and aspirations as he was for his own. He praised her penmanship and compositions, encouraged her studies, urged her to set high ideals, and hoped that she too would receive a thorough education. He wished he could "visit and hold sweet converse with those so dearly loved, but. . . . manhood, with its stern and complicated duties [calls me]. . . . I am no longer that little boy that used to scale the rugged mountains and travel through the vallies of old Brookfield . . . now if ever, I must prepare for meeting the responsibilities of life. . . . Would that you and all of my brothers and sisters could have the advantages that would secure for you a thorough education. But my good wishes are all the means at my command to aid you for I am penniless."[6]

He promised to send her "a copy of the best grammar extant when the new postage law comes into effect" and encouraged her to strive daily in her quest for knowledge: "let me urge you to improve every golden moment as it flies. . . . let your time be employed in gather[ing] priceless gems from the rich storehouse of knowledge. Be *hopeful* and *prayerful*— aim *high*, for the old maxim is that he (or she) 'who aims at the sun, to be sure his arrow will not hit it but will fly higher than if it were aimed at an object on a level with himself.'"[7] As the youngest child, Artemesia was expected to care for her aging parents, but they did not hold her back; she enrolled in 1854. Sadly, manhood's "stern and complicated duties" called Daniel to Civil War service as a lieutenant and he died during the war.

Not only did students receive profound support from their families, they also had help from village residents, rooming with a friend or cousin, living with an aunt, visiting neighbors. "The college life was very closely associated with the community life. Indeed it could not well be otherwise. The students largely were housed in the homes of the community. In these homes they found a large part of their social life. They were, in no restricted sense, members of the family. There were no student fraternities."[8]

Rooming together in the village and boarding as cheaply as possible helped reduce expenses. "One group of young men, John Hoffman and Edwin Bliss being among the number, roomed in the Luke Green house across the street from the village church. They started the year with a barrel of crackers. These with milk was practically all they had till the barrel was empty. Occasionally a pie from home enlivened their diet." Alice Vinette Wells and Sarah Ayars cooked for themselves even when they lived in "The Brick," making pies, baking bread, and receiving "a box of victuals from home." Their parents or grandparents occasionally drove over to visit, bringing more provisions. Cortez Clawson remembered low-budget boarding arrangements from the end of the century. "Days before college opened wagons would be seen coming into town with pieces of furniture for light housekeeping. There were several boarding clubs. The steward was appointed for each club and the food could be made to cost as little as possible. . . . Members of the club frequently brought in from the farms potatoes, cabbage and other vegetables which helped materially to reduce the cost of board per week."[9]

Students sought work in the village or on campus. The forests slowly fell as aspiring scholars sought cash. Jonathan Allen cut firewood for tuition in the winter of 1836. Boothe Davis worked in the 1880s "cutting wood, doing such jobs as janitor of the grammar school . . . janitor of the church." Daniel Willard walked to Alfred from Friendship in 1883, a single silver dollar in his pocket earned by sawing wood, pleased that Alfred did not require tuition in advance. John Prosser split wood for twenty-two cents a cord, worked for a cheese box manufacturer in 1886, and milked six cows each evening for one cent each. Cleaning carpets, washing windows, ringing the hourly school bells, filling wood boxes, feeding the "capacious mouths" of the immense wood stoves in the Chapel, doing housework—all brought cash.[10]

Most colleges were poorly funded and had few residential facilities. As Potts points out, income from boarders helped ensure community favor for the colleges in their midst. But beyond that, townspeople helped students set up housekeeping, brought them butter and pies, conveyed them to church, and watched over them during illness. Asa Burdick sat up all night in October 1870 with "two sick young students." Diaries record visit after visit to village families—the Crandalls, the Burdicks, Mr. Sheppard—for talk, singing, or cider. Maria and Samuel Whitford helped many students, driving them back and forth to their rooms, carrying furniture, flour and other provisions, and taking them on excursions. Numerous students visited them, sometimes staying for days, helping to make maple sugar, visiting neighbors. The Whitfords lent them furniture and Maria baked pies and cakes for the students' journeys home to Rhode Island or Wisconsin. Their generosity was remarkable. On January 6, 1861, with the two Saunders girls already sleeping over, Thomas Saunders and three more students, including Asher Williams (who would soon make the "radical" speech at Chapel on April 26 as war broke out), arrived unexpectedly at three a.m. Maria and her husband got up, giving the students their bed. "I knit on my mitten till daylight. . . . The company went off about noon."[11]

Most "Sunday-keepers" were soon drawn in to share the Saturday Sabbath while they attended Alfred and almost the entire student body—Sabbath and Sunday students alike—attended the Sabbath morning service (although students were not required to attend if they preferred Sunday). "First-day" (Sunday-keeping) families who moved to the area also were sometimes drawn into Sabbatarian practices. Ida Reveley, a "Sunday-keeper," recalled fondly: "My three years in Alfred gave me a great deal to recall happily, and very little that was not pleasant. . . . the calm of the sunset hour as I sat by my window and looked up the valley to the west, the beautiful services and the devoted pastors who ministered to all of us alike, the democratic spirit that made no account of what a person did for a living provided he was a worthy individual."[12]

Neither labor nor play was permitted on the Sabbath for Sabbatarians and non-Sabbatarians alike. Reveley remembered being caught in the darkroom making photographs for a school assignment on Friday evening. As late as 1898, Sabbath observance was strict, as she found when she went skating one evening:

> One incident impressed me very much, for a number of reasons, an example of the retort courteous, the reply that left no more to be said, and so on. I had gone to skate on the pond on the side hill below the village, and, arriving late had skated only seven minutes when the word came to clear the rink, owing to the time of day, as it was Friday. "Oh, Mr. Langworthy, I have only just come. I do not keep 'sun down,' so please let me stay just a few minutes." He looked at me solemnly and began to recite that portion of scripture that begins, "Honor the Sabbath Day to keep it holy," and ends, "nor thy man-servant, nor thy maid-servant nor thy cattle nor the stranger that is within thy gates." Needless to say I went home, directly and meekly.[13]

Students were reminded daily to make something of themselves, to serve humanity, and they reflected these high goals. From the earliest valedictory speech, they insisted that only education could bring the world closer to perfection and idealized the profession of teaching, chosen by so many. Hannah Simpson, who taught eight years before attending Alfred and would teach again after leaving, preserved this encouraging message written in her autograph book by a friend, Samuel Tann: "My friend, Ours is an awful responsibility. No doubt you often think of it. And do you never feel how truly we as Teachers are doing God's Holy will, & never will you turn back from the arduous task you have entered upon till your mission is accomplished & then do we not know that our reward is promised hereafter.[14]

Mary Taylor Burdick's daughter, Leona, enrolled in 1872. She remembered a strong commitment to education for its own sake: "Things were not approached from the practical side. We did not study that we might later have a way and means of employing talents or earning our living, but we did study almost entirely to cultivate our minds. Later I was to realize that it all made for that intangible something—unconscious growth and culture." Leona loved Latin: "The Latin I learned in those years—the training received—gave me a never failing secure foundation for my daily speech as well as a thorough knowledge of the English language that has been a joy to me all the years." She was competitive, proud to get a higher mark than a male student: "There were some fine scholars in those old classes. One Sylvanus Aeneas Peavy, for instance, who never knew where the lesson ended, but would ramble on indefinitely if he were not stopped. One of the proud moments of my life was when I received a higher mark than he in a Regents examination."[15]

Despite their enthusiasm, Alfred's women occasionally became enmeshed in self-doubts. Although higher education was rare for nineteenth-century women, their fears were focused not on that unusual experience but on ordinary matters—uncertainty of future happiness, disappointment in love. Despite her confident challenge of the "crack" geometry scholars, Myra McAlmont wrote her mother of her confusion: "I am not quite as discontented as I was, for my lessons do not give me time to think of future prospects, which, although I know to be hopelessly hid from our curious gaze, I am forever, at the enormous price of happiness, striving to throw aside and behold the picture. But were we privileged to read our destinies, would not our very hearts sometimes grow sick and faint, at the disappointments, withered hopes, and the heart trial before?" Hannah Simpson, agitated by the attentions of one man and unrequited love for another, struggled with her feelings: "I became *O so wild.* . . . Father; *help me* to be *strong* and *meek!* Oh, *give* me *wisdom - strength.*" Bombarded by perfectionist ideals, Hannah found it difficult to live as she wished: "I am not doing much that is really elevating—am not thorough in what I do & seem almost devoid of real earnest thought. Shall I *ever* arouse and again have high holy feelings?"[16]

In this community of turbulent youthful feelings, discipline was strict as at all colleges, but often meted out with flexibility. Though their purpose was serious and students lived under the restrictions governing all proper nineteenth-century behavior, the environment was more relaxed than that reported at similar schools. These were not the stiff, distanced relationships described by Carroll Smith-Rosenberg—men and women strangers to one another—"a world in which men made but a shadowy appearance." While female academies are portrayed as engendering a sense of sisterhood, reinforcing the developing ideology of separate spheres, students at Alfred approached the peer relationship that Cott asserts most women were denied. Clearly these relationships were not simply the function of a coeducational setting, for at other schools interactions between men and women failed to reach a comfortable level. Alfred's student recollections and diaries record a multitude of cross-gender relationships. Tales of disciplinary infractions also attest to these friendships.[17]

Parents were reassured that "the Government of the students will be in the hands of the Principals, and will be strictly and steadily exercised, and at the same time, strictly parental. The object of our academic government being to secure the greatest possible amount of physical, intellectual, and moral good to the students themselves, regularity and order of exercises, and good and wholesome citizens to society."[18] Tobacco, games of chance, profanity, and alcohol were forbidden. Chapel bells divided the day into class periods, meal times, study period, and rest. The morning bell rang at five; lights were out at ten. Faculty patrolled the halls to make sure residents adhered to study hours and other demands of the bells. Students and faculty long remembered one winter when Kenyon, fearing discipline was slipping, imposed a five thirty chapel hour:

> Professor Kenyon, our grandest of leaders, was the embodiment of the value of every golden moment. Four o'clock seldom, and five o'clock never, found him in bed. . . . The rising bell for all rang at five. Prof. Kenyon began to think some did not heed its call, so conceived the idea of having the chapel exercises at half past five, where every one was expected to answer to his name when the roll was called. The winter of '48 was a severe one, snow coming on in November and staying till April, but the *fiat* went forth for this early gathering of the clans. The Chapel was in the fourth story of the Ladies' Hall. . . . A bee line of a road and walk led from this building to town. East, west, north, and south, muffled figures came forth from every doorway, into the dark and the cold. No street lights cheered the path of the wayfarer; no fine walks above the drifts, or glorious pines for wind breaks; no snow plows to clear the way, and snow sometimes two feet deep. . . . Many of the students, gentlemen as well as ladies, boarded themselves, and this arrangement interfered with the morning duties and was discontinued after one term's experiment. We went back to the 8 o'clock chapel hour.[19]

Disciplinary violations were handled in dreaded meetings between the miscreant and the entire faculty or a solo conference with the president. "Woe to the student who wilfully disobeyed the traditions and regulations of the college. Before the entire student body the offender's name would be called out and invited to the white house on the hill for a conference. No student knew at what hour day or night he might expect a call from the president." Parents were also called in on occasion. Asa Burdick recorded a lengthy conference with President Allen: "Spent some 2 hours in forenoon in conversation with Proff. Allen relative to Adelle's conduct in school." Sometimes, students not sufficiently serious were encouraged to leave school before wasting further time or money.[20]

Daily chapel lectures guided student behavior. Hannah Simpson wrote in her diary, "This morning Prof. Allen spoke to us about keeping the regulations. Not because they were rules of this school but Life rules." Although twenty-six years of age, Abram Burt dutifully recorded Kenyon's admonitions: "Sept. 1st Prof. K lectured in Chapel on profanity. . . . He then spoke of Civillity of manners, 'Bow to every person you meet & pass the time of day. . . . September 2nd another Lecture in Chapel by Prof K contents was Thou shalt not steal; This repeated twice with emphasis constituted our lecture; (Sequel was, the night before the boys stole his Apples and green corn; At night four of us started on our first foraging expedition; went about a mile, found good apples & green corn and the boys would have taken a turkey, but I persuaded them not to do it, Had on an overcoat and had about 1/2 B. [bushel] in the pockets.)" Not surprisingly, Burt had roast corn the next day. Kenyon did not quickly forget his stolen apples. On September 16, the student assembly "Rec'd a lecture in chapel on malignant dispositions [who would] knock off all the green apples they could find."[21]

Occasionally the faculty asked the village pastor to help regulate behavior: "When following the opening of a skating rink in the fall of 1884, it became a menace to the University - students neglected their lessons to skate in the rink, and the lyceums were deserted, - [Pastor Wardner] Titsworth was appealed to and preached a sermon on amusements. Not long after, the rink went out of business. . . . [W]hen discipline in the Brick went completely to pieces as to the girls entertaining boys in their rooms in face of regulations to the contrary, Titsworth was again appealed to. Again he preached a sermon on ethics as applied to such a situation, and the problem was solved."[22]

In fact, the problem was probably not solved for long; the school's strict discipline co-existed with good-hearted testing of the rules, particularly the very unpopular rule prohibiting "Unpermitted Association" between male and female students. In the school's early years, when most students roomed in the village and their encounters were under community supervision, some freedom of manners was permitted. In 1840 Luke Green Maxson wrote Cordelia Hartshorn (whom he later married) describing a party where male students held female students on their laps "from a want of room for seats."[23]

Such privileges disappeared when the school added extensive residential facilities. With this responsibility, the faculty took care to regulate their charges' behavior, leading to the prohibition of "Unpermitted Association." Abigail Allen recalled, "To fit the new order of things unheard-of regulations became necessary, and it took time and patience with both teachers and students to overcome the friction." Ellis Witter remembered the many attempts to circumvent this regulation: "If a young man wished to call on a young lady, or take her out for a ride, or to a concert or an entertainment he was to get permission from the president or some member of the faculty. Many interesting incidents grew out of this order; sometimes the young folks would take matters in their own hands for a season of stolen sweets. Many times these seasons were broken up by the president or some member of the faculty rapping at the door or walking in to the presence of the culprets. President Allen was a very sure detective in such cases even when the windows had been darkened and the lights turned down."[24]

Mrs. Isaac B. Brown recalled that the rule against unpermitted association appealed to parents but was "honored more in the breach than the observance." Marion Lucretia Brown (Nicholson) agreed: "Boys and girls were not supposed or allowed to walk on the same side of the street in those Alfred days, but *often did.*"[25] Lydia Langworthy Palmer recounted a famous incident that occurred after President Kenyon "got very angry about gentlemen and ladies going up and down the walk together. They claimed it was accidental. But one morning he gave them a bad talk and threatened to demerit 48 [of a total of 60 points for good behavior] any gentleman and lady he saw go up or down the walk together."

> The next morning, he was coming up from the post office and started to pass a lady on the walk. He lifted his hat with great gallantry, but *did not pass her.* She kept up with him. He walked as fast as he could, till she fairly ran beside him. Thus they came up the stairs and into the chapel. It was only two or three minutes before chapel exercises commenced, so nearly all the students were in their seats. Many had seen it all and just got their places; but the joke was plain in their flushed faces and breathlessness. A round of applause greeted them, and was several times repeated. Pres. Kenyon qualified his threat of the day before, as, if the like happened to any gentleman as did to him that morning, he would not be demerited. Miss C., the lady, was a merry little witch, who was beloved by all, and was a great favorite with Pres. Kenyon.
>
> In the winter term following, she and two or three other girls from the building got into a big snow-balling frolic with Pres. Kenyon. He took it in good part and paid them back in their own coin. So they all came into chapel powdered with snow and flushed and laughing. This occurred several times that term, and they were always sure of a cheer from the school.[26]

Later, in the 1880s, the rule against walking together was "relaxed, or more strictly defined, forbidding the men not to walk nearer the women than so many feet, the exact number of feet I don't recall. . . . but some of the young people had poles cut the exact length and carried them, boy at one end and girl at the other." Others remember the regulation, and the distance, as "The Five Foot Rule."[27]

The rules were identical for men and women, although at other schools women's conduct was more severely regulated than men's, and Alfred's faculty tolerated fairly active socializing. Theodore Thacher recorded in his diary on December 21, 1861, "this afternoon we helped the Ladies trim the Brick Hall for which I got my shame by cutting my arm with an ax. The Ladies intend I believe to have a merry time of it on Christmas Eve." And so they did. On December 26 Thacher wrote, "Last teusday evening (or Christmas eve) was a time that I probably never shall forget as long as I live. The Ladies of the Brick Hall gave an entertainment to the other students of this institution & a good time it was. it all went off very nicely. they served up coffee crackers, cheese Pickles & three different kinds of cake. I never spent an evening in more lively yet gentlemanly & Ladylike company in my Life!"[28]

Students rooming in village homes also had an extensive social life. Hannah Simpson frequently spent time with male students (particularly

Joseph Whiting, a close friend who was fond of her friend Diana), often walking and sitting together, entertaining them and engaging in joint activities. To take just a few examples from her 1861 diary,

> January 3. At night went to the Crandall's. Met Whiting. Sung.
>
> January 4 . . . At night having an excuse from Prof. Kenyon, called on Mr. Whiting to invite him to take a ride to Hornellsville the next morning. He called on us during the evening.
>
> March 4 . . . Was examined in Latin and Chemistry. The result was satisfactory. By invitation went to stay with Sophy. Found Buffrum and Whiting there.
>
> April 11 . . . Evening Mr. Whiting called but I left him and Dinah while I went to sit again with Com[mittee of her literary society] Presume that neither of we three were sorry for the coincidence.
>
> June 1. We did up the work then went up on the hill to write. . . . Just as I was thinking of the closing sentence I saw Mr. Hill. He had been writing not more than two rods away. He came and we sat and talked for a long time.
>
> June 23 . . . Mr. N. B. Maxson called. While he was here the boys came with strawberries for us.

Cortez Clawson remembered, "there was no way by which to a certain extent this mingling could be prevented. So many of the students lived about town and while they were to a certain extent under the supervision of the different homes the boys and girls did the best they could to get together. . . . While the regulations regarding the sexes might be considered rather lax I am inclined to think that no serious problem resulted from it."[29]

President Kenyon's attempts to enforce the rules involved him inadvertently in a memorable incident:

> There were rules in those days, too, forbidding young men from entering the upper floors of the Brick [women's residence]. Nothing daunted, the girls rigged up a clothes basket which they lowered from the top floor on the west side of the building [more than thirty feet above the ground]. At a given signal, they would let it down and draw up someone's date, as we would say today. Prexy suspected some sort of foul play, so investigated the mysterious incidents at the Brick. After some detective work, he discovered the code, so decided to try the ascent himself. He chose a dark night for the expedition, and after exchanging the prearranged signal, found himself being drawn up the side of the building. All went well until the girls saw a shiny head scantily covered with sandy hair appear above the window sill. Paralyzed with astonishment, they gave a horrified shriek and dropped the startled dignitary to the ground. Why he wasn't killed, I don't know, but he did live to tell the tale to a very select coterie of friends.
>
> Incidentally, I might add here, that President Kenyon was noted for his prying habits. The result was that the college boys of that generation used to string wires and ropes all around the campus to trip him. It seems to have been a case of dog eat dog.[30]

Fig. 8.1. Students in their boarding hall, "The Brick." 1870s.

Presidential prying and prescience repeatedly interfered with student pleasures. Sneaking back into town from a jaunt, students would find President Allen standing in the stream they hoped to use for a hidden approach. Jarvis Kenyon, President Kenyon's half-brother, told of a prank played on his brother: "There came a night when a group of young bloods, smarting under the severe restrictions which forbade them to call upon girls at the Brick in the evening, determined to steal the wagon of their great academic enemy. They stole it, and dragged it with great labor up the precipitous slope of Pine Hill, over the crest, and almost down to what was known in my day as the Isaac Lewis farm. There they paused to rest and exult. But not for long. Some hay in the wagon suddenly showed animation. The hay sat up, and from it there emerged the bald head, the square spectacles, and the twinkling eyes of Boss Kenyon. "Gentlemen," said he, "I have had a fine ride. Now pull me back home please."[31]

At times, teacher joined students in a little adventure. Mary Emma Darrow told of one spring night in 1871, when after the Alfriedian lyceum session "one glorious moon light night two 'brick' girls with our friendly art teacher [probably Amelia Stillman, who began teaching in 1870] took blankets and slipped away to spend the night on Pine Hill. Are the pines there now? Their music lulled us to sleep, and the soulful song of a hermit thrush entranced our morning hours." They came down late Sunday morning, hiding their basket and blankets in a closet in the Chapel. "A lengthy paper was read in a ladies lyceum asking most pointedly How we secured such an unheard-of privilege as to be allowed out all night!" Soon the Orophilian men discovered their hiding place and "next morning our basket crowned a point of the Chapel tower to which our attention was called. The closet was empty."[32]

Pine Hill and other steep hills surrounding the campus provided a beloved if hazardous sport shared by men and women (in February 1885 Asa Burdick went to the funeral of a female student killed while sledding on "Chapel hill"). Abram Burt wrote in his diary one November day, "We still have sleighing & the boys are trying to improve it sliding down hill every night and snowballing through the day, girls and boys both taking part in the play."[33] Leona Burdick Merrill remembered the sledding too:

> Student recreation included innocuous but jolly early evening parties with coasting in winter. To go out in a clear, moonlit evening with a long bob sled, trek to the top of a high hill, and roar down through the village like an express train, was a winter sport of parts.
>
> There were some serious accidents and at least one in which a serious village doctor suffered the separation of his horse from the cutter in which he was riding, but the exhiliration never failed.[34]

Fig. 8.2. Art class in Kenyon Memorial Hall, instructor Amelia Stillman standing right of center. 1880s.

These were dangerous pleasures. One sled carrying a male and female student missed the wide bridge for horse and wagon, and sailed across the creek thirty feet to the other bank, without serious injury: "He said that he would not have tried this feat again for all the money on earth."[35] Even the dignified President Allen joined in the sport. One student recalled "sliding down the big Hill on a Bobsled. . . . I can recall one ride President Allen took with us and can still see his sparkling black eyes as we flew down the Hill."

The informality of these relationships, the deep connections between students and faculty or students and townspeople, and the mutual affection among men and women surely seemed to them "the most natural way in the world." In these simple ways, the community's intellectual life—particularly in the exuberant literary societies—and its social life— jaunts, oyster suppers, flying down the hill on sleds—made known to us through archival evidence, reflected Abigail Allen's belief that "life work means co-work of the sexes" and Jonathan Allen's assertion—"The essential powers of the spirit are neither masculine nor feminine, but human, sexless. Thought knows no sex."

Chapter Nine

"The Past Lives and Shines In and Through Us"

I have no memory of ever being cold though the winters were frigid, the snows deep and lasting, and house fires extinguished at bedtime, and re-built early mornings. . . . Education seemed the desirable thing, its price being considered above precious stones.

—Leona Burdick Merrill, "Recollections of Alfred"

T oward the end of the century, the "circle of knowledge," as Jonathan Allen termed it, grew rapidly. Freedom and experimentation first seen in literary societies became integrated into the curriculum with the elective system, championed by Harvard's Charles Eliot; students were no longer required to pursue a fixed course of study. Fields intro-duced in the Ladies' Course—modern literature, modern languages, art history, studio arts—or the Scientific Course became increasingly impor-tant. By the 1880s, Alfred University offered a wide range of degrees, including civil engineering, a B.F.A. program, and business education. Its curriculum reflected increased diversity of purpose, which Allen described as a "universal law" of advancing civilization.

The "Procrustean bed" of the invariant B.A. course must give way to new needs, declared Allen in 1891, during his last major address to the campus: "the circle of knowledge has become so enlarged in its sweep, by the rapid increase of new sciences, new literatures, new industries, creat-ing complexity and diversity, demanding diversity of culture, that it is no longer possible to include even the rudiments of these demands within the compass of a single course, and most colleges have been compelled to institute either electives leading to the same degree, or different courses leading to different degrees."[1]

New programs brought a stronger emphasis on science. The first large gift to Alfred University, $10,000 from Mrs. Ann Lyon in 1867, endowed a department of Industrial Mechanics in memory of her son who died at twenty-one, just as he was beginning an engineering career. Sympathetic with the Allens' reform views, Mrs. Lyon was an energetic woman who worked with freedmen later in her life. She requested among the gift's conditions that the university add $5,000 to the departmental endowment and that its courses parallel those of Yale's Sheffield Scientific School.

The university built an outstanding observatory through the efforts of William A. Rogers, who made and purchased an array of equipment, including a nine-inch telescope. In 1870 he was invited to work at the Harvard observatory and left for Cambridge, taking equipment purchased with his own funds, but leaving behind a fine facility. Strained relations between Rogers and Allen may have spurred his departure. Both men were described as "possessed of a certain type of jealousy, and . . . highly sensitive."[2] They healed the breach fifteen years later and, after teaching at Harvard and Colby, Rogers intended to return in 1898 to teach in Alfred's new Babcock Hall of Physics (built for him), when he suddenly died.

The Ladies' Course, last listed in the 1871 catalog, and the Scientific Course were replaced by the Course in Science and Literature, which offered several languages—French, German, and Greek, with electives in Anglo-Saxon and Hebrew—and numerous sciences—chemistry, physiology, botany, astronomy, psychology, zoology, geology—as well as rhetoric, elocution, law, history, logic, and ethics. Students soon requested that the Laureate of Arts degree be dropped and graduates after 1883 received either the B.A. or the B.Phil.

The Allens' natural history collection grew quickly as they continued "geologizing," traveling with horse and carriage for weeks, laden with specimens. Thousands of rocks, plants, birds, animals, and anthropological curios were stored in cabinets in their large "White House" (the old "Middle Building"). Eventually the collection spilled out of their home and in 1876 the Allens bought Ida Kenyon's partially constructed stone home, the "Steinheim," and began to build a small museum. "It was Mr. Allen's idea to have the exterior of the building an exponent of the geological formation of this region, and the finish of the interior representative of the native woods, and also of as many kinds as could be gathered from other parts of the world. There are between seven and eight thousand samples of different rocks in the outside walls and several hundreds of woods, including that of fruit trees and shrubs, worked into the rooms of the building."[3]

The museum contained one of the earliest university scientific collections at a time when Spencer Baird, Secretary of the Smithsonian Institution, was encouraging colleges to build such collections. In fact, as Kim Tolley notes, "achievements in natural history appeared to dominate the

Fig. 9.1. Steinheim Museum. 1880s.

field of American science during the post-Civil War decade." Botany became "the most popular science in America for recreational and pedagogical purposes"; women were particularly drawn to "botanizing" and the study of natural history. The Allens were tireless, going far beyond genteel "botanizing" in their expeditions; coins, archaeological relics, fossils raked up with the help of hired teams of horses, 10,000 seashells filled the space. Their finds and friends' donations eventually became part of the New York State Geological Survey and the Smithsonian collections.[4]

A Conservatory of Music was opened and emphasis increased on the studio arts, which President Allen encouraged by hanging paintings in all the halls and classroom buildings. A gymnasium (reflecting colleges' growing interest in physical education) was constructed in 1875 and another building started, Kenyon Memorial Hall, which would contain classrooms, a laboratory, and the library. Additional space was obtained when the home built by Ira and Serena White Sayles was sold to the university; the "Gothic" housed classes and then the Theological Seminary for many years. Purchase of the Gothic was fortuitous since construction of Kenyon Hall took nine years, as funds were raised very slowly.

The constant search for funds to support chemistry and mechanics laboratories, Kenyon Hall's construction, building repairs, and other programs was exhausting. Still weak from a bout of smallpox in 1879, Allen was, like Kenyon before him, growing fatigued from overwork. He was persuaded to go abroad in summer 1882 with three friends, visiting historic and scientific sites in seven countries. One companion remembered that if Allen was napping, they had only to say "geological formation!" and he would spring to his feet to see the passing peat bog or scarp. One memorable morning, the group went inside Vesuvius's crater amid jets of sulphurous gas, fresh lava, and sharp explosions. Allen suddenly appeared from behind a lava flow, blood streaming from his head. "Full of scientific enthusiasm," he had gashed his head badly when he tried to leap across a chasm, his hands full of specimens. A few days later, Allen confided to his friends, "If I had found that I was fatally hurt, I intended to ask you to cremate me there. . . . It was but a little way below there that Byron cremated Shelley."[5]

The expansion of science and creation of new disciplines meant that many more books and journals were being published; new teaching methods drew on this variety. As a result, colleges began to establish comprehensive libraries, integrating free-standing collections and setting regular hours. After much debate, Alfred's students urged creation of such a library, combining the individual collections of the four literary societies, the theology department, and the university. Allen added his personal collection to these and, as Kenyon Hall reached completion in 1885, they were all moved to the new building, with a periodical reading room in the tower. This constricted the space that Professor Larkin was counting on for *his* scientific specimens. The morning after the new library opened, the

Fig. 9.2. Jonathan Allen in his handmade rocking chair on the porch of his home, the "White House." The Steinheim Museum is in the background. About 1885.

campus awoke to find that the irascible Larkin had thrown the periodicals out the tower windows, shoved the furniture into the hallway, and locked the door. The students, who had helped pay for the new facility, appealed to the trustees, who backed them in the fray. Ultimately the library was moved to Kenyon Hall's spacious second floor and arranged according to the soon-to-be-famous system devised by an Alfred student, Melvil Dewey, leaving Larkin his tower room.

Throughout his presidency, Jonathan Allen continued on the university's nonsectarian path; the theology school remained subordinate to the College of Liberal Arts and the teacher-training mission was perpetuated. He was less active in denominational affairs (except for his long campaign to include women in governance) than some would have liked; his attention was more absorbed in his natural history collection.[6] Like Kenyon, Allen must have felt he best served the church through education. Addressing the campus in 1891, he delivered a magnificent summary of his aspirations for the university, stressing the great themes of his life—the pleasure of learning, the joy of teaching, reform, and the rights of women. Fifty-five years after joining the first class, he recalled the "common soil" from which it had grown:

[the University] did not start into being to satisfy the wishes of any particular class, calling, profession, or pursuit, but to meet a felt want, voicing itself, irrespective of calling, class, race, color, or sex. . . .

Alfred University had its origin in a response to the cry of the people for more light. It has grown up naturally as the trees grow, from the common soil of the common wants of the people.

. . . it has been from the start deeply religious, earnestly, even radically, reformatory. It imbued its students more or less with the same spirit, preparing them to go forth as evangels, reformers, leaders in all the enterprises having for their end the bettering of human conditions or doing away with evil and wrong that blind and bind men.

In this, his valedictory, Allen reiterated themes Kenyon had outlined forty years earlier—Alfred's education was not "decorative" but for active work; its chief mission, determined by location and needs of its people, was to "the poor" who had to work their way through school; its students would be independent thinkers and go forward to reform the world; he embraced the nobility of the teaching profession. Allen paid teaching one last tribute: "the teacher should come to his profession in the spirit of consecration, not as to a mere livelihood or handicraft. . . . the teacher needs the true up-gush of the soul, fresh and buoyant, the outright flash of spontaneous fervor, simplicity, clearness, strength, directness, force, effectiveness, which, like sacred tongues of flame, shall kindle what is best in each. Whoever fulfills this high calling is faithful to one of the most important and sacred trusts coming to man."[7] Yet for all they shared, Allen always went further than Kenyon in one important area, asserting women's inalienable rights. Caustic as ever toward those blind to the need—"more pathetic than wise"—he did see progress in this long struggle:

In meeting these all-pervasive human needs the first demand was for the recognition of the needs and the consequent rights of woman. From the year 505 A.D., when a great council of divines gravely debated the question whether woman ought to be called a human being; to the time when she was reluctantly permitted to eat at the same table with man; to the time when she was grudgingly allowed to learn the alphabet, the same as man; to the present, when, amid no little opposition, she has been admitted to all, or nearly all, of the more progressive colleges of the land—though many of the older ones, founded on the monastic plan, hold to their celibate condition with a tenacity which is "more pathetic than wise"—has this struggle been going on. From the start, woman has had here equal rights and privileges with man. At its founding no woman in all the land, if in any land, held a collegiate or professional degree. None were regularly licensed physicians, lawyers, or ordained ministers of the gospel. Now there are thousands bearing such degrees, and thousands more in training for them—hundreds of women in the professions, and hundreds more preparing to enter them. In all this, Providence has manifestly been guiding and helping woman, and will help on

Fig. 9.3. President Jonathan Allen with the class of 1892.

to still broader and higher equalities; and woman, we doubt not, will in the future, as in the past, amply vindicate her right to these. In all this Alfred has ever sought to follow the lead of Providence and do what it could to fulfill the divine intent.[8]

Allen had long wished to see America's West and in the summer of 1891 friends, concerned for his health, helped organize a trip with Abigail through the Rockies to California. A traveling companion marveled as Allen gathered specimens at every scenic stop: "It is a constant surprise to see the freshness of his enthusiasm." The following winter he had new cases made for the Steinheim and spent many evenings "classifying new specimens and rearranging the old ones." His health was failing and although he prepared for fall classes, he was too ill to begin teaching. He weakened rapidly and died the morning of September 21, 1892, his family standing near. "I am happy," he said to the sorrowing faces about him, "why cannot you be so?"[9]

At his death, Alfred University encompassed the College of Liberal Arts, Schools of Fine Arts, Industrial Mechanics, and Theology, the Normal School, and the Academy. The university continued to carry heavy debt. Its income barely covered teachers' salaries, not building maintenance or equipment purchases, nor were there adequate funds for capital projects. Despite gifts for professorships in physics, Greek, and history, the endowment remained small, not much larger than accumulated debt, and the school's finances, always straitened, became dangerously extended in the last decade of the century. One student, Cortez Clawson, remembered, "Changes came slowly in those days. Pres. Allen was philosopher and scholar and not a financier." Though he was not a talented executive, Jonathan Allen, in partnership with his wife, left an unparalleled legacy. Allen in turn always acknowledged his debt to the school's history, to a continuity of purpose and values that culminated in the Allens' activism: "Though we live in the present, the past lives and shines in and through us."[10]

New pressures soon transformed the university. Arthur E. Main, elected president in 1893, served a brief, conflicted, and disappointing term. Accepting his resignation, the trustees turned to Alfred's young, energetic, and much-admired pastor, Boothe Colwell Davis, who had graduated from Alfred and Yale Divinity School. As Davis recalled, their "insistence" that he accept the position "swept Mrs. Davis and me irresistibly to a consideration of duty, opportunity, and adaptability, on the one side; and the problems, risks, and dangers on the other." Denominational enrollment could not sustain the school and as free public high schools were created in neighboring towns and villages, academy enrollment fell off rapidly. (In 1915 the academy closed; the university helped fund a high school in its place.) A severe depression in the 1890s pushed numerous colleges near ruin and by 1895, Alfred was on the brink of bankruptcy. Davis reluctantly concluded that his duty lay in accepting the post—at his request, for a five-year term, commencing September 1895. (In fact, he served until 1933, nearly forty years.)[11]

The new president—only thirty-two years old—had a painful choice. "Seventh Day Baptists simply could not support two or three good colleges. He must either go into bankruptcy or return to the original non-sectarian basis and appeal to Sunday keepers for money and students. . . . Nobody not born a Seventh Day Baptist can quite appreciate what his struggle must have been. The smaller a group, especially a religious group, the stronger the natural appeal for group loyalty." Davis proposed that the two newer Seventh Day Baptist colleges, Milton (chartered 1867) and Salem (chartered 1890), disband in favor of Alfred since there were not enough students to go around. After being pressured to withdraw this proposal, Davis reluctantly turned away from the denominational base and deliberately broadened the student body by personally recruiting (visiting up to fifty high schools a year) and seeking state support to expand the art and engineering offerings.[12]

As a result, the New York State College of Ceramics was added to the university in 1900 and a School of Agriculture was funded by the state in 1908 (this school later separated from the university). Seventh Day Baptist representation fell off quickly as the university increased in size from its dangerously low 1895 enrollment of 159, of whom about 80 percent were Seventh Day Baptist. By 1901, enrollment was 275 and less than one-third of students were Seventh Day Baptist; by 1928 only about 10 percent of its 705 students were. Still, the symbolic importance of the Sabbath was relinquished with difficulty. Even when vastly outnumbered, townspeople and trustees resisted Saturday football games and it became increasingly difficult to find opponents who would schedule days other than Saturday. When Alfred at last began to play away on Saturday (with players that were Sunday-keepers), the Theology School threatened to secede from the university. Not until lights were installed in the 1930s were home games permitted, on Saturday evening, after the Sabbath.

Abigail's influence, like her husband's, kept Alfred on its egalitarian path throughout the nineteenth century, and for several decades after her death, pride in this tradition continued. Elsewhere, the reaction against coeducation intensified during what was regarded, ironically, as the Progressive Era. As women's enrollment increased (by 1900, 35 percent of total enrollment nationally; by 1920, 47 percent), fears grew that they would "take over" collegiate culture and win academic prizes that would otherwise go to men. The newly created research universities established a system of admission quotas, credential requirements, and prestige hierarchy that restricted women's enrollment. The democratizing power represented by antebellum colleges diminished and a newly exclusive monolithic model arose. "Many new barriers had arisen even faster than the best women of the time could scramble over them. . . . The coming of professionalism in the 1880s and 1890s had contained and circumscribed the women and restricted them to the fringes of science, almost as far from the real involvement and leadership as they had been decades before." The antebellum ethos of opening opportunities for "the poor" became a distant memory. As Reuben concludes, "leaders of research universities strengthened their institutions' commitment to the advancement of knowledge, but they were never able to recapture university reformers' faith in the power of knowledge to elevate individuals and the world." By the late nineteenth century, M. Carey Thomas felt college women were viewed as creatures with "hoofs and horns," "fearsome toads." At times, echoed a Wellesley faculty member, "the bright woman feels like an 'intellectual Frankenstein.'" The "great withdrawal" of the twentieth century followed and not until the resurgence of the equal rights movement in the 1960s did women begin to fight their way back into prestigious male schools, graduate study, the professions, and faculty positions.[13]

Rationalization for the backlash against women took such forms as discovery of "natural forces"—"sex repulsion" (numerical dominance of classrooms by one sex would drive out the other; no such fears, of course, had operated when women were in the minority) and its converse, "sex attraction." At the University of Chicago (founded 1892), women rose from 24 percent to 52 percent of enrollment within a decade and formed a majority in Phi Beta Kappa. In 1901, President Harper instituted segregated instruction. Within a few years, women and men again shared classrooms, but that integration was accompanied by a weaker position for women as the culture shifted to venerate varsity sports and emphasize preparation for business and the professions, worlds mostly closed to women. Hostility was evident at most research universities: Berkeley's disdain for its "ugly pelicans" mirrored Wesleyan's dismissal of its women as "quails"; Michigan and Stanford set quotas.

Small liberal arts colleges, particularly those not originally coeducational, followed suit. Enmity at Wesleyan became intense at the end of the century; campus life moved to emphasize football and fraternities, "islands of untainted masculinity." Student newspapers declared coeducation "a menace to the welfare of the college." Contemptuous remarks were replaced by positively offensive language, ridicule, and harassment. In 1909, to position Wesleyan with Amherst, Dartmouth, and Yale and cement relations with urban businessmen, women were eliminated entirely.

Colby and Middlebury were among those that segregated women in this period. Like Wesleyan, Colby admitted its first woman in 1871. In 1890 President Albion Small announced a plan for "coordinate education," establishing a women's division to eliminate the "original ungenerous prejudice" against women and "the undesirable competition between young men and young women." "The normal woman," he said, "is not the school teacher, nor the organizer of philanthropies, nor the reform agitator, but the wife and mother." Alumnae protests were to no avail. In 1900, equal numbers of women and men entered Colby, spurring an alumni crusade to eliminate women entirely. Although this did not succeed, a quota was in place for decades.[14]

Middlebury (founded 1800) first admitted women in 1883 due to low enrollment and townspeople's desire to educate their daughters at "the town's college." In 1901 more women than men entered the freshman class and women were taking many academic prizes; fears for the college's reputation led the trustees to limit female numbers and place them in a Women's College in 1902. "The result was a semisegregated community in which ill-defined and changing role expectations produced a nebulous and uneasy relationship between the men and the women."[15]

Despite this increasingly corrosive climate, Alfred's attitude toward its women continued to be supportive. In 1899, one of the men's literary societies, the Orophilians, scheduled a debate on the question "Resolved, that co-education should be abolished from Alfred University." It was decided in the negative. The student paper noted disapprovingly in 1901 that Cornell's freshman class proposed to exclude women from its class organization, and the paper continued to print women's rights arguments in later years.

Abigail Allen ceased teaching in 1892 but remained involved in reform activities until her death. She reported on Allegany County suffrage activities to the 1892 Woman Suffrage Convention and maintained ties with foremost feminists. In 1895 she visited Elizabeth Cady Stanton, whom she had met many times. "We felt it a great privilege to be able to greet her in her pleasant winter quarters" in New York City. "She remembered Alfred and its thoroughly advanced educational work." They talked of the suffrage struggle, improvement of tenement housing with Mrs. Russell Sage, children's playgrounds, and other social issues. "Mrs. Stanton does not expect to help usher in the millennium, but does not doubt that she shall see the fulfillment of most of the reforms that she has so long advocated. We left her feeling that a benediction had descended upon us." In the same year, Allen praised Julia Ward Howe: "her facile pen has done important service for every right that should be proclaimed, every wrong that should be righted." In 1900 Abigail was recognized as "one of the band of early workers for this noble reform [suffrage]" and invited to Susan B. Anthony's eightieth birthday celebration in Washington, D.C.[16]

Long after the Civil War, the plight of uneducated black children in the South distressed her; at the age of seventy-six, only two years before her own death, she made up her mind to go South with a friend, "make a little home there and day by day, gather in the children for instruction. She was sure she had the strength for it. But the way did not open so she renewed her efforts to help in other ways and to influence others to go. Again and again her call went out for good text books and literature. . . . Mrs. Allen superintended the packing of the barrels, collected the money for freight, and sent them to home-missionaries in different parts of the South. One such barrel was sent on its way but two months before she died."

Fig. 9.4. Abigail Allen in the studio, with a
portrait of Jonathan Allen in the background. 1890s.

Abigail also continued her involvement in the school, offering assistance to President Davis in August 1902, just weeks before her death. She wrote, "Dear friend, If you could come in for a few moments I think I could save you many hours of time. Giving you the bones that you can put the flesh on as you please. Hastily, A. A. Allen."[17]

A reformer to the end, Allen believed women should exert their local voting rights. New York's women were given the right to vote in school district elections in 1880, but opponents fought it immediately. Decades of confusion, restrictions, intimidation, court battles, and legislative battles followed. By 1890, nineteen states offered such partial suffrage but "it never brought enough women to the polls to constitute a convincing demonstration that women wanted the ballot; on the contrary, it furnished the opposition with the argument that women were simply not interested in voting." Those women who did attempt to exert even this limited right could face harassment and threatening behavior. "Small wonder," Eleanor Flexner concluded, that turnout was low. In 1901, New York's property-owning women were allowed to vote on tax issues in towns and villages. Proponents like Abigail Allen continued to encourage women to use their limited rights to vote.[18]

A few months before Abigail's death, nearly blind, "feeling that women did not realize their responsibility in this direction, she undertook long drives over Alfred's beautiful hills, which she loved so dearly, to persuade all she could to attend the approaching school meetings and to live up to their high privilege of having a voice and influence in school matters. The roads had been badly cut out and washed by heavy floods and there were frequent rains, but no one ever heard her complain of weariness, though she was seventy nine years old, and there was no thought of giving up until all had been done which seemed to her desirable."

Abigail Allen died on October 26, 1902, the same day as her respected friend, Elizabeth Cady Stanton. Like Stanton, Allen had "joined herself heart and hand with great causes in the struggle for right, and she watched with profound interest the progress of truth in the vast world."[19]

Abigail's death marked the end of an era; she was the last of the founding faculty. Their dedication, their strengths (with their failings), their commitment to learning were honored by those who shared with them the early days of women's higher education. "Educators and students alike," as Nash concluded, "held an ideal of learning as one of life's great pleasures, a pleasure that was of equal value to women and men."[20] The affection of past students for the school and its valley setting was extraordinary. Leona Burdick Merrill grew up in Alfred. Her recollections form a moving elegy to the high ideals and friendly warmth of this educational community:

> The University library on the first floor of the Chapel was pleasant and light with its atmosphere of quiet warmth and the singing coal fire—papers, magazines and not too many books.
>
> The Chapel, itself, at Commencement time or Anniversary, as we called it, is the pleasantest memory. Decorated with great ropes of evergreen stretched diagonally from opposite corners of the room, the effect and the perfume and sweetness were never to be forgotten. . . .
>
> The long, cold winters heaped with snow and the (then) long, warm, dry summer months when the sound of the mowing machine in the

meadows, with the scent of wild strawberries, the sound of building and the ringing of an anvil, then the pleasant excitement of school beginning, the Chapel bell, new and interesting faces and personalities, friendships formed immediately upon sight that were to continue always and forever, experiences that blended to make an elusive intangible something, that is yet more real and tangible than any element of the combination. . . .

I have no memory of ever being cold though the winters were frigid, the snows deep and lasting, and house fires extinguished at bedtime, and rebuilt early mornings. The sense of warmth and comfort within and the sound of the wind roaring through the big pines on Pine Hill will last forever and a day. Food was plain and good and plentiful.

There was no want nor lack unless it were the lack of money. People were well fed, decently and comfortably clothed and industrious, with books to read.

Education seemed the desirable thing, its price being considered above precious stones.[21]

Fig. 9.5. Students relaxing on Pine Hill. About 1904.

Conclusion

The essential powers of the spirit are neither masculine nor feminine, but human, sexless. Thought knows no sex.

—Jonathan Allen, "Mixed Schools"

Diversity is the hallmark of antebellum and mid-nineteenth-century higher education. Its contours were notably variegated—pious conservatism reigned at many evangelical colleges; numerous colleges did not admit women until years or even decades after their founding; progressivism and principles of equality were evident at a few institutions. For the pioneering generation of women, a combination of cultural factors, economic impulses, educational philosophies, and personal beliefs shaped their education. It is no simple task to sort through the complex array of contributing factors. Clearly no one influence created Alfred's environment; individuals, regional factors, and local needs mingled in unusual ways.

Alfred University's teaching mission is not a sufficient explanation for its egalitarian environment or its support for women's rights. Antioch, for example, also emphasized teacher training but President Mann was opposed to the women's rights movement. Although teaching offered economic independence and some level of autonomous status to women, early advocates of female teachers tended to frame their arguments within the doctrine of separate spheres.

Nor did reform activity often lead to explicit support for women's rights. Reformers of all stripes embraced temperance, and many came to be antislavery, but only a few advocated extending principles of equality to women. Oberlin and Knox were strongly abolitionist, for example, but their women were subordinate. While the commitment to reform was, like the teaching mission, a crucial platform for egalitarianism, it too was insufficient.

The relationship of education to organized religion was even more complicated. Some denominations founded exclusively male colleges; others established coeducational ones, but these ran the gamut from conservative to progressive in their treatment of women. Among Baptists,

171

only the breakaway Seventh Day and Free Will Baptists established coeducational schools, mingling ideological motives and the cost savings important to small sects. The value Seventh Day Baptists placed on basic education and their emphasis on training teachers opened opportunities for women, but these did not spring from explicit precepts of gender equality within the denomination itself. Of Seventh Day Baptist schools, only Alfred was notably egalitarian.

If Seventh Day Baptist beliefs did not directly support women's equality and if church governance excluded them until late in the century, what characteristics might have indirectly contributed? Surely the desire, shared with other Baptists, to educate both sexes was an important foundation, but it too was insufficient; all colleges founded by Baptists before 1860 were male. Alfred's avoidance of denominational control, deemphasis of ministerial training, and maintenance of a secular mission were critical in providing a framework for liberal views. More secular values were important: need for educated children and teachers of both sexes; strong commitment to certain reform movements; aversion to dogma; rural way of life; extended family networks.

Rural work patterns contributed to a blurring of gender boundaries. Numerous historians have found mutuality between the sexes, significant economic contributions from women, and early feminist values in "the back country." The normal school students studied by Ogren, predominantly from farms and very small towns, "created a comfortable public sphere with few gender boundaries." Even they "tended, however, to stop short of full support for women's rights." Rural egalitarianism took a particularly progressive path at Alfred.[1]

The Allens clearly went beyond these influences to push for women's innate equality. Ironically, two characteristics that most affected the environment for women—refusal to be dominated by ministerial training and a vision of equal rights—although not fully supported by the denomination may have derived indirectly from it, for resistance to dogmatism was also a Seventh Day Baptist value. Baptist lack of dogma allowed the Allens to form their belief that sexual equality was a divine command when their denomination did not.

The milieu in which their equal rights convictions developed offers significant parallels to the rural cultures studied by Jensen, Hewitt, and Osterud, in which reciprocity and mutuality between the sexes led to early stands on equal rights. The university drew its students from a region of homogeneous villages with limited class stratification. Like the 1848 Declaration of Sentiments signers, the school and its community exhibited dense kinship networks, large flexible households, and cooperative gender roles.[2] While Quaker reformers espoused precepts of sexual equality derived from their religious beliefs, the Allens moved well beyond Seventh Day Baptist beliefs in promulgating women's rights. In so doing they joined Stanton,

Stone, Dall, and Howe by drawing their convictions from Enlightenment values and a keen sense of the need for meaningful employment.

Even the contribution of individuals must be qualified. Though Abigail and Jonathan Allen were unquestionably crucial in defining and articulating the school's philosophy, their advanced views were for the most part embraced by their community. Abigail Allen's beliefs could not have prevailed alone. We have only to remember that Oberlin President Finney's wife, supportive as she was of Susan B. Anthony's work, nonetheless had to whisper that support outside her husband's hearing. The family model of coeducation, first expressed in their student years, was refined by the Allens and linked by them to an ideology of equality drawn from Enlightenment thought, yet that model was also intrinsic to this culture.

And so we return to the question that initiated this research: How was women's public speaking handled at Alfred? Jonathan Allen spoke more truly than he knew in responding, "The most natural way in the world." Egalitarianism seemed natural because it was rooted in factors associated with these people's childhood homes—their farming origins, family structure, and the regional economy—as well as in the ideology of natural rights. Shared labor, a dense kinship system, a separatist denomination, independence from that denomination, liberal theology, a secular mission—all combined to support an explicit ideology of equality in this early collegiate environment.

Alfred's story is just one of many, of course, and the variety of student experiences was extraordinary. Nash has shown that three women's schools in a single town—Oxford, Ohio—varied considerably in purpose and student affluence, with "alternate visions of education for women co-existing in the same time and place." Similarly, in just one Western New York region examined by Kerns, five colleges, each educating women, located within a hundred miles and founded within twenty years of each other, differed remarkably. Two were women's colleges. LeRoy Female Seminary (later Ingham University) was founded in 1835 by two sisters who modeled their school on Zilpah Grant's Ipswich Female Seminary, and was supported by a group of LeRoy businessmen and lawyers. Elmira Female College (founded 1855) was modeled on Mount Holyoke Female Seminary, founded in 1837 by Mary Lyon, who collaborated with Grant at Ipswich. Three were coeducational. Genesee College (which later moved, forming the nucleus of Syracuse University) was chartered in 1849 from Genesee Wesleyan Seminary, a coeducational school which opened in 1832. New York Central College (founded 1849, closed 1859) was a manual labor school, like Oberlin modeled on Oneida Institute. Alfred University was the third.[3]

These five exhibited a rich variety of founding impulses, drawing on differing educational models, or no model at all. Three were inspired by earlier schools (Ipswich, Mount Holyoke, Oneida). Genesee was fairly large and eclectic, combining denominational with local support; Beadie traces its growth and competition with Cornell for land grant funds. Alfred was "home-grown," with no recognizable predecessor. Women's influence on the five schools' philosophies and practices ranged from dominating to nearly nonexistent. LeRoy was initially run by women—the Ingham sisters; at Alfred, women did not govern but were very influential; men dominated the other three colleges. Students' origins also differed. Only one-third of Elmira's students came from farm families; at LeRoy one-half; at Alfred three-quarters. The two women's schools were located in urban areas; the three coeducational ones were in small towns.[4]

Founded in the "denominational era" (a term we must recognize as misleading at best), only two of the five had formal denominational ties and these two were otherwise quite dissimilar. Genesee College was sponsored by a mainstream group, the Methodist General Conference; New York Central College was established by the breakaway American Baptist Free Missionary Society, a reformist abolitionist sect, at a time when antislavery students were being expelled from other schools. Typical of women's schools, LeRoy and Elmira were free of denominational ties, but evangelical in spirit. The Ingham sisters were strongly influenced by Zilpah Grant's conversion practices and wished to educate their students to become "missionary teachers"; Elmira's trustees intended it to be "highly evangelical." In contrast, Alfred was secular in spirit and free of formal denominational ties, but as we have seen was in complicated ways both dependent on and independent of a denomination.

Finally, the five schools varied dramatically in their views on women's education and their proper societal role. At three, the mainstream Methodist college and the two evangelical women's colleges, conservative beliefs about gender roles and the doctrine of separate spheres prevailed. For instance, Elmira's President Reverend Augustus Cowles believed "woman's mission was 'a loving subjection of the wife . . . to her husband.'" In contrast, it appears (on scant evidence) that New York Central's attitude toward women was very progressive. One of its founding principles was "to contribute to the settlement of the equality of the sexes" and its first annual report excoriated "the disgraceful doctrine, so dishonorable both to the head and the heart of its advocates, that woman is the intellectual inferior of man." Given the relationship between dissent and women's rights advocacy, it is not surprising that this small dissenting group nurtured progressive views on women's rights. Alfred and New York Central were also the most assertively antislavery communities, while the other three appeared to favor women's benevolent activities but not more radical stances.[5]

In surveys of women's educational history, it has become common to describe the Progressive Era women of 1890–1920 as the "second generation" of college-educated women and those who attended women's colleges opening after the Civil War as the "first generation." That odd convention completely overlooks the true pioneers—women who enrolled at the early coeducational schools opening between 1833 and 1865. These schools offer fascinating variety and insight into the impulse to higher education, particularly when diaries, letters, society minutes, and other archival resources allow students to speak for themselves, recording daily events or simply musing on their hopes.

Recent work on academies has overturned many preconceptions and "new scholarship," as Geiger asserted, "has shown that the familiar stereotypes of the nineteenth-century college are seriously deficient." The history and environment of early colleges have not been fully explored; even fewer studies are grounded in student experiences. Examination of other pioneering colleges (New York Central's egalitarianism is a compelling example) will bring fresh insights into the diversity of schools that educated women in the hopeful early days when students like Leona Burdick Merrill could revel in the scent of wild strawberries and new-mown hay—and in an education whose price was above precious stones.[6]

Notes

Introduction

1. Abigail Allen, *Life and Sermons of Jonathan Allen*, 51–52. Lucy Stone (1818–1893) attended Oberlin with her earnings from several years of teaching. She began lecturing for an antislavery society after graduation and became one of the nineteenth century's best-known reformers.

2. Conable, *Women at Cornell*; McGuigan, *A Dangerous Experiment*; Miller-Bernal, *Separate by Degree*; Miller-Bernal & Poulson, *Going Coed*; Solomon, *In the Company of Educated Women*; Hogeland, "Coeducation of the Sexes at Oberlin College"; and Rury and Harper, "The Trouble With Coeducation," for example, emphasize the conservative aspects of coeducation. Ogren, *The American State Normal School*, 65, also stresses the "climate of hostility" at coeducational colleges.

3. Nash, *Women's Education in the United States, 1780-1840*, 116; Beadie and Tolley, *Chartered Schools*, 6; Tolley, *The Science Education of American Girls*, 1; Ogren, *State*, 5; Ogren, "'Not Necessarily Bloomer Women,'" 3.

4. The newly settled areas of New York and Ohio were considered the western frontier at the time.

5. Jonathan Allen, "Mixed Schools"; Abigail Allen, "Co-education," 14.

6. Solomon, *Company*, xix; 15; Conway, "Perspectives on the History of Women's Education in the United States," 6, 8.

7. Hogeland, "Coeducation," 167 quotes Fletcher, *A History of Oberlin College*, 1: 291. Fletcher's thorough and discerning history of Oberlin is an exception to the usual superficial inclusion of women in older institutional histories; Hogeland, "Coeducation," 172; Fairchild, "Coeducation of the Sexes," 395. Lucy Stone was one of the three "strong-minded" alumnae.

8. Rury and Harper, "Trouble," 500; Mann, *Life of Horace Mann*, 527; Joan Zimmerman, "Daughters of Main Street: Culture and the Female Community at Grinnell, 1884-1917," in Kelley, ed., *Woman's Being, Woman's Place*, 154.

9. Boas, *Woman's Education Begins*, 56; Solomon, *Company*, xxi.

10. Solomon, *Company*, 27, quoting Catherine H. Birney, *The Grimké Sisters* (Boston: Lee and Shepard, 1885), 275; Rury and Harper, "Trouble," 502; J. W. Scott, "Women's History as Women's Education," 7.

11. Hofstadter and Metzger, *The Development of Academic Freedom in the United States*, 212, 209–10; Leslie, *Gentlemen and Scholars*, xv; Burke, *American Collegiate*

Populations, 242; Reuben, "Writing When Everything Has Been Said," 415; Leslie, *Gentlemen and Scholars*, 2.

12. Beadie and Tolley, eds., *Chartered Schools*, ix; Beadie, "Internal Improvement," in Beadie and Tolley, eds., *Chartered Schools*, 109; Nash, *Women's Education*; Malkmus, "Small Towns, Small Sects, and Coeducation in Midwestern Colleges, 1853–1861," 33.

13. Welter, "The Cult of True Womanhood: 1820–1860," 173; Cott, *The Bonds of Womanhood*, 17. Smith-Rosenberg, on the other hand, found a subculture of "love and ritual" in women's sphere that extolled gender differences, "The Female World," in *Disorderly Conduct*. Studies of single-sex education have often stressed this view. Among the studies of rural egalitarianism, see Jensen, *Promise to the Land*, Osterud, *Bonds of Community*, and Hewitt, *Women's Activism and Social Change*.

14. Hewitt, *Women's Activism*, 19; Hewitt, "Feminist Friends," 29.

15. Tewksbury, *The Founding of American Colleges and Universities Before the Civil War*, 4.

16. Tyack and Hansot, *Learning Together*, 36; Noble, *A World Without Women*, 256; Cott, *Bonds*, 140, 159.

17. Cott, *Bonds*, 204; see Isenberg, "Coequality," and Hersh, *The Slavery of Sex*.

One. Gender and Higher Education

1. Lerner, "Placing Women in History," 7.

2. J. W. Scott, "Women's History as Women's Education," 38; Welter, "Cult of True Womanhood"; Lerner, "The Lady and the Mill Girl"; Cott, *Bonds*, 200

3. George B. Emerson, "On Motives to be Addressed in the Instruction of Children," *Common School Journal* (1839), 374, quoted by Nancy Green, "Female Education and School Competition," 136; "Cassandra," in Abrams, ed., *The Norton Anthology of English Literature*, 2: 1734.

4. Cott, *Bonds*, 15; Kerber, "'Nothing Useless or Absurd or Fantastical'" in Lasser, ed., *Educating Men and Women Together*, 40.

5. Cott, *Bonds*, 119; Woody, *A History of Women's Education in the United States*, 1: 311. Woody's encyclopedic history of women's education, published in 1929, stands as the most thorough overview; it has yet to be updated.

6. Le Roy J. Halsey, ed., *The Works of Philip Lindsley* (Philadelphia, 1864) 1: 254, quoted in Tewksbury, *The Founding of American Colleges and Universities Before the Civil War*, 4, 76; Katz, "The Role of American Colleges in the Nineteenth Century," 215; Veysey, *Emergence*, 3, 8.

7. Henry P. Tappan, *University Education* (New York: 1850), 64, quoted in Tewksbury, *Founding*, 3.

8. Kerns, "Antebellum Higher Education for Women in Western New York State," 44. There were many more unincorporated academies. Sizer, ed., *The Age of the Academies*, 12, notes the difficulty of making an accurate count. One source listed 286 New York State academies in 1850; another found 887 in 1855.

9. Tewksbury, *Founding*, 5n17; Sizer, *Age of the Academies*, 47.

10. Sizer, *Age of the Academies*, 1.

11. The high school movement began in Massachusetts under Horace Mann's urging. After the Civil War, high schools spread rapidly, appearing in rural areas. In 1870, 160 high schools were reported; by 1900, there were more than 6,000. A. T. Smith, "Coeducation in the Schools and Colleges of the United States," in Office of Education, *Annual Report*, 1903: 1054, 1061; Rury and Harper, "Trouble," 485; Messerli, *Horace Mann*, 553; Palmieri, *In Adamless Eden*, 13; Leslie, *Gentlemen and Scholars*, 51.

12. Fairchild, *Oberlin*, 174, 178.

13. Welter, "Cult of True Womanhood," 151.

14. M. Carey Thomas, "Notes for the opening address at Bryn Mawr College, 1899," quoted in B. M. Cross, ed., *The Educated Woman in America*, 141–42.

15. Ehrenreich and English, *For Her Own Good*, 127–28; Smith-Rosenberg and Rosenberg, "The Female Animal," 335; Clarke, *Sex in Education*, 127.

16. Clarke, *Sex in Education*, 94, 93, 63.

17. M. Carey Thomas, "Present Tendencies in Women's Colleges and University Education," *Educational Review* 25 (1908): 69.

18. Alice Freeman Palmer, "A Review of the Higher Education of Women," in Brackett, ed., *Woman and the Higher Education*, 104, 106, 129. For the debate over nineteenth-century coeducation and gender roles, see Woody, *History of Women's Education*, and Tyack and Hansot, *Learning Together*. Miller-Bernal, *Separate by Degree*, summarizes the continuing debate over single-sex education vs. coeducation.

19. Two rare exceptions were New York Central College (founded 1849, closed 1859) and Antioch College, which opened as colleges with large preparatory departments. New York Central was a manual labor school, modeled like many others on Oneida Institute. Founded by the militantly abolitionist American Baptist Free Mission Society, it was open to women and blacks. It failed to achieve financial stability. Another pattern was presented by Grinnell, which opened its doors in 1861 to men and women but denied women the bachelor's degree for decades. Palmer in Brackett, ed., *Woman and the Higher Education*, 108.

20. Turner, *The Frontier in American History*, 38; Kerns, "Antebellum Higher Education," 190.

21. Olin, *Women of a State University*, 31.

22. McGuigan, *Dangerous Experiment*, 20.

23. McGuigan, 20, 18.

24. Olin, *Women of a State University*, 101–2; Ogren, "Where Coeds Were Coeducated"; G. J. Clifford, "'Shaking Dangerous Questions from the Crease,'" 25; Conable, *Women at Cornell*, 122.

25. Harper, *The Life and Work of Susan B. Anthony*, 1: 155–57.

26. McLachlan, "The American College in the Nineteenth Century," 296; Rudolph, *Curriculum*, 102.

27. Olin, *Women of a State University*, 163.

28. Hewitt, "Beyond the Search for Sisterhood," 300; Kerber et al., "Beyond Roles, Beyond Spheres," 565.

29. Nash, *Women's Education*, 10; Ogren, "'Not Necessarily Bloomer Women,'" 4.

30. Nash, for example, found Enlightenment beliefs articulated in the post–Revolutionary War rationale for expanding female education, "Rethinking Republican Motherhood," 171–72; Kerber, *Women of the Republic*, 269.

Two. Seventh Day
Baptist and Farm Roots

1. A. Allen, *Life and Sermons*, 381. "Fiat Lux" became the school's motto.
2. Tewksbury, *Founding of American Colleges*, 2.
3. McNall, *An Agricultural History of the Genesee Valley*, 2, 76.
4. Minard, *History of Allegany County*, 624.
5. *History of Allegany County*, 96.
6. Seventh Day Baptists periodically sent missionaries to Jews in New York City or Palestine, thinking their shared Sabbath might give them a recruiting edge in the long-running Christian attempt to convert the Jews; these efforts were fruitless. One hopeful agent reported that although he was treated civilly, the erstwhile converts declined prayer sessions and, permitting "none but Jews" in their synagogues, the agent could not instruct them there. Since the agent could not understand Hebrew, he had to acknowledge that "their expertness in the original [gave them] a decided advantage in verbal debate." All in all, the agent concluded, he could "hope for but little success in our undertaking"—"Society For the Promotion of Christianity Among the Jews," Seventh Day Baptist General Conference, *Year Book*, 1839, 21–27. Sanford, *Conscience Taken Captive*, 1.
7. Dall, "Syllabub."
8. Rowe, *Thunder and Trumpets*, 80–81, 73–74.
9. *Manual of the Seventh-Day Baptists*, 53.
10. E. H. Lewis, "Remarks of Dr. Edwin H. Lewis at the Alfred Dinner." Chicago, 1933.
11. Minard, *History of Allegany County*, 633.
12. Daniel Maxson to Artemesia Maxson.
13. Sanford, *A Choosing People*, 374. This preference for rural lives probably had a significant effect on the university's ability to raise funds and build a sustaining endowment. Booming new economic possibilities in the cities were denied Alfred's overwhelmingly rural supporters. In consequence, while many colleges could turn to wealthy urban members of their denomination to build endowment, Alfred University had few such resources among its coreligionists or local donors. Jonathan Allen wrote in 1875, "even [the] staunchest friends of the Institution will, mayhap, be surprised to learn how little, on the whole, has been done for Alfred, except what she has done for herself." The relatively minuscule size of the Seventh Day Baptist sect also made it an insubstantial base for major fund raising. Thus, size and rural orientation ensured that the university's financial resources would be slender.
14. C. H. Maxson, "A Chapter of Family History in Relation to Alfred and Alfred University," 17; Minard, *History of Allegany County*, 626, 627; *History of Allegany County*, 316.
15. Ellis, "The Yankee Invasion of New York," 5, 3.

16. Clawson, *History of the Town of Alfred*, 77; Minard, *History of Allegany County*, 630.

17. C. H. Maxson, "Chapter," 18; Minard, *History of Allegany County*, 634.

18. Jonathan Allen, "Alfred University Historic Sketch—First Decade," *Sabbath Recorder*, July 28, 1881.

19. McNall, *Agricultural History*, 184; Orra Stillman to Bradford Manchester; J. Collins to Amorilla C. Babcock and Daniel C. Babcock, November 25, 1843; Minard, *History of Allegany County*, 128.

20. Phelan, ed., *And a White Vest for Sam'l*, 233.

21. Phelan, 39.

22. Phelan, 195, 10–12, 34–35.

23. Ryan, *Womanhood in America*, 156; Kerns, "Farmers' Daughters," 24–25.

24. Barkun, *Crucible of the Millennium*, 118.

25. Jensen, *Promise to the Land*, 174, 180; Jensen, *Loosening the Bonds*, 130.

26. Osterud, "The Valuation of Women's Work," 19; Jensen, *Promise to the Land*, 10; Osterud, *Bonds of Community*, 275.

27. Osterud, *Bonds of Community*, 286.

28. Hewitt, *Women's Activism and Social Change*, 18–19, 242; W. R. Cross, *The Burned-over District*, 222; Jensen, *Promise to the Land*, 256–57.

29. Kerns, "Antebellum Higher Education," 309–10. "Alfred drew the greatest percentage of its students from farm families—76.3%, as opposed to 68.5% for Genesee, 52.9% for LeRoy and 36.0% for Elmira. . . . Alfred is most rural with 96.3%, then Genesee 93.3%, LeRoy 79.8%, and Elmira 51.7%," Kerns, "Antebellum Higher Education," 219–20.

Three. Origins:
The Select School, 1836–1843

1. Tyack and Hansot, *Learning Together*, 57.

2. *History of Allegany County*, 143; C. H. Maxson, "Chapter," 26; James Lee Gamble, "Alfred University," in *Seventh Day Baptists in Europe and America*, 1: 488.

3. A. Allen, *Life and Sermons*, 28.

4. J. Allen, "Alfred University: Historic Sketch—First Decade," *Sabbath Recorder*, July 21, 1881, 3; Orra Stillman to Bradford Manchester, January 12, 1837; Norwood, "Bethuel Cooley Church," 6; Norwood, *Fiat Lux*, 7.

5. "Women at Alfred: Co-education," *The Alfred Sun*, May 16, 1895, 1.

6. A. Allen, *Life and Sermons*, 30.

7. Baker, "Alfred University."

8. Sizer, *The Age of the Academies*, 22; Larkin, "History of Alfred University," 3. In Greek mythology, Cadmus was a sun god; King of Thebes, he introduced the Phoenician alphabet to the Greek people. He was thus known as the giver of letters and the light of learning.

9. Halsey H. Baker, "About Alfred University," *Sabbath Recorder*, August 19, 1886.

10. D. Stillman to Maxson Greene, September 7, 1837.

11. Irish, "Sketch of the Early Life of Rev. James R. Irish," 262.

12. Ibid., 278. R. S. Fletcher, *History of Oberlin College*, 1: 184 reports that in 1835 fifty students left Phillips Andover because they were not permitted to form an antislavery society. Phillips Academy archives reveal that the student rebellion followed two administrative rejections of their request to form an antislavery society. On July 22, 1835, fifty men asked to be dismissed honorably from the academy, Irish among them.

13. Sanderson, "J. R. Irish"; "Alfred University and Union."

14. P. E. Johnson, *A Shopkeeper's Millennium*, 5.

15. Barkun, *Crucible of the Millennium*, 4; W. R. Cross, *Burned-over District*, 88, 219. Weld (1803–1895) attended the experimental manual labor school, Oneida Institute, then helped found Cincinnati's Lane Seminary and went on to Oberlin. Stanton (1805–1887) went to Lane with Weld; both became agents for the American Anti-Slavery Society.

16. A. H. Lewis, *Seventh-Day Baptist Hand Book*, 38–39; Kerns, "Farmers' Daughters," 17.

17. Seventh-Day Baptist General Conference. *Year Book*, 1836, 10.

18. Lovejoy was a newspaperman, Presbyterian preacher, and abolitionist who was killed by a mob that was attempting to destroy his press.

19. R. S. Fletcher, *History of Oberlin College*, 1: 184–85; Aptheker, *Abolitionism*, 94.

20. McPherson in *Battle Cry of Freedom*, 54, defines abolitionists as the most radical reformers, believing that slavery was a sinful violation of human rights that should be immediately expiated. The antislavery reformers viewed bondage as an evil—socially, economically, and politically repressive—but were willing to let it die a slower death by a firm prohibition on extending slavery to new territories.

21. Lane Seminary was founded in Cincinnati in 1831 through the agency of Theodore Weld, student leader from Oneida Institute, and funding from the wealthy reforming Tappan brothers. Conservative trustees attempted to suppress the student abolitionist society in 1834 and threatened Weld with expulsion. In response nearly all eighty students withdrew in protest, thirty-eight organizing another seminary in makeshift quarters. Coincidentally Reverend John Shipherd, founder of Oberlin Collegiate Institute (1833), passed through in search of funds for his school and met a group of "Lane Rebels" at Asa Mahan's home. The parties negotiated a merger of students, funds, and facilities, adding Mahan as president of Oberlin and their evangelistic leader, Charles Grandison Finney, as professor of theology. The deal brought funding to a failing enterprise and, as a condition, black students from Lane Seminary (which like Oneida Institute, and as the Tappans insisted, admitted blacks). After rancorous debate and near-riotous meetings, Oberlin trustees accepted the black students. While the trustees were antislavery, they had not expected to actually associate with blacks. The Lane Rebels moved to Oberlin in the spring of 1835.

22. Irish, "Sketch of the Labors of Rev. James Irish," 294; "Alfred University and Union," *Union Alumni Monthly*, May 1928; J. Allen, "Divine Guidance and Help," in A. Allen, *Life and Sermons*, 379.

23. Norwood, *Fiat Lux*, 12; Irish, "Sketch of the Labors of Rev. James Irish," 294, 278.

24. Irish, "Sketch of the Labors of Rev. James Irish," 294.

25. Ibid., 278. Irish's roommate was William C. Kenyon.

26. Greene, "History of the First Seventh Day Baptist Church of Alfred"; Irish, "Sketch of the Labors of Rev. James Irish," 294; James Irish data sheet, April 29, 1855, Union College files. HMLA.

27. In 1846 Irish became principal at DeRuyter Institute and pastor of the Seventh Day Baptist church there. He was a missionary pastor in various places and, in 1869, moved to Rockville, Rhode Island, where he continued to teach, preach, and serve as school committeeman. Irish died in Rockville, March 3, 1891. Kenyon to "M," April 3, 1839.

28. Ibid.

29. Mary A. Sheldon Powell, "A Few Reminiscences of Early School Days in the Town of Alfred."

30. Powell.

31. C. H. Maxson, "Chapter," 28–29.

32. Gamble, "Alfred University, Condensed History," 25; *Fiat Lux*, October 13, 1914, 4; J. Allen, "Life and Labors of Pres. Wm. C. Kenyon," 6.

33. J. Allen, "Life and Labors of Pres. Wm. C. Kenyon," 6–7.

34. Kenyon to "M."

35. Ibid.

36. Biography, anonymous, undated. HMLA.

37. J. Allen, "Life and Labors of Pres. Wm. C. Kenyon"; Dall, "Syllabub," 8; Miller, *The Academy System of the State of New York*, 123. "Boss" was a word newly coined in the early nineteenth century.

38. Minard, *History of Allegany County*, 182.

39. J. Allen, "Life and Labors of Pres. Wm. C. Kenyon," 2–3.

40. Nash, "Rethinking Republican Motherhood," 176; Tomlinson, "Motives and Ideals of President W. C. Kenyon," 4–5.

41. J. Allen, "Life and Labors of Pres. Wm. C. Kenyon," 4–5.

42. "Alfred University and Union"; Child, *Gazetteer and Business Directory of Allegany County, N.Y. for 1875*, 35; Seventh-Day Baptist General Conference, *Year Book*, 1837, 18.

43. W. C. Kenyon, October 14, 1838, letter quoted in *Alfred Student* 3 (February 1876): 51 and *Sabbath Recorder*, August 4, 1881. Nott, an influential, reforming educator also counted Francis Wayland, Brown president, and Henry Tappan, University of Michigan president, among his protégés, Marsden, *Soul*, 102, 106.

44. Tomlinson, "Motives and Ideals," 3–4; Nathaniel M. Hubbard to William F. Place, July 4, 1896. HMLA.

45. Tomlinson, "Motives and Ideals," 4, 6.

46. Ibid., 8; J. Allen, "The Kenyon Memorial Hall," quoted in Gamble, "Alfred University, Condensed History," 24.

47. Ogren, *American State Normal School*, 82; Larkin, "History of Alfred University," 11.

48. "Alfred University: Points of Interest." While this recollection may seem hopelessly idealistic, it was not uncommon for financially strapped schools to reduce salaries. The 1849 Compact is the most famous, but not the only, example of the spirit of self-sacrifice that permeated Alfred's faculty. Like Alfred, Oberlin featured low tuition and low salaries. Most of its faculty were Oberlin alumni,

partly to ensure the proper theological training, partly because institutional loyalty meant they would accept low pay.

49. Minard, 174.
50. "Alfred's Teachers"; J. Allen, "Life and Labors of Pres. Wm. C. Kenyon," 9.
51. Minard, 174.
52. "Melissa B. Ward Kenyon, Teacher 1840–1863."
53. "Melissa Bloomfield Ward Kenyon." HMLA; "Alfred's Teachers."
54. "Valedictory," undated, anonymous. "Valedictory" here is the final speech in a public program; because only one teacher apparently is employed, this talk must have been given about 1840.

Four. Alfred Academy: Educational Reform

1. Miller, *Academy System*, 131; Tomlinson, "Founders' Day Address, December 1909," 2–3.
2. *History of Allegany County*, 67–68.
3. Kaestle, *Pillars of the Republic*, 104–5, 21; *History of Allegany County*, 67–68; Hoffman, *Woman's "True" Profession*, 39. Tyack and Hansot also describe the low wages, poor preparation, and high turnover among common school teachers, *Learning Together*, 60–67.
4. Irish, "Sketch of the Early Life of Rev. James R. Irish," 262.
5. Thacher, *Thirty Years Out of School*, 4. About 10 percent of teachers were female in 1800; by 1920 86 percent were—Hoffman, xv. Kaestle reports that during the antebellum period women's pay was 44 percent of men's in Michigan, 53 percent in Wisconsin, 40 percent in Massachusetts, *Pillars*, 123; Jensen, "Not Only Ours But Others," 3–4.
6. Minard, 164–65.
7. "Valedictory"; Tomlinson, "Founders' Day Address," 3.
8. A. Allen quoted in Minard, 185; Pink and Delmage, eds., *Candle in the Wilderness*, 11.
9. Leslie, *Gentlemen and Scholars*, 74.
10. J. Allen, "Caroline B. Maxson Stillman," 63.
11. "Alfred's Teachers."
12. Powell, "A Few Reminiscences."
13. Carolyn B. Maxson Stillman.
14. Sizer, *Age of the Academies*, 12; Miller, *Academy System*, 172, 82, 85, 24; Beadie, "Internal Improvement: The Structure and Culture of Academy Expansion in New York State in the Antebellum Era, 1820–1860," in Beadie and Tolley, *Chartered Schools*, 89–115. From 1835 to 1843, $3,500 was appropriated annually to support teacher training, while from 1850 to 1886, about $15,000 annually was shared among the academies, Miller, *Academy System*, 78.
15. Norwood, *Fiat Lux*, 17.
16. Potts, *Wesleyan University, 1831–1910*, 163.
17. Collins to Babcock and Babcock.
18. Norwood, *Fiat Lux*, 19; *Catalogue*, 1848, 19, 21.

19. J. Allen, "Alfred University: Historic Sketch—First Decade, 1836–1846," *Sabbath Recorder*, August 11, 1881, 3.

20. J. Rockwell to "Brother"; "Alfred Academy in 1855"; Davis, "Response to questions," 17.

21. "Alfred Academy in 1855."

22. Ibid.; Tomlinson, "Founders' Day Address," 7.

23. "Alfred Academy in 1855."

24. LeRoy Female Seminary was opened by Marietta and Emily Ingham in 1837. Modeled on Emily's alma mater, Zilpah Grant's Ipswich Female Seminary, in 1857 it was chartered as Ingham University. It closed in 1892.

25. Champlin and Babcock, *An Offering to the Memory of Abigail Ann Allen by the Ladies' Literary Societies of Alfred University*, 18–19.

26. Emily E. Ingham to Abigail A. Maxson, September 14, 1844, LeRoy Historical Society, LeRoy, New York. Thanks to Kerns, "Antebellum Higher Education," 39, who first noted this source. Ingham records list Abigail A. Maxson as an 1845 graduate.

27. Minard, 170; Tolley and Beadie, "Socioeconomic Incentives," 55. Ellis et al. report that in 1846 "the average wage per month for male teachers was $14.00, and for females, $7.50," *History of New York State*, 319.

28. Abigail Allen, *Sabbath Recorder*, August 24, 1893.

29. Champlin and Babcock, *Offering to the Memory*, 9.

30. "Death of Mrs. Allen," *Alfred Sun*, October 29, 1902.

31. Champlin and Babcock, *Offering to the Memory*, 52, 56.

32. Blanche Glassman Hersh, "The 'True Woman' and the 'New Woman' in Nineteenth-Century America: Feminist-Abolitionists and a New Concept of True Womanhood," in Kelley, *Woman's Being, Woman's Place*, 272, 279.

33. Champlin and Babcock, *Offering to the Memory*, 66.

34. Champlin and Babcock, 14.

35. Norwood, *Fiat Lux*, 30; James Marvin quoted in A. Allen, *Life and Sermons*, 55–56.

36. William C. Kenyon, "Progress and Education," *Sabbath Recorder*, May 11, 1882; Irish, "Sketch of the Early Life of Rev. James R. Irish," 278.

37. Tewksbury, *Founding of American Colleges*, 89–91; *Seventh Day Baptists in Europe and America*, 1: 568; Sanford, *A Choosing People*, 209. Coeducational DeRuyter never reached college status and, hampered by financial difficulties, was sold to the public school district in 1874; James Lee Gamble, "Alfred University," in *Seventh Day Baptists in Europe and America*, 1: 519.

38. Kenyon to A. C. Spicer, February 19, 1849. Spicer never received this letter.

39. William C. Kenyon, May 1849 letter, reprinted in Seventh-Day Baptist Education Society, *Twelfth Annual Report*, 36–37.

40. A. Allen, *Life and Sermons*, 52.

41. Numerous early academies and colleges hired their own graduates for the faculty. See the histories of Oberlin and Wesleyan, for example.

42. A. Allen, "President Jonathan Allen," in Minard, 185; Ira Sayles left in 1850 and returned in 1860 for two more years. Relations between him and Kenyon became very hostile. Writing in "the spirit of Christian candor" many years later, Sayles listed Kenyon's "fatal defects": unreasonable demands on his students;

severe drills; "Failure to Teach Through Fundamental Practices and Principles"; "shallowness"—"where he needed to be an eagle, he was a very sparrow"; "failure to recognize the weaknesses of childhood"; "ungovernable irritability"; "treacherous." Finally Sayles charged Kenyon with being a reckless financier—Sayles to William F. Place, April 29, 1879.

43. Place to Ida F. Kenyon.

44. Hislop, *Eliphalet Nott*, 421, 398–99.

45. Kenyon to Spicer.

46. M. C. McAlmont to Mrs. S. McAlmont, August 27, 1852.

47. Beadie, "Female Students and Denominational Affiliation," 89, 95–96. Beadie defines Regents students as "enrolled in higher level subjects for at least four months of the year and thus eligible to earn their institution per-pupil funding from the state," 89.

48. Mary E. Goff (Cone) to Mrs. Samantha McAlmont, August 26, 1859; J. W. Howe, "An Idyl of Mid-Summer and Middle Age," 446.

49. In the 1850s, "more than twice as many permanent colleges were founded as in the preceding ten years." Tewksbury counted thirty-five permanent colleges founded in the 1830s, thirty-two in the 1840s, and sixty-six in the 1850s, *Founding of American Colleges*, 16–17.

50. D. Maxson to A. Maxson, January 10, 1851, July 25, 1851; "A Mirror," *Literary Star*, October 27, 1855.

51. E. A. Witter, "The Literary Societies—Alfred University: Historic Sketch—Alleghanian Lyceum," *Sabbath Recorder*, September 22, 1881, 3; *History of Allegany County*, 83–84.

52. A. Allen, *Life and Sermons*, 46.

53. *Seventh Day Baptists in Europe & America*, 1: 348, 466. Several Seventh Day Baptist academies existed at this time: Alfred, Brookfield, and DeRuyter in New York, Milton Academy in Wisconsin, Union and New Market in New Jersey. Most closed or merged as public school systems developed. Sanford, *A Choosing People*, 221. Even given its rural roots, it is not clear why the school did not employ an agent to raise funds, a common device elsewhere. Apart from Jonathan Allen's unrewarding experience, there is no record of Alfred using one.

54. Leslie, *Gentlemen and Scholars*, 52.

55. Leslie, 74.

56. Dating of early schools is always difficult because of their idiosyncratic development. St. Lawrence, which also claims to be the first coeducational college in New York, was chartered April 3, 1856 as a theological school and college. Its first students arrived in 1858. None were prepared for college, so a preparatory department was established. College work began in a few years and the first graduates finished in 1865. Founded in 1855 and receiving its college charter in 1862, Bates College became the first coeducational college in New England. The founder's mother and wife, both spirited people, supported women's education. Nevertheless, Bates's first small group of female students was ridiculed and all dropped out. Women's numbers remained small at Bates for many years and a quota limiting their enrollment continued into the twentieth century. Leslie, *Gentlemen and Scholars*, 27.

57. William C. Kenyon, "Address to Class of 1851." HMLA.

58. ms. journal, Oberlin College Archives. Quoted in Lawrence, "The Teaching of Rhetoric and Composition in Nineteenth-Century Women's Colleges," 57.

59. Hosford, *Father Shipherd's Magna Charta*, 87; Fletcher, *History of Oberlin College*, 209, 252.

60. Fletcher, *History of Oberlin College*, 296.

61. Anthony to Stanton, May 26, 1856, quoted in DuBois, *Feminism and Suffrage*, 50; Cott, *Bonds of Womanhood*, 159.

62. Champlin and Babcock, *Offering to the Memory*, 25.

Five. Kenyon's University Years

1. Kerns, "Antebellum Higher Education," 47–62.

2. Kerns, "Farmers' Daughters," 18–19; Vandelia Varnum to Charles W. Eliot, May 11, 1880, Box 1, Gilman Papers, 1870-1910, Massachusetts Historical Society. (No response from Eliot was found.) Varnum went on to become Professor of Modern Languages at Mount Carroll Ladies Seminary and a temperance lecturer.

3. F. L. Greene, "History."

4. Townsend, "Gender Effect," 88.

5. A. Allen, *Life and Sermons*, 105.

6. Potts, *Baptist Colleges in the Development of American Society, 1812-1861*, 323.

7. Anne Firor Scott, "Education of Women: The Ambiguous Reform," in A. F. Scott, *Making the Invisible Woman Visible*, 298; Veysey, *The Emergence of the American University*, 38.

8. J. Allen, "Divine Guidance and Help," in A. Allen, *Life and Sermons*, 386.

9. Kerns, "Antebellum Higher Education," 68.

10. Ibid., 77. Since women's presence on other faculties was rare, comparable information on salaries earned at other colleges is not available.

11. Larkin, "History of Alfred University," 26–27.

12. Randolph, "President Allen and William A. Rogers."

13. *Seventh Day Baptists in Europe and America*, 1: 550.

14. A. Allen, *Life and Sermons*, 81.

15. Davis and Davis, "Memoirs," 52.

16. A. C. Burdick diary; Cazden, *Antoinette Brown Blackwell*, 192. Experience FitzRandolph was probably the first woman to enroll in the theology school.

17. Cott, *Bonds of Womanhood*, 204; Isenberg, "'Coequality of the Sexes,'" 186–87.

18. Sanford, *A Choosing People*, 355. Alfred's theology school closed in 1963; St. Lawrence's closed in 1965. Potts, *Baptist Colleges*.

19. "The Celebration of the One Hundredth Anniversary of the Founding of Alfred University," 11.

20. *Alfred Student* 1 (January 1874): 11. The first woman to earn an M.D. in the United States was Elizabeth Blackwell, who graduated from Geneva College in 1849. In 1850 a second woman earned her M.D. from Central Medical College in Rochester.

21. M. A. T. Burdick, "Fifty Years Ago." Frederick Douglass (1817?–1895) was born into slavery as Frederick Bailey. In 1838, Bailey escaped to the North with his wife Anna, emerging as Frederick Douglass. He began working against slavery, then moved on to a wider field of oratory and alliance with William Lloyd Garrison. In 1846 Douglass's freedom was purchased by friends. The first issue of his

well-known paper, *North Star*, was published in 1847. Douglass became the best-known spokesman for the black cause.

22. A. Allen, *Life and Sermons*, 69.

23. Sanford, *A Choosing People*, 156.

24. Converted to abolitionism by Theodore Weld, Smith (1797–1874) also involved himself in temperance, peace, dietary reform, and dress reform. He funded Frederick Douglass's *North Star* whenever it faced difficulties. He also supported women's rights, praising the Grimké sisters when they were attacked, attending Antoinette Brown's ordination, assisting his cousin, Elizabeth Cady Stanton, and encouraging his daughter, Elizabeth Smith Miller, in her advocacy of the "Bloomer costume." He included Oberlin, Hamilton, Cornell, and Howard as well as Alfred in his philanthropy.

25. J. W. Howe, *Reminiscences*, 253–55.

26. Nathan V. Hull to Gerrit Smith, November 10, 1868, cited in Harlow, *Gerrit Smith*, 483; E. H. Lewis, *Allen of Alfred*, 23. Allen may have met John Brown at Oberlin, where Brown's father was a trustee and his younger brothers and a sister were students.

27. McAlmont to McAlmont.

28. William W. Brown, "Founder's Day Ceremony," *Fiat Lux*, December 8, 1914, 6; Alfriedian Society, *Minutes*; W. R. Prentice, "Orophilian Lyceum," *Alfred University*, August 1888: 2; Alleghanian Lyceum, *Minutes*.

29. Muelder, *Missionaries and Muckrakers*, 23; Kerns, "Antebellum Higher Education," 264.

30. M. A. T. Burdick, "Fifty Years Ago."

31. Gamble, "Alfred University, Condensed History," 28.

32. Ladies' Literary Society box. HMLA.

33. John P. Herrick, "Alfred University Thirty Years Ago," *Elmira Advertiser*, March 3, 1932.

34. D. Lewis, "Memoir of President Allen," 5.

35. M. A. T. Burdick, "Fifty Years Ago."

36. D. Lewis, "Memoir of President Allen," 5.

37. Ibid., 6; Abram Burt diary, August 28 and 29; September 8; October 9; November 3, 1864.

38. Copp autograph book. Sojourner Truth (ca. 1797–1883) was freed in 1827 and first spoke at an abolitionist meeting in the 1840s. Six feet tall, with natural strength and dignity, she impressed listeners by her powerful speech, wit, and calm, reasonable manner; Champlin and Babcock, *Offering to the Memory*, 43.

39. Norwood, *Fiat Lux*, 49, 50. Enrollment problems were widespread in this period. Mount Union also reached an enrollment peak in 1857, then lost nearly 50 percent of its student numbers by 1860—Osborne, *A Select School*, 59.

40. H. P. Burdick, "Recollections"; J. Allen, "Alfred University: Historic Sketch," *Sabbath Recorder*, August 25, 1881; *Alfred Student* 1 (January 1874): 11. Mary Wager is still honored for her literary accomplishments by Alfred University's Mary Wager Fisher prize.

41. Burt diary.

42. *Alfred Year Book*, 1903–04, 119; Bliss, "Recollections."

43. Kenyon to H. P. Burdick, September 17, 1865.

44. H. P. Burdick, "Recollections."

45. T. R. Williams to William and Ida Kenyon, January 7, 1867.

46. Norwood, *Fiat Lux*, 60.

47. Place to Ida Kenyon, January 31, 1895.

48. William Rogers to W. F. Place, May 7, 1886. HMLA.

49. Palmer to Abigail Allen, May 1896.

50. Larkin, "History of Alfred University," 12.

51. W. C. Kenyon to Jarvis Kenyon, May 22, 1867. HMLA.

52. Norwood, *Fiat Lux*, 54.

Six. "No More Thought of Changing": Women's Equality

1. Davis, "Response to questions," 7.

2. Mary Setchel Haight, "Reminiscences of Alfred" in A. Allen, *Life and Sermons*, 188.

3. A. Allen, *Life and Sermons*, 21–22.

4. Ibid., 33–34.

5. A. Allen, "President Jonathan Allen," in Minard, 184.

6. W. R. Cross, *Burned-over District*, 101.

7. A. Allen, *Life and Sermons*, 49–51.

8. A. Allen, "President Jonathan Allen," in Minard, 184; Donald M. Love to John Nelson Norwood, February 15, 1939 and March 6, 1939. HMLA. Oberlin followed the common practice of conferring a master's degree "in course," three years after the bachelor's degree with no requirements beyond payment of a fee and demonstration of good character. The earned master's degree did not become common until later in the century.

9. "Re-Dedication of the Old Chapel." HMLA.

10. D. Lewis, "Memoir of President Allen," 9; Davis and Davis, "Memoirs," 50.

11. Boothe Colwell Davis, "Address on Behalf of the Students" in "Memorial Service," 20; M. A. T. Burdick, "Fifty Years Ago"; J. Allen, "The College Community." See Veysey, *Emergence of the American University*, 28, for the importance of character development to nineteenth-century educators.

12. D. Lewis, "Memoir of President Allen," 3–4.

13. A. Allen, *Life and Sermons*, 95.

14. Alfred Allen to John Nelson Norwood, May 9, 1935.

15. Merrill, "Recollections of Alfred"; Alfred Allen to Norwood.

16. A. Allen, "President Jonathan Allen," in Minard, 185; L. C. Rogers, "Address on Behalf of the Faculty," 13, in "Memorial Service"; P. A. Burdick, "Address on Behalf of Moral Reform," 29, in "Memorial Service."

17. Potts, *Wesleyan University*, 287; J. W. Scott, *Women's History as Women's Education*, 7; Conable, *Women at Cornell*, 62.

18. "The College World," *Alfred Student* 1 (June 1874): 72.

19. Conable, 117, 127, 122.

20. Hersh in Kelley, *Woman's Being, Woman's Place*, 272.

21. All quotations from this address are drawn from Abigail Allen, "Co-education."

22. Thomas Higginson, "Colonel Higginson," was a reformer, author, member of the "Secret Six" that plotted with John Brown, and Colonel of the first black regiment in the Civil War.

23. J. Allen, "Mixed Schools," 1-2.

24. Isenberg, "'Coequality of the Sexes,'" 136, 165, 385.

25. Potts, *Wesleyan University*, 104.

26. *Alfred Student* 4 (January 1877): 43.

27. Born in 1822, Dall involved herself in religion and good works from an early age. After her marriage to Charles Dall, she became increasingly interested in women's rights and employment issues. In her husband's biography, Abigail Allen asserted the honorary degree had been awarded, and the book's title page carries a quotation from "Caroline H. Dall, LL.D." *Who's Who in America* 1908-1909 reported the degree. Ray A. Smith, *Women Recipients of Honorary Degrees in the United States* (master's thesis, New York University, 1935), was unable to find any record of an honorary degree conferred on a woman before 1882.

28. Dall, "Syllabub."

29. Dall, *The College, the Market, and the Court*, 6, 135, 138, 207-8.

30. Ibid., 207-8.

31. J. Allen, "Caroline H. Dall," 14-15.

32. Daniel B. Sass, "Caroline H. Dall: The Curious Story of a Doctorate of Laws," in Littell, ed., *Sesquicentennial History of Alfred University*, 75-76.

33. *Alfred University* 3 (May 1891): 27.

34. A. Allen, "Co-education," 2-3.

35. J. Allen, "Education for Women," 53.

36. *Sabbath Recorder* 48 (1892): 274, quoted in Kerns, "Antebellum Higher Education," 285-86.

37. Hewitt, "Feminist Friends," 41; Jensen, *Promise to the Land*, 183.

38. J. Allen, "Education for Women," 53.

39. Quoted in Lutz, *Susan B. Anthony*, 127.

40. "Who Should Vote?" *Alfred Student* 3 (October 1875): 2-3.

41. J. Allen, "Suffrage," 73-75.

42. Stanton, *Eighty Years and More*, 465-66; Gordon, *Gender and Higher Education in the Progressive Era*, 194; Lutz, *Susan B. Anthony*, 306.

43 "The Woman Who Dared"; Cottrell, "Alfred History"; Attorney's brief.

44. Cottrell, "Alfred History"; Champlin and Babcock, *Offering to the Memory*, 57.

Seven. "The Exercise of Equity": A Voice for Women

1. James McLachlan, "The *Choice of Hercules*: American Student Societies in the Early 19th Century," in Stone, ed., *The University in Society*, 2: 472; Geiger, ed. *The American College in the Nineteenth Century*, 13; Rudolph, *Curriculum*, 97.

2. See Ogren, *American State Normal School*, and M. Kelley, *Learning to Stand & Speak*.

3. Quoted in N. Johnson, *Nineteenth-Century Rhetoric*, 244.

4. Solomon, *Company*, 28. See Nash, "Rethinking Republican Motherhood," for a close look at student speakers at the Young Ladies' Academy.

5. Yellin, *Women & Sisters*, 38.

6. Hall, *Julia Ward Howe*, 136.

7. McFeely, *Frederick Douglass*, 34; Sterling, *Ahead of Her Time*, 108.

8. Cazden, *Antoinette Brown Blackwell*, 26; Lawrence, "Teaching of Rhetoric and Composition," 61; Fairchild, *Oberlin*, 182; Fairchild, "Woman's Rights and Duties," quoted in Cazden, *Antoinette Brown Blackwell*, 27.

9. Hogeland, "Coeducation of the Sexes," 172; Hymowitz and Weissman, *A History of Women in America*, 98. William Lloyd Garrison (1805-1879) was a leader of the most radical wing of the antislavery movement and editor of *The Liberator*. Garrison believed in immediate abolition, distrusted the solutions of government (arguing that it was founded on a corrupt Constitution that accommodated slavery), and urged his followers to withdraw from churches that did not denounce slavery. His beliefs were anathema to many clergymen and too extreme for most antislavery factions who wished to work for change within existing institutions; Cazden, *Antoinette Brown Blackwell*, 28; Lasser, *Educating Men and Women Together*, 84.

10. A. Allen, *Life and Sermons*, 51; Cazden, *Antoinette Brown Blackwell*, 39; Conable, *Women at Cornell*, 34. Corinthians I, 14:34-35—"Let your women keep silence in the churches; for it is not permitted unto them to speak; but *they are commanded* to be under obedience, as also saith the law. And if they will learn any thing, let them ask their husbands at home: for it is a shame for women to speak in the church."

11. Blackwell, *Lucy Stone*, 67-71.

12. A. Allen, *Life and Sermons*, 51-52. The 1848-1849 Oberlin catalog shows that Jonathan Allen roomed at the home of Professor Fairchild, later President of Oberlin.

13. A. Allen, *Life and Sermons*, 51-52; Fairchild, *Oberlin*, 181. "Heated discussion" was reported in *The Oberlin News*, February 14, 1917, quoted in Lawrence, "Teaching of Rhetoric and Composition," 80.

14. Blackwell, *Lucy Stone*, 34.

15. Coté, *Olympia Brown*, 30. Olympia attended the St. Lawrence Theological School and was ordained by the Universalist Association in 1863, the first woman ordained by a denomination. Antoinette Brown was ordained by her church in South Butler, New York, in 1853 but not by its Congregational denomination.

16. Mann to Sophia Hawthorne, May 18, 1858, quoted in Rury and Harper, "The Trouble With Coeducation," 496.

17. Rury and Harper, 497, 495.

18. Hosford, *Father Shipherd's Magna Charta*, 83.

19. J. Allen, "Alfred University: Historic Sketch—First Decade, 1836-1846," *Sabbath Recorder*, August 11, 1881; Luke Green Maxson to Cordelia Hartshorn, November 3, 1840, quoted in C. H. Maxson, "A Chapter of Family History," 32.

20. A. Allen, *Life and Sermons*, 88-89.

21. Ibid., 46.

22. *Hornellsville Tribune*, July 13, 1854, 2 (thanks to Kerns, "Farmers' Daughters," 17, who first noted this comment); Kerns, "Antebellum Higher Education," 252.

23. Harper, *Life and Work of Susan B. Anthony*, 1: 98-100.

24. Abigail Allen, "The Rochester Teachers' Convention," *Sabbath Recorder*, August 24, 1893. Writing forty years later, Allen has placed this event in 1854, rather than 1853.

25. Harper, *Life and Work*, 1: 101; quoted in Lutz, *Created Equal*, 96.

26. Norwood, *Fiat Lux*, 48.

27. J. Allen, "Divine Guidance and Help," in A. Allen, *Life and Sermons*, 380; S. M. Burdick to John Nelson Norwood, April 25, 1935.

28. Davis, "Response to questions," 4.

29. S. M. Burdick to Norwood; Bliss, "Recollections."

30. Simpson diary.

31. McLachlan, in Stone, *The University in Society*, 2: 472; Clawson to John Nelson Norwood, February 19, 1935.

32. A. Allen, *Life and Sermons*, 46.

33. "The Literary Societies—Alfred University," *Sabbath Recorder*, September 8, 1881, 3.

34. M. Allen, "Literary Societies."

35. Prentice to Arta Place, December 8, 1902; M. Allen, "Literary Societies."

36. M. Allen, "Literary Societies."

37. Merrill, "Recollections at Alfred." The Alleghanian's motto drew from one of Kenyon's favorite sayings, "Perseverance conquers all things."

38. Bliss, "Recollections."

39. "Lyceums—Organization, History, and Present Work," *Alfred Sun*, May 16, 1895, 3.

40. Athenaean Lyceum, *Minutes.*

41. Lawrence, "Teaching of Rhetoric and Composition," 66.

42. McLachlan, in Stone, *The University in Society*, 2: 467; Clawson to Norwood.

43. "The Seminary Method," *Alfred University* 1 (June 1889): 29.

44. Davis and Davis, "Memoirs," 41; Rudolph, *Curriculum*, 12–13; Ogren, *American State Normal School*, 108.

45. Osborne, *Select School*, 57.

46. W. R. Prentice, "The Literary Societies—Alfred University: Orophilian Lyceum," *Sabbath Recorder*, September 15, 1881, 3.

47. Ibid.

48. "Assembly Address," *Fiat Lux*, April 28, 1914, 7; E. A. Witter, "The Literary Societies—Alfred University . . . Alleghanian Lyceum," *Sabbath Recorder*, September 22, 1881, 3; Lincoln to Eunice H. Howell, February 17, 1860.

49. Simpson diary; A. C. Burdick diary.

50. Alleghanian Lyceum, *Minutes.*

51. Orophilian Lyceum, *Minutes.*

52. Ibid.

53. Norwood, *Fiat Lux*, 36.

54. Lawrence, "Teaching of Rhetoric and Composition," 82; Olin, *Women of a State University*, 34; Ogren, *American State Normal School*, 110; Radke, "'Can She Not See,'" 369–75.

55. Ladies' Literary Society, *Minutes*, June 18, 1859.

56. Simpson diary, June 11, 1861.

57. *Alfred Student* 4 (June 1877): 103–4.

58. J. W. Howe, "Idyl," 448, 330.

59. Mary Setchel Haight, "Reminiscences of Alfred," in A. Allen, *Life and Sermons*, 188.

60. Athenaean Lyceum, *Minutes.*

61. M. Allen, "Literary Societies."

62. J. W. Howe, "Idyl," 444–45.

63. Ibid., 448.

64. M. Allen, "Literary Societies."

65. "Man Suffrage," *Alfred Student* 3 (March 1876): 61–62; 3 (April 1876): 73–75.

66. McLachlan in Stone, *The University in Society*, 2: 485.

67. Potts, *Baptist Colleges*, 225.

68. Miller-Bernal, *Separate by Degree*, 142; Leslie, *Gentlemen and Scholars*, 105.

69. "The College World," *Alfred Student* 1 (June 1874): 72; A. Allen, "Co-education," 13; "College Secret Societies," *Alfred Student* 1 (February 1874): 20. Ironically, the first secret fraternity arose in 1832 at Union College, Kenyon's alma mater. Despite President Nott's vehement opposition, the society could not be suppressed, Hislop, *Eliphalet Nott*, 389.

Eight. Student Ties

1. Nash, *Women's Education*, 116; Kerns, "Antebellum Higher Education," x. Gordon, *Gender and Higher Education*, 20, also comments on family support for "their daughters' efforts to get the best education possible and move into the professions" somewhat later in the century.

2. Goff (Cone) to Mrs. Samantha McAlmont, August 26, 1859.

3. Wells, "Alice at Alfred."

4. Randolph, *History of Seventh Day Baptists*, 356.

5. A. C. Burdick diary.

6. D. Maxson to Artemesia Maxson, January 10, 1851.

7. D. Maxson to Artemesia Maxson, September 13, 1852.

8. Witter, "Alfred University."

9. Bliss, "Recollections"; Clawson to John Nelson Norwood, February 19, 1935.

10. Davis and Davis, "Memoirs," 6; Prosser to Curtis F. Randolph, October 3, 1936.

11. Potts, *Baptist Colleges*, 172–73; A. C. Burdick diary; Phelan, *And a White Vest for Sam'l*, 10, 58, 17, 60–61, 211.

12. Reveley to John Nelson Norwood, February 11, 1936.

13. Ibid. The passage is from Exodus, 23: 12: "Six days thou shalt do thy work, and on the seventh day thou shalt rest: that thine ox and thine ass may rest, and the son of thy handmaid, and the stranger, may be refreshed."

14. Simpson (Spencer) autograph book.

15. Merrill, "Recollections of Alfred."

16. McAlmont to Mrs. S. McAlmont, August 27, 1852; Simpson (Spencer) diary, 1861.

17. Smith-Rosenberg, "The Female World of Love and Ritual," in *Disorderly Conduct*, 53; C. E. Kelly, "Between Town and Country," 62; Cott, *Bonds of Womanhood*, 188.

18. *Catalogue*, 1848, 26.

19. A. Allen, "Alfred in Olden Times," *Alfred Monthly* 1 (February 1899): 6.

20. Clawson to John Nelson Norwood, February 19, 1935; A. C. Burdick diary, November 29, 1872.

21. Burt diary.

22. Randolph, "President Allen and William A. Rogers."

23. Luke Green Maxson to Cordelia Hartshorn, November 3, 1840, quoted in C. H. Maxson, "A Chapter of Family History," 32.

24. A. Allen, *Life and Sermons*, 45; Witter, "Alfred University."

25. Rededication of the Chapel. HMLA; Brown (Nicholson) to John Nelson Norwood, December 13, 1935.

26. Palmer to Abigail Allen, May 1896.

27. Randolph to John Nelson Norwood, March 1, 1942; Cottrell, "Alfred History." Oberlin students had their own methods of circumventing a similar rule, pretending urgent business that took them in the same direction, or walking extremely slowly, a gait called the "Oberlin step"—Barnard, *From Evangelism to Progressivism*, 23.

28. Theodore Thacher diary. HMLA.

29. Clawson to John Nelson Norwood, February 19, 1935.

30. M. F. Greene to M. Ellis Drake, July 16, 1934.

31. E. H. Lewis to John Nelson Norwood, March 12, 1935.

32. Mary Emma Darrow Almy to Ellis Drake, July 27, 1934. HMLA.

33. Burt diary.

34. Merrill, "Recollections of Alfred."

35. E. H. Lewis to John Nelson Norwood, March 12, 1935; Brown (Nicholson) to Norwood, December 13, 1935.

Nine. "The Past Lives and Shines In and Through Us"

1. J. Allen, "Divine Guidance and Help," in A. Allen, *Life and Sermons*, 385.

2. Randolph, "President Allen and William A. Rogers."

3. A. Allen, *Life and Sermons*, 96–97.

4. Tolley, *Science Education*, 112; Keeney, *The Botanizers*, 1.

5. A. Allen, *Life and Sermons*, 144–46.

6. "Memorial Service," 14.

7. J. Allen, "Divine Guidance and Help," in A. Allen, *Life and Sermons*, 384–90.

8. Ibid., 378–82.

9. A. Allen, *Life and Sermons*, 158–60.

10. Clawson to John Nelson Norwood, February 19, 1935; J. Allen, "Divine Guidance and Help," in A. Allen, *Life and Sermons*, 391.

11. Davis, "Response to questions," 14.

12. E. H. Lewis, "Remarks." Ultimately Davis's judgment was correct. Milton closed in 1982 after several years of financial pressures. Salem merged with Teikyo University of Japan in 1989.

13. Rossiter, *Women Scientists in America*, 99; Reuben, *Making of the Modern University*, 265; M. Carey Thomas, "Present Tendencies," 66, 68; Palmieri, *In Adamless Eden*, 96, quoting Ethel Puffer, "The College Girl," *Boston Transcript*, June, 23, 1900.

14. Potts, *Wesleyan University*, 199, 203; Mavrinac, "Genteel Conflict," 12–13.

15. Stameshkin, *The Town's College*, 273.

16. A. Allen, "Report from Alleghany County"; A. Allen, "A Call on Mrs. Elizabeth Cady Stanton," *Alfred Sun*, May 16, 1895, 9, 14; Kerns, "Antebellum Higher Education," 79.

17. Champlin and Babcock, "Offering to the Memory," 43–44; Abigail Allen to B. C. Davis. HMLA.

18. Amy M. Gilbert, "The Woman's Movement," in Flick, *History*, 8: 353–54; Flexner, *Century of Struggle*, 179–80.

19. Champlin and Babcock, "Offering to the Memory," 41; "Death of Mrs. Allen," *Alfred Sun*, October 29, 1902.

20. Nash, *Women's Education*, 116.

21. Merrill, "Recollections of Alfred."

Conclusion

1. Ogren, *American State Normal School*, 175.

2. Judith Wellman, "Women and Radical Reform in Upstate New York," in Mabel E. Deutrich and Virginia C. Purdy, eds., *Clio Was a Woman: Studies in the History of American Women* (Washington, D.C.: Howard University Press, 1980), 113–27, cited by Osterud, *Bonds of Community*, 287.

3. Nash, "'A Salutary Rivalry,'" 28.

4. Beadie, "From Academy to University."

5. Kerns, "Antebellum Higher Education," 135, 100–101. Men's colleges also exhibited diversity, some drawing on the Yale model, others on the seminary; Methodist schools copied Wesleyan, while Union sought a more secular education.

6. Geiger, ed., *American College*, vii.

General Bibliography

Abrams, M. H., ed. *The Norton Anthology of English Literature.* 7th ed. 2 vols. New York: Norton, 1986.

Allen, Abigail A. *Life and Sermons of Jonathan Allen, President of Alfred University.* Oakland, Calif.: Pacific Press Publishing, 1894.

Allmendinger, David F., Jr. "New England Students and the Revolution in Higher Education, 1800–1900." *History of Education Quarterly* 11 (Winter 1971): 381–89.

———. *Paupers and Scholars: The Transformation of Student Life in Nineteenth-Century New England.* New York: St. Martin's, 1975.

Anthony, Alfred Williams. *Bates College and Its Background: A Review of Origins and Causes.* Philadelphia: Judson, 1936.

Aptheker, Herbert. *Abolitionism: A Revolutionary Movement.* Boston: Twayne, 1989.

Barkun, Michael. *Crucible of the Millennium: The Burned-over District of New York in the 1840s.* Syracuse, N.Y.: Syracuse University Press, 1986.

Barnard, John. *From Evangelism to Progressivism at Oberlin College, 1866-1917.* Columbus: Ohio State University Press, 1969.

Beadie, Nancy. "Female Students and Denominational Affiliation: Sources of Success and Variation among Nineteenth-Century Academies." *American Journal of Education* 107, no. 2 (February 1999): 75–115.

———. "From Academy to University in New York State: The Genesee Institutions and the Importance of Capital to the Success of an Idea, 1848–1871." *History of Higher Education Annual* 14 (1994): 13–38.

Beadie, Nancy, and Kim Tolley, eds. *Chartered Schools: Two Hundred Years of Independent Academies in the United States, 1727-1925.* New York: Routledge-Falmer, 2002.

Blackwell, Alice Stone. *Lucy Stone: Pioneer of Woman's Rights.* 2nd ed. Norwood, Mass.: Alice Stone Blackwell Committee, 1930.

Boas, Louise Schutz. *Woman's Education Begins: The Rise of the Women's Colleges.* Norton, Mass.: Wheaton College Press, 1935.

Brackett, Anna C., ed. *Woman and the Higher Education.* New York: Harper & Brothers, 1893.

Burke, Colin B. *American Collegiate Populations: A Test of the Traditional View.* New York: New York University Press, 1982.

Cazden, Elizabeth. *Antoinette Brown Blackwell: A Biography.* Old Westbury, N.Y.: Feminist Press, 1983.

Champlin, Eva St. Clair, and Frances Babcock. *An Offering to the Memory of Abigail Ann Allen by the Ladies' Literary Societies of Alfred University.* Alfred, N.Y.: Sun Publishing, n.d.

Child, Hamilton. *Gazetteer and Business Directory of Allegany County, N. Y. for 1875.* Syracuse, N.Y.: The Journal, 1875.

Clarke, Edward. *Sex in Education; or, A Fair Chance for the Girls.* Medicine & Society in America. 1874. Reprint, New York: Arno & The New York Times, 1972.

Clawson, Cortez R. *History of the Town of Alfred, New York, from the Earliest Times to the Present.* Alfred, N.Y.: Sun Publishing, 1926.

Clifford, Geraldine Jonçich. "'Shaking Dangerous Questions from the Crease': Gender and American Higher Education." *Feminist Issues* 3 (Fall 1983): 3–62.

Conable, Charlotte Williams. *Women at Cornell: The Myth of Equal Education.* Ithaca, N.Y.: Cornell University Press, 1977.

Conway, Jill Ker. "Perspectives on the History of Women's Education in the United States." *History of Education Quarterly* 14 (Spring 1974): 1–12.

Coté, Charlotte. *Olympia Brown: The Battle for Equality.* Racine, Wis.: Mother Courage Press, 1988.

Cott, Nancy F. *The Bonds of Womanhood: "Woman's Sphere" in New England, 1780-1835.* New Haven: Yale University Press, 1977.

Cross, Barbara M., ed. *The Educated Woman in America: Selected Writings of Catharine Beecher, Margaret Fuller, and M. Carey Thomas.* New York: Teachers College Press, Columbia University, 1965.

Cross, Whitney R. *The Burned-over District: The Social and Intellectual History of Enthusiastic Religion in Western New York, 1800-1850.* New York: Harper & Row, 1965.

Dall, Caroline H. *The College, the Market, and the Court; Or, Woman's Relation to Education, Labor, and Law.* 1867. Reprint, New York: Arno, 1972.

——. "Syllabub.—VII." *New Age* 8 (1876).

DuBois, Ellen Carol. *Feminism and Suffrage: The Emergence of an Independent Women's Movement in America, 1848-1869.* Ithaca, N.Y.: Cornell University Press, 1978.

Ehrenreich, Barbara, and Deirdre English. *For Her Own Good: 150 Years of the Experts' Advice to Women.* Garden City, N.Y.: Anchor/Doubleday, 1979.

Ellis, David M. "The Yankee Invasion of New York, 1783–1850." *New York History* 32 (January 1951): 3–17.

Ellis, David M., James A. Frost, Howard C. Syrett, and Harry J. Carman. *A History of New York State.* Rev. ed. of *A Short History of New York State.* Ithaca, N.Y.: Cornell University Press, in cooperation with New York State Historical Association, 1967.

Fairchild, James H. "Coeducation of the Sexes." *American Journal of Education* 17 (January 1868): 385–99.

——. *Oberlin: The Colony and the College, 1833-1883*. Oberlin, Ohio: Goodrich, 1883.

Fletcher, Robert Samuel. *A History of Oberlin College: From Its Foundation through the Civil War*. 2 vols. Oberlin, Ohio: Oberlin College, 1943.

Flexner, Eleanor. *Century of Struggle: The Woman's Rights Movement in the United States*. Cambridge, Mass.: The Belknap Press of Harvard University Press, 1959.

Flick, Alexander C., ed. *History of the State of New York*. 10 vols. New York: Columbia University Press, 1933-1937.

Geiger, Roger, ed. *The American College in the Nineteenth Century*. Nashville, Tenn.: Vanderbilt University Press, 2000.

Gordon, Lynn D. *Gender and Higher Education in the Progressive Era*. New Haven: Yale University Press, 1990.

Green, Nancy. "Female Education and School Competition: 1820-1850." *History of Education Quarterly* 18 (Summer 1978): 129-42.

Hall, Florence Howe. *Julia Ward Howe and the Woman Suffrage Movement*. 1913. Reprint, New York: Arno & The New York Times, 1969.

Harlow, Ralph Volney. *Gerrit Smith: Philanthropist and Reformer*. New York: Holt, 1939.

Harper, Ida Husted. *The Life and Work of Susan B. Anthony*. 3 vols. Indianapolis: Bowen-Merrill, 1898-1908.

Hersh, Blanche Glassman. *The Slavery of Sex: Feminist-Abolitionists in America*. Urbana: University of Illinois Press, 1978.

Hewitt, Nancy A. "Beyond the Search for Sisterhood: American Women's History in the 1980s." *Social History* 10 (October 1985): 299-321.

——. "Feminist Friends: Agrarian Quakers and the Emergence of Woman's Rights in America." *Feminist Studies* 12 (Spring 1986): 27-49.

——. *Women's Activism and Social Change: Rochester, New York, 1822-1872*. Ithaca, N.Y.: Cornell University Press, 1984.

Hislop, Codman. *Eliphalet Nott*. Middletown, Conn.: Wesleyan University Press, 1971.

History of Allegany County, N.Y. 1879. Reprint, Ovid, N.Y.: Morrison, 1978.

Hoffman, Nancy. *Woman's "True" Profession: Voices from the History of Teaching*. New York: Feminist Press, 1981.

Hofstadter, Richard, and Walter P. Metzger. *The Development of Academic Freedom in the United States*. New York: Columbia University Press, 1955.

Hogeland, Ronald W. "Coeducation of the Sexes at Oberlin College: A Study of Social Ideas in Mid-Nineteenth-Century America." *Journal of Social History* 6 (Winter 1972-73): 160-76.

Hosford, Frances Juliette. *Father Shipherd's Magna Charta: A Century of Coeducation in Oberlin College*. Boston: Marshall Jones, 1937.

Howe, Julia Ward. "An Idyl of Mid-Summer and Middle Age." *Old and New* (1871): 330-33; 443-49.

——. *Reminiscences, 1819-1899*. 1899. Reprint, New York: Negro Universities Press, 1969.

——, ed. *Sex and Education: A Reply to Dr. E. H. Clarke's "Sex in Education."* Boston: Roberts Brothers, 1874.

Hymowitz, Carol, and Michaele Weissman. *A History of Women in America*. New York: Bantam, 1978.

Isenberg, Nancy Gale. "'Coequality of the Sexes': The Feminist Discourse of the Antebellum Women's Rights Movement in America." Ph.D. diss., University of Wisconsin-Madison, 1990.

Jensen, Joan M. *Loosening the Bonds: Mid-Atlantic Farm Women, 1750-1850*. New Haven: Yale University Press, 1986.

———. "Not Only Ours But Others: The Quaker Teaching Daughters of the Mid-Atlantic, 1790-1850." *History of Education Quarterly* 24 (Spring 1984): 3-19.

———. *Promise to the Land: Essays on Rural Women*. Albuquerque: University of New Mexico Press, 1991.

Johnson, Nan. *Nineteenth-Century Rhetoric in North America*. Carbondale: Southern Illinois University Press, 1991.

Johnson, Paul E. *A Shopkeeper's Millennium: Society and Revivals in Rochester, New York, 1815-1837*. American Century Series. New York: Hill and Wang, 1978.

Kaestle, Carl F. *Pillars of the Republic: Common Schools and American Society, 1780-1860*. American Century Series. New York: Hill and Wang, 1983.

Katz, Michael B. "The Role of American Colleges in the Nineteenth Century: Essay Review 1." *History of Education* 23 (Summer 1983): 215-23.

Keeney, Elizabeth B. *The Botanizers: Amateur Scientists in Nineteenth-Century America*. Chapel Hill: University of North Carolina Press, 1992.

Kelley, Mary. *Learning to Stand & Speak: Women, Education, and Public Life in America's Republic*. Chapel Hill: Published for the Omohundro Institute of Early American History and Culture, Williamsburg, Virginia, by the University of North Carolina Press, 2006.

Kelley, Mary, ed. *Woman's Being, Woman's Place: Female Identity and Vocation in American History*. Boston: Hall, 1979.

Kelly, Catherine E. "Between Town and Country: New England Women and the Creation of a Provincial Middle Class, 1820-1860." Ph.D. diss., University of Rochester, 1992.

Kerber, Linda K. *Women of the Republic: Intellect and Ideology in Revolutionary America*. Chapel Hill: Published for Institute of Early American History and Culture, Williamsburg, Virginia, by the University of North Carolina Press, 1980.

Kerber, Linda K., Nancy F. Cott, Robert Gross, Lynn Hunt, Carroll Smith-Rosenberg, and Christine M. Stansell. "Beyond Roles, Beyond Spheres: Thinking about Gender in the Early Republic." *William and Mary Quarterly*, 3d series, 46 (July 1989): 565-85.

Kerns, Kathryn M. "Antebellum Higher Education for Women in Western New York State." Ph.D. diss., University of Pennsylvania, 1993.

———. "Farmers' Daughters: The Education of Women at Alfred Academy and University Before the Civil War." *History of Higher Education Annual* (1986): 11-28.

Lasser, Carol, ed. *Educating Men and Women Together: Coeducation in a Changing World*. Urbana: University of Illinois Press in conjunction with Oberlin College, 1987.

Lawrence, LeeAnna Michelle. "The Teaching of Rhetoric and Composition in Nineteenth-Century Women's Colleges." Ph.D. diss., Duke University, 1990.

Lerner, Gerda. "The Lady and the Mill Girl: Changes in the Status of Women in the Age of Jackson." *Mid-Continent American Studies Journal* 10 (1969): 5-15.

———. "Placing Women in History: Definitions and Challenges." *FS: Feminist Studies* 3 (Fall 1975): 5-14.

Leslie, W. Bruce. *Gentlemen and Scholars: College and Community in the "Age of the University," 1865-1917.* University Park: Pennsylvania State University Press, 1992.

Lewis, A. H. *Seventh-Day Baptist Hand Book.* Rev. ed. Plainfield, N.J.: American Sabbath Tract Society, 1896.

Lewis, E. H. *Allen of Alfred: Some of His Words to Students Which Are as Steady Candles Set in Homeward Windows.* Milton, Wis.: Davis-Greene, 1932.

Littell, Alan, ed. *A Sesquicentennial History of Alfred University: Essays in Change.* Alfred, N.Y.: Alfred University Press, 1985.

Lutz, Alma. *Created Equal: A Biography of Elizabeth Cady Stanton, 1815-1902.* New York: Octagon Books, 1974.

———. *Susan B. Anthony: Rebel, Crusader, Humanitarian.* Boston: Beacon Press, 1959. Reprint, Washington, D.C.: Zenger, 1975.

Malkmus, Doris. "Small Towns, Small Sects, and Coeducation in Midwestern Colleges, 1853-1861." *History of Higher Education Annual* 22 (2002): 33-65.

Mann, Mary Peabody. *Life of Horace Mann.* Boston: Walker, Fuller, 1865.

Manual of the Seventh-Day Baptists; Containing an Historical Sketch of the Denomination, and Reasons for Emphasizing the Day of the Sabbath. New York: George B. Utter, 1858.

Marsden, George M. *The Soul of the American University: From Protestant Establishment to Established Nonbelief.* New York: Oxford University Press, 1994.

Mavrinac, Marilyn. "Genteel Conflict: The Early Years of Coeducation at Colby College." *Colby Alumnus* 76 (December 1986): 12-17.

McFeely, William S. *Frederick Douglass.* New York: Norton, 1991.

McGuigan, Dorothy Gies. *A Dangerous Experiment: 100 Years of Women at the University of Michigan.* Ann Arbor: Center for Continuing Education of Women, University of Michigan, 1970.

McLachlan, James. "The American College in the Nineteenth Century: Toward a Reappraisal." *Teachers College Record* 80 (December 1978): 287-306.

McNall, Neil Adams. *An Agricultural History of the Genesee Valley, 1790-1860.* Philadelphia: University of Pennsylvania, 1952. Reprint, Westport, Conn.: Greenwood Press, 1976.

McPherson, James M. *Battle Cry of Freedom: The Civil War Era.* New York: Ballantine Books, 1988.

Messerli, Jonathan. *Horace Mann: A Biography.* New York: Knopf, 1972.

Miller, George Frederick. *The Academy System of the State of New York.* Albany, N.Y.: J. B. Lyon, 1922.

Miller-Bernal, Leslie. *Separate by Degree: Women Students' Experiences in Single-Sex and Coeducational Colleges.* New York: Peter Lang, 2000.

Miller-Bernal, Leslie, and Susan L. Poulson. *Going Coed: Women's Experiences in Formerly Men's Colleges and Universities, 1950-2000.* Nashville, Tenn.: Vanderbilt University Press, 2004.

Minard, John S. *History of Allegany County, New York: A Centennial Memorial.* Alfred, N.Y.: W. A. Fergusson, 1896.

Muelder, Hermann R. *Missionaries and Muckrakers: The First Hundred Years of Knox College.* Urbana: University of Illinois Press, 1984.

Nash, Margaret A. "Rethinking Republican Motherhood: Benjamin Rush and the Young Ladies' Academy of Philadelphia." *Journal of the Early Republic* 17, no. 2 (Summer 1997): 171–91.

———. "'A Salutary Rivalry': The Growth of Higher Education for Women in Oxford, Ohio, 1855–1867." *History of Higher Education Annual* 16 (1996): 21–38.

———. *Women's Education in the United States, 1780–1840.* New York: Palgrave Macmillan, 2005.

Noble, David F. *A World Without Women: The Christian Clerical Culture of Western Science.* New York: Knopf, 1992.

Norton, Mary Beth. *Liberty's Daughters: The Revolutionary Experience of American Women, 1750–1800.* Boston: Little, Brown, 1980.

Norwood, John Nelson. *Fiat Lux: The Story of Alfred University.* Alfred, N.Y.: Alfred University, 1957.

Ogren, Christine A. *The American State Normal School: "An Instrument of Great Good."* New York: Palgrave Macmillan, 2005.

———. "'Not Necessarily Bloomer Women': The Gender Attitudes and Life Choices of Female Normal-School Graduates." Presented at the Canadian History of Education Association/History of Education Society joint conference, Toronto, Canada, October 17, 1996.

———. "Where Coeds Were Coeducated: Normal Schools in Wisconsin, 1870–1920." *History of Education Quarterly* 35, no. 1 (Spring 1995): 1–26.

Olin, Helen R. *The Women of a State University: An Illustration of the Working of Coeducation in the Middle West.* New York: Putnam's Sons, 1909.

Osborne, Newell Yost. *A Select School: The History of Mount Union College and an Account of a Unique Educational Experiment, Scio College.* n.p.: Mount Union College, 1967.

Osterud, Nancy Grey. *Bonds of Community: The Lives of Farm Women in Nineteenth-Century New York.* Ithaca, N.Y.: Cornell University Press, 1991.

———. "The Valuation of Women's Work: Gender and the Market in a Dairy Farming Community during the Late Nineteenth Century." *Frontiers* 10, no. 2 (1988): 18–24.

Palmieri, Patricia Ann. *In Adamless Eden: The Community of Women Faculty at Wellesley.* New Haven: Yale University Press, 1995.

Phelan, Helene C., ed. *And A White Vest for Sam'l: An Account of Rural Life in Western N.Y. from the Diaries of Maria Langworthy Whitford of Alfred Station, N.Y., 1857–1861.* Almond, N.Y.: Phelan, 1976.

Pink, Louis H., and Rutherford E. Delmage, eds. *Candle in the Wilderness: A Centennial History of the St. Lawrence University, 1856–1956.* New York: Appleton-Century-Crofts, 1957.

Potts, David B. *Baptist Colleges in the Development of American Society, 1812–1861.* Harvard Dissertations in American History and Political Science. New York: Garland, 1988.

———. "'College Enthusiasm!' As Public Response, 1800–1860." *Harvard Educational Review* 47 (February 1977): 28–42.

———. *Wesleyan University, 1831–1910: Collegiate Enterprise in New England.* New Haven: Yale University Press, 1992.

Radke, Andrea G. "'Can She Not See and Hear, and Smell and Taste?': Women Students at Coeducational Land-Grant Universities in the American West, 1868–1917." Ph.D. diss, University of Nebraska, 2002.

Randolph, Corliss Fitz. *A History of Seventh Day Baptists in West Virginia.* Plainfield, N.J.: The American Sabbath Tract Society, 1905.

Reuben, Julie A. *The Making of the Modern University: Intellectual Transformation and the Marginalization of Morality.* Chicago: University of Chicago Press, 1996.

———. "Writing When Everything Has Been Said: The History of American Higher Education Following Laurence Veysey's Classic." *History of Education Quarterly* 45, no. 3 (Fall 2005): 412–19.

Rorabaugh, W. J. *The Alcoholic Republic: An American Tradition.* New York: Oxford University Press, 1979.

Rossiter, Margaret W. *Women Scientists in America.* Baltimore, Md.: Johns Hopkins University Press, 1982.

Rowe, David L. *Thunder and Trumpets: Millerites and Dissenting Religion in Upstate New York, 1800–1850.* Chico, Calif.: Scholars Press, 1985.

Rudolph, Frederick. *The American College and University: A History.* New York: Knopf, 1962.

———. *Curriculum: A History of the American Undergraduate Course of Study Since 1636.* San Francisco: Jossey-Bass, 1977.

Rury, John, and Glenn Harper. "The Trouble With Coeducation: Mann and Women at Antioch, 1853–1860." *History of Education Quarterly* 26 (Winter 1986): 481–502.

Ryan, Mary P. *Womanhood in America: From Colonial Times to the Present.* New York: New Viewpoints, 1975.

Sanford, Don A. *A Choosing People: The History of Seventh Day Baptists.* Nashville, Tenn.: Broadman, 1992.

———. *Conscience Taken Captive: A Short History of Seventh Day Baptists.* Janesville, Wis.: Seventh Day Baptist Historical Society, 1991.

Scott, Anne Firor. *Making the Invisible Woman Visible.* Urbana: University of Illinois Press, 1984.

Scott, Joan Wallach. "Women's History as Women's Education," in *Women's History as Women's Education,* Essays by Natalie Zemon Davis and Joan Wallach Scott, from a Symposium in Honor of Jill and John Conway, Smith College, April 17, 1985. Northampton, Mass.: Sophia Smith Collection and College Archives, Smith College, 1985.

Seventh Day Baptist General Conference. *Year Book.* Janesville, Wis.: Seventh Day Baptist General Conference, 1808–.

Seventh Day Baptists in Europe and America. 3 vols. Plainfield, N.J.: Printed for the Seventh Day Baptist General Conference by the American Sabbath Tract Society, 1910.

Sizer, Theodore R., ed. *The Age of the Academies.* New York: Bureau of Publications, Teachers College, Columbia University, 1964.

Smith, Anna Tolman. "Coeducation in the Schools and Colleges of the United States." In Office of Education *Annual Report,* 1903, 1047–78.

Smith-Rosenberg, Carroll. *Disorderly Conduct: Visions of Gender in Victorian America.* New York: Knopf, 1985.

Smith-Rosenberg, Carroll, and Charles Rosenberg. "The Female Animal: Medical and Biological Views of Woman and Her Role in Nineteenth-Century America." *Journal of American History* 60 (September 1973): 332–56.

Solomon, Barbara Miller. *In the Company of Educated Women: A History of Women and Higher Education in America.* New Haven: Yale University Press, 1985.

Stameshkin, David M. *The Town's College: Middlebury College, 1800–1915.* Middlebury, Vt.: Middlebury College Press, 1985.

Stanton, Elizabeth Cady. *Eighty Years and More: Reminiscences, 1815–1897.* 1898. Reprint, with a new introduction by Gail Parker, New York: Schocken Books, 1971.

Sterling, Dorothy. *Ahead of Her Time: Abby Kelley and the Politics of Antislavery.* New York: Norton, 1991.

Stone, Lawrence, ed. *The University in Society.* 2 vols. Princeton, N.J.: Princeton University Press, 1967.

Tewksbury, Donald G. *The Founding of American Colleges and Universities Before the Civil War.* New York: Bureau of Publications, Teachers College, Columbia University, 1932.

Thacher, Timothy Dwight. *Thirty Years Out of School: An Address Delivered During the Celebration of the 50th Anniversary of the Founding of Alfred Academy, Alfred, New York, June 28, 1886.* Topeka: Kansas Publishing House, 1886.

Thomas, M. Carey. "Present Tendencies in Women's College and University Education." *Educational Review* 25 (1908): 64–85.

Tolley, Kim. *The Science Education of American Girls: A Historical Perspective.* New York: RoutledgeFalmer, 2003.

Tolley, Kim, and Nancy Beadie. "Socioeconomic Incentives to Teach in New York and North Carolina: Toward a More Complex Model of Teacher Labor Markets, 1800–1850." *History of Education Quarterly* 46, no. 1 (Spring 2006): 36–72.

Townsend, Lucy. "The Gender Effect: The Early Curricula of Beloit College and Rockford Female Seminary." *History of Higher Education Annual* 10 (1990): 69–90.

Turner, Frederick Jackson. *The Frontier in American History.* New York: Holt, Rinehart, and Winston, 1962.

Tyack, David, and Elisabeth Hansot. *Learning Together: A History of Coeducation in American Public Schools.* New York: Russell Sage Foundation, 1992.

Veysey, Laurence R. *The Emergence of the American University.* Chicago: University of Chicago Press, 1965.

Welter, Barbara. "The Cult of True Womanhood: 1820–1860." *American Quarterly* 18 (Summer 1966): 151–74.

Woody, Thomas. *A History of Women's Education in the United States.* 2 vols. 1929. Reprint, New York: Octagon Books, 1974.

Yellin, Jean Fagan. *Women & Sisters: The Antislavery Feminists in American Culture.* New Haven: Yale University Press, 1989.

Works Cited from the
Alfred University Archives
Herrick Memorial Library
(HMLA)

Alfred Academy and University Catalogs. 1843–1900.
"Alfred Academy in 1855."
The Alfred Monthly (later, *The Alfred University Monthly*). vols. 1–15 (1898–1913).
The Alfred Student. 1874–1878.
The Alfred Sun, May 16, 1895. "The Woman's Edition."
"Alfred University: Points of Interest in Connection with That Institution of
        Learning." Unidentified newspaper clipping, 1903.
"Alfred University and Union." *Union Alumni Monthly,* May 1928.
Alfred Year Book.
"Alfred's Teachers."
Alfriedian Society. *Minutes.* 1853–1920.
Alleghanian Lyceum. *Minutes.* 1856–1906.
Allen, Abigail A. "Co-education." *Alfred Student* 1 (January 1874): 1–3; 1 (February
        1874): 13–15.
———. "Report from Alleghany County." 1892.
Allen, Alfred to John Nelson Norwood, May 9, 1935.
Allen, Jonathan. "Alfred University: Historic Sketch—First Decade." *Sabbath
        Recorder,* July 21, 1881; July 28, 1881; August 11, 1881; August 25, 1881.
———. "Caroline B. Maxson Stillman." *Alfred Student* 1 (June 1874): 63.
———. "Caroline H. Dall." *Alfred Student* 5 (November 1877): 14–15.
———. "The College Community." *Alfred University,* August 1888, 5.
———. "Education for Women." *Alfred Student* 3 (February 1876): 53.
———. "The Kenyon Memorial Hall." *Alfred Student* 3 (October 1875): 7.
———. "Life and Labors of President Wm. C. Kenyon." *Catalogue of Alfred Univer-
        sity for the Year Ending June 30, 1869.*
———. "Mixed Schools." *Alfred Student* 4 (October 1876): 1–2.
———. "Suffrage." *Alfred Student* 4 (April 1877): 73–75.

Allen, May. "The Literary Societies—Alfred University: Historic Sketch—Athenaean Lyceum." *Sabbath Recorder*, October 13, 1881.

Athenaean Lyceum. *Minutes.* 1859–1915.

Attorney's brief.

Baker, Halsey H. "Alfred University: Interesting Sketch of the Beginning of This School." Unidentified newspaper clipping, 1901.

Bliss, Edna M. "Recollections," October 30, 1935.

Brown (Nicholson), Marion Lucretia to John Nelson Norwood, December 13, 1935.

Brown (Tomlinson), Mary Ellen. "Stepping Stones," 1868.

Burdick, Asa C. Diaries.

Burdick, Hiram P. "Recollections."

Burdick, Mary A. Taylor. "Fifty Years Ago." *Alfred Sun*, June 14, 1911.

Burdick, Susan M. to John Nelson Norwood, April 25, 1935.

Burt, Abram. Diary. 1864.

"The Celebration of the One Hundredth Anniversary of the Founding of Alfred University." *University Bulletin* 13 (June 1937).

Clark, Martin Marion to Eslie Langworthy, June 7, 1870.

Clawson, Cortez R. to John Nelson Norwood, February 19, 1935.

Collins, John B. to Amorilla C. Babcock and Daniel C. Babcock, November 25, 1843.

Copp, Josephine M. Autograph Book.

Cottrell, Helen. "Alfred History—A Sketch." *Alfred Historical Society Monograph #2*, February 7, 1968.

Davis, Boothe Colwell. Response to questions submitted by President Norwood and commentary by Dr. Corliss F. Randolph. 1935.

Davis, Boothe Colwell, and Estelle Hoffman Davis. "Memoirs."

"Death of Mrs. Allen." *Alfred Sun*, October 29, 1902.

Gamble, James Lee. "Alfred University, Condensed History, December 5, 1836 to June 30, 1903."

Goff (Cone), Mary E. to Mrs. Samantha McAlmont, August 26, 1859.

Greene, Frank L. "History of the First Seventh Day Baptist Church of Alfred, New York, 1816–1916."

Greene, Maxson F. to M. Ellis Drake, July 16, 1934.

Irish, James. "A Sketch of the Early Life of Rev. James R. Irish." *Sabbath Recorder,* April 23, 1891, 262–63; April 30, 1891, 278.

———. "Sketch of the Labors of Rev. James R. Irish in Alfred Academy." *Sabbath Recorder,* May 7, 1891, 294.

Kenyon, William C. Presidential Papers.

——— to A. C. Spicer, February 19, 1849.

——— to Hiram P. Burdick, September 17, 1865.

——— to "M.," April 3, 1839. Reprinted in *Alfred Student* 3 (April 1876): 77.

Ladies' Literary Society. *Minutes.* 1853–1858. 1858–1867.

Larkin, Ethan H. "History of Alfred University."

Lewis, Daniel. "Memoir of President Allen."

Lewis, Edwin H. "Remarks of Dr. Edwin H. Lewis at the Alfred Dinner." Chicago, 1933.

——— to John Nelson Norwood, March 12, 1935.

Lincoln, Abraham to Eunice E. Howell, February 17, 1860.

The Literary Star.

Maxson, Charles Hartshorn. "A Chapter of Family History in Relation to Alfred and Alfred University."

Maxson, Daniel to Artemesia Maxson. Letters.

McAlmont, Myra C. to Mrs. S. McAlmont, August 27, 1852.

"Melissa B. Ward Kenyon, Teacher 1840–1863."

"Memorial Service, September 24, 1892."

Merrill, Leona Burdick. "Recollections of Alfred."

Norwood, John Nelson. "Bethuel Cooley Church." 1951.

——. Presidential Papers.

Orophilian Lyceum. *Minutes.* 1859–1920.

Palmer, Lydia Langworthy to Abigail Allen, May 1896.

Place, William F. to Ida F. Kenyon, October 30, 1895; January 15, 1895.

Powell, Mary A. Sheldon. "A Few Reminiscences of Early School Days in the Town of Alfred."

Prentice, Mary Greene to Arta Place, December 8, 1902.

Prosser, John M. to Curtis F. Randolph, October 3, 1936.

Randolph, Corliss F. "President Allen and William A. Rogers."

—— to John Nelson Norwood, March 1, 1942.

Reveley, Ida to John Nelson Norwood, February 11, 1936.

Rockwell, Joseph G. to "Brother," November 1, 1847.

Sanderson, Reg. "J. R. Irish."

Sayles, Ira to William F. Place, April 29, 1879.

Simpson (Spencer), Hannah A. Autograph book.

——. Diary, 1861.

Smith, Elizabeth Oakes. "A College for Both Sexes." Letter to the editor of the *United States Magazine,* July 3, 1854.

Stillman, Caroline B. Maxson.

Stillman, David to Maxson Greene, September 7, 1837.

Stillman, Orra to Bradford Manchester, January 12, 1837.

Tomlinson, E. M. "Founder's Day Address, December 1909."

——. "Motives and Ideals of President W. C. Kenyon."

"Valedictory." Undated, anonymous.

Wells, Alice Vinette. "Alice at Alfred." Diary edited by Gertrude Wells Seaman.

Williams, Thomas R. to William and Ida Kenyon, January 7, 1867.

Witter, Ellis Adelbert. "Alfred University."

"The Woman Who Dared." Newspaper clipping [1888].

Index

Made in the USA
Lexington, KY
16 December 2013